Effective
Technical
Communication

Effective Technical Communication

Anne Eisenberg
Polytechnic Institute of New York

McGraw-Hill Book Company
New York St. Louis San Francisco Auckland Bogotá Hamburg
Johannesburg London Madrid Mexico Montreal New Delhi
Panama Paris São Paulo Singapore Sydney Tokyo Toronto

Library of Congress Cataloging in Publication Data

Eisenberg, Anne, date
    Effective technical communication.

    Includes bibliographies and index.
    1. Communication of technical information.
2. Technical writing.   I. Title.
T10.5.E36   808'.0666021   81-12354
ISBN 0-07-019096-8   AACR2
ISBN 0-07-019097-6 (pbk.)

EFFECTIVE TECHNICAL COMMUNICATION

    2 3 4 5 6 7 8 9 0   DODO   8 9 8 7 6 5 4 3 2

ISBN 0-07-019096-8 HC

ISBN 0-07-019097-6 SC

This book was set in Baskerville by Black Dot, Inc.
The editors were Julienne V. Brown and David A. Damstra;
the designers were Charles A. Carson and Caliber Design Planning;
the production supervisor was John Mancia.
The part opening and soft cover illustrations were done by Anne
Canevari Green; new drawings were done by ECL Art Associates, Inc.
R. R. Donnelley & Sons Company was printer and binder.

About the Author

Anne Eisenberg is an Assistant Professor at the Polytechnic Institute of New York, where she directs the graduate program in scientific and technical writing. Her earlier book, *Reading Technical Books* (1978), is widely used in college classrooms. Her articles on writing have appeared in the *Journal of Chemical Education, Trends in Biochemical Sciences, Journal of Basic Writing, Graduating Engineer,* and other publications. She is the author of the American Chemical Society film, *Technical Writing,* and gives a course in technical writing for that society. She is a graduate of Barnard College, the University of Iowa, and New York University.

Contents

Preface   xi

1 Overview   1
Types of Scientific and Technical Communication   2
Style in Scientific Communication   3
Audience—A Key Issue   5
Five Basic Guidelines   6
Summary   8
Literature Cited   8
Exercises   9

PART ONE   PARTS OF THE WHOLE: BASIC PATTERNS IN TECHNICAL AND SCIENTIFIC WRITING

2 Writing Definitions   29
Definition by Class and Differentiation   30
Definition by Form and Function   31
Definition by Etymology   31
Definition by Analysis   32
List of Properties   32
Use of Synonyms   33
Expanded Definition   33
Academic Information   34
Techniques in Definition: Contrast, Comparison, and Example   35
Summary   37
Literature Cited   37
Exercises   38

3 Writing a Technical Description   41
Difference between Technical and Literary Description   42
How to Write a Technical Description: Three Examples   43
Describing a Process   46
Five Examples of Analysis by Process   46
Three Techniques in Process Writing   53
Guidelines for Describing a Process   55
Summary   55
Literature Cited   56
Exercises   56

4 Writing Instructions   65
Writing Instructions for Tying a Necktie   67
Use of Illustration in Technical Instructions   72
Summary   74
Literature Cited   76
Exercises   77

5 Basic Rhetorical Patterns: The Art of Arrangement   85
Analogy   86
Comparison and Contrast: Two Examples   87

Problem-Solution: Two Examples   90
Cause and Effect: Two Examples   93
Inductive Order: Specific to General   95
Deductive Order: General to Specific   96
Enumeration and Classification   98
Summary   101
Literature Cited   102
Exercises   102

PART TWO   PREPARATORY WORK: STAGES IN THE PROCESS

6 The Writing Process   107
Entering the Data: First Assemble, Then Assimilate   108
Beginnings   110
First Draft   113
Second Draft: Persuasiveness   116
Third Draft: Mechanics   117
Summary   118
Literature Cited   118
Exercises   119

7 Using the Library: Keeping Up in
      Science and Engineering   124
General Sources   126
Secondary Sources   129
Other Important Sources   138
Patent Information   139
Summary   141
Literature Cited   142
Exercises   142

8 Style   145
Accuracy   146
Brevity   146
Clarity   146
Seven Ways to Trim Useless Language   148
Summary   153
Exercises   154

PART THREE   REPORTS AND PROPOSALS

9 Writing an Abstract   159
Definitions and Formats   160
Two Types of Abstracts   161
An Exercise in Writing an Abstract   164
Commercial Abstracts   169
Summary   171
Exercises   171

10 Report Writing   179
Types of Reports   180
Technical Business Report   182
Format for Formal Business Reports   183
Format for Informal TBR: Memo and Letter   189

Journal Report   192
Contract Report   194
Handling Sources in a Report   194
Summary   198
Exercises   200

11 Effective Illustration   212
Graphs and Charts   213
Callouts and Instructions   218
Photographs   220
Tables   222
Summary   228
Exercises   229

12 Preparing a Proposal   234
What's a Proposal?   235
Who Is the Audience?   235
Parts of the Proposal   236
Section 1: The Problem Statement   236
Section 2: Objectives   237
Section 3: Procedure   237
Section 4: Evaluation   238
Section 5: Follow-Up   239
Section 6: Qualifications   240
Section 7: Budget   241
The Abstract   242
Summary   242
Exercises   243

PART FOUR   ORAL PRESENTATION AND SHORT FORMS

13 Preparing and Giving a Speech   259
Before You Begin   260
Writing Out the Speech   262
Rehearsing   264
On Machinery   265
Delivery Using Slides or Transparencies   268
Blackboards, Easels, and Tagboards   270
Audience Participation   271
Polishing Your Delivery   271
The Speech as a Whole   273
Summary: A Checklist   276
Exercises   277
Appendix: Working with Transparencies and Slides   278

14 Letter Writing   282
Ten Suggestions for Letter Writing   285
Courtesy in Letter Writing   297
Dictation   298
On Cover Letters and "No" Letters   299
Summary   300
Literature Cited   301
Exercises   301
Appendix: Sample Letters and Corrections   303

15 Résumés 305
Getting Started 306
Basic Categories 306
Summary 311
Sample Résumés 313

APPENDIXES

A Keeping a Laboratory Notebook 323
For Authentication: Purpose and Format 325
In a University Setting 326
What to Include 327
Summary 328
Literature Cited 328
Exercises 329

B Prosefalls 330
Grammar: Four Trouble Spots 331
Punctuation 335
Ten Usage Demons 340
Numbers: Numerals or Spelled Form? 342
Exercises 343
Test Answers 345

Index 347

Preface

This book is based on my experience teaching technical writing to undergraduates at the Polytechnic Institute of New York, and to working scientists and engineers through the American Chemical Society.

The focus is on clear, direct presentation of technical and scientific information, beginning with such components of report writing as definitions and descriptions, and ending with their use in reports, proposals, and oral presentations. The vehicle is discussion, example, and exercises. Together, the parts of the book are intended to take the reader from an overview to specific and detailed practice in writing and speaking using technical content.

The overview discusses the basic questions of audience and the ways writers of technical and scientific prose adjust the amount and flow of detail depending upon the reader's background, knowledge, and experience.

Part 1 addresses the parts of the whole: definitions, physical descriptions, process analyses, and instructions. Basic organizational patterns are discussed with attention to devices of particular use in scientific writing such as cause-effect, analogy, and problem-solution format.

Part 2 deals with preparatory work. The writing process described in Chapter 6 is drawn in part from interviews with scientists. None considered themselves exceptional writers, yet all learned to handle the writing process efficiently as part of their jobs. Their insights into ways to organize and proceed may be useful to others embarking on similar careers. Chapter 7 provides a discussion of reference sources with an eye toward the preparation of reports or proposals.

The longer forms in technical writing—reports and proposals, and their accessories, abstracts and illustrations—are presented in Part 3. There is a variety of exercises.

Since oral presentations are increasingly important for working scientists and engineers, the subject is developed separately and in detail.

As a reference for such errors as faulty parallelism and misplaced modifiers, an appendix on common grammatical errors is included. A section on laboratory notebooks is also appended for those who may need to keep them.

I've quoted a great many people in this book. In so doing, I have tried to draw upon a breadth of technical and scientific writing, from the *McGraw-Hill Encyclopedia of Science and Technology* to Leonardo's notebooks. Aristotle wrote well on marine biology; Joseph Lister's landmark paper on the antiseptic principle reads as powerfully today as it did in

1867. There are also many commercial and industrial examples, from a well-presented description of a mousetrap to instructions for dry column chromatography.

I have introduced the great set pieces of technical and scientific writing—the proposal one does to get the job, the report one writes when it is done—in a sequence that begins with the building blocks of definition, description, and rhetorical patterns. The stress is on the language of the presentation and on the logical arrangement of that presentation.

Many people helped in the preparation of *Effective Technical Communication*. At McGraw-Hill, George Barlow read and commented upon the chapter on library resources, Sylvia Warren the appendix on prosefalls. Mel Haber, McGraw-Hill, and Edward Bell, *Scientific American*, kindly helped with information on technical illustration. David Damstra, McGraw-Hill, ably orchestrated these and other matters. Elizabeth Schofield typed the manuscript; Nancy Warren copyedited. They were both patient and proficient, and I thank them. Max Quackenbos of Union Carbide and Ken Chapman of the American Chemical Society were both quite helpful as was Julienne Brown of McGraw-Hill. O. Allan Gianniny, Jr., of the University of Virginia and Beth A. Nilsson read early versions of the manuscript and commented upon them. Professor Bruce Garetz, Chemistry Department, Polytechnic Institute of New York, read many chapters for technical accuracy, and I thank him in particular.

Anne Eisenberg

1
Overview

We do not admire what we cannot understand.
Marianne Moore

An undergraduate came to my office some months ago. He said he didn't need to take a report writing class because "my secretary can do my writing for me."

I told him not to count on it.

Scientists, engineers, and people in related technical fields do a lot of writing. A productive worker easily generates 800 to 1000 pages a year in laboratory notebooks, technical reports, proprietary reports, patent applications, abstracts, articles, memos, and correspondence.

That means that if you work in a scientific, engineering, or technical field, you will probably find yourself spending anywhere from 10 to 20 percent of your time writing; further, the quality of this writing will influence your professional growth.

There may be the grand occasions when you will sit down to write a long and complicated paper or report—and when the quality of your work is judged by your success in communicating the findings—or there may be the innumerable smaller occasions when you sit writing a letter or memo, trying to make a point simply and clearly. It may be to bring in income, to persuade a business or research associate of an argument, to keep an orderly notebook, or to begin the essential task of organizing and focusing thinking.

Scientists and engineers do many sorts of writing. "We like to think of exploring in science as a lonely, meditative business," Lewis Thomas comments in *Lives of a Cell*, "but always, sooner or later . . . we call to each other, communicate, publish, send letters to the editor, present papers, cry out on finding" [1].*

Not only do scientists, engineers, and technical staff members write. As their careers develop, they find themselves doing a lot of public speaking, too, in the form of technical briefs and presentations for colleagues, clients, and members of the public.

Finally, they spend a lot of time on literature searches, since many writing and speaking jobs begin not in the laboratory but in the library. For the beginning researcher, it is a daunting place; as E. Bright Wilson comments, it may sometimes appear easier to rediscover a fact that to look it up, so vast and spiraling are the secondary and primary sources available in scientific literature.

Using computerized or manual references; delivering technical speeches and briefs; writing abstracts, reports, and proposals —these are all part of technical communication.

If the chemist could stick to symbols and the physicist to the language of mathematics, they would avoid many difficulties. But they cannot. As Werner Heisenberg points out in *Across the Frontiers*, "The physicist . . . has to speak about his results also to nonphysicists who will not be satisfied unless some explanation is given in plain language. Even for a physicist the description in plain language would be a criterion of the degree of understanding that has been reached" [2].

The scientist is in the same position as T. S. Eliot's character who exclaims, "I gotta use words when I talk to you!"

Types of Scientific and Technical Communication

There are certain forms of scientific and technical writing that are as basic to the mode as short stories are to literary writing.

The Report of an Investigation   Leeuwenhoek looked into the single-lens microscopes he'd built, saw "wee small animals" in the

---

*Bracketed numbers refer to notes in the "Literature Cited" section at the end of the chapter.

scrapings from his teeth, and wrote of his extraordinary findings in hundreds of letters to the Royal Society of England. They duly had them translated from Leeuwenhoek's Dutch to the English and Latin of their membership and pondered his exact descriptions of the protozoa.

Today scientists typically present the results of their investigations in journals in the form of research papers. These are highly formal accounts of the *procedure, results, conclusions,* and *implications.* These papers, and the accompanying letters that shuttle back and forth between workers in the field, are the keystone of the scientific communications network.

Technical Business Report   An adaptation of the classic report of an investigation, this form takes the standard parts of procedure, results, and conclusion and shapes them to commercial objectives. A recent industrial survey by IBM disclosed that report writing can be crucial to employees' careers, providing the personal visibility that results in recognition from both management and peers, and more responsibility.

Laboratory Notebooks   These documents, irreplaceable for establishing patents, are also a superb source for detailed procedural information not available in the more compressed accounts that appear in scholarly journals.

The Proposal   After you finish the job, you write a report, but to get the job, you will often write a proposal. A proposal is a formal offering to do a particular job on particular terms, and it is a basic literary form in the scientific marketplace. It is actually a hybrid that ideally combines the persuasiveness of a sales pitch with the formality and rigor of a research paper.

Daily Commercial Applications   New product releases, specification sheets, preparation of technical information for advertising or marketing people, letters and memos, oral technical presentations—these are just a few of the daily applications.

Style in Scientific Communication

Whether you are speaking or writing, there are certain constraints in the rhetoric of scientific and technical writing that will influence how you present your ideas.

Literary writing is the search to create what Marianne Moore calls "imaginary gardens with real toads in them"—to present a flashing, psychologically correct setting in which readers suddenly come upon their own experiences with the shock of recognition.

Scientific writing does not speak in this tongue. Instead, one finds an avoidance of impressionistic detail, of language which is obviously emotive or suggestive. In other words, the science writer struggles to *reduce* the emotional involvement of the reader's response rather than to *evoke* it.

Elaborate prose is rare. The author attempts to transmit information as objectively as possible, with language the admitted enemy in this endeavor. Language is rife with ambiguity; emotional associations cluster around words. It is the scientist's job to cut away at this ambiguity, using mathematics and other symbols when possible, and the language of daily life as the last resort.

Precision and consistency are hallmarks of the style.

As an aid, scientists often invent words which are not in everyday usage and therefore not so likely to evoke irrelevant associations in the reader's mind. For example, when Faraday finished his work on electrolysis, he visited William Whewell, at that time professor of moral philosophy at Cambridge, to have an untarnished set of words coined for his results. That is how the terms *anode* and *cathode* came into existence.

The language of science is also distinguished by what Leonard Bloomfield, the linguist, calls its "translatability." Because the meaning of many words has been sharply fixed by agreement, many terms—such as *absolute, critical,* and *fundamental*—have precise meanings which do not vary from user to user as they do in popular language. Nor do they vary from language to language. It is a commonplace that in scientific translation the amount of one-for-one translation that can be done is striking, the differences being of negligible magnitude. There is only one choice when the translator is dealing with such words as *solution, precipitate, crystallize.*

This translatability is one example of the consistency and rigor of the language. Another is found when linguists trace developments in the meaning of terms. Scientific terms do not change their meanings so rapidly as do terms in daily use. "Constancy in form and function gives to scientific words a character which distinguishes them sharply from other words, but relates them to the symbols of mathematics," Savory writes in *The Language of Science.* [3]

The rigor and consistency of scientific vocabulary distinguishes the prose from general writing. Another stylistic variation occurs in the pattern of explication.

Less is better in scientific writing. "More is in vain when less will serve," Newton said in his *Rules of Reasoning in Philosophy*. Science is parsimonious not only in its method; this thrift is carried over into its prose style. Watson and Crick took 900 words to expound their extraordinary discovery of the double helix; that brevity is a model for scientific style. Examples and explanations are used sparingly. One finds instance after instance in which a single word is seized upon to do the work of many. Sentences are collapsed, one into another, with labor-saving use of pronouns and other references, all to compact the prose.

In response to problems of ambiguity in language, scientists have developed their own style of writing. The tone tends to be undecorated. There are exceptions: R. W. Wood, for instance, describes spectra as "furrowed," and in the *Journal of the American Chemical Society*, Woodward describes the "tangled skein of atoms" that constitutes the strychnine molecule.

But such touches of color are rare: in general the language is austere. Figurative language is infrequent, narrative voice hardly occurs. Usually the speaker is shoved firmly in the background, and prose is not used to create effect.

Audience—A Key Issue

The issue of audience—the nature of your reader or listener—is always crucial in writing, but it is particularly thorny in scientific and technical writing. Because the content is by definition highly specialized, people who write about science are forced to live in divided and distinguished worlds, sometimes writing for their peers, and sometimes for supervisors, clients, or members of the public who know less than they about the subject.

This means that rhetorical stance—where the writer stands in relation to the audience—shifts. For instance, you may write the same information one way for your peers, another way for the public.

If the audience were solely peers, there might be no problem. But this situation rarely arises outside the readership of specialized journals. The typical science writing job, instead, is instructions for a worker, a budget justification for a manager unfamiliar with the specific procedures, preparation on a new product for marketing staff. The acronyms and familiar phrases of one's profession can't stand alone. Instead, the writer has to define terms, explain to a larger audience.

Usually you will write against the tide: for busy people who may not be experts and who need to have complex information served up in a brief, clear, and forceful way.

This is never an easy job, and it grows more difficult as the complexity of the information increases. William Stockton, science editor of *The New York Times*, has much experience in presenting scientific topics to a general readership. He does the following conjugation: "Biology is possible, physics becomes difficult, and mathematics impossible."

To write about science is to struggle with complex, inherently abstract information: the reasons are probably related to the development of scientific knowledge.

The history of science has been a history of abstraction. Werner Heisenberg writes that abstraction in science has an inherent inevitability. For instance, in zoology and botany scientists started with broad units but were inevitably drawn to the smallest parts of the organism, the history of inheritance in chemical script. "To see individuals as a case of something more general is always a step into abstraction," Heisenberg writes, "for the more general unites the wealth of diverse, individual things under a unitary point of view . . . in other words, it abstracts from them" [4].

Presenting difficult or technical content means one needs to take special note of the background of the audience. In most cases, it will mean extra care with definitions and explanations. And while it's true that many ideas are so complex that it simply is not possible to clarify every nuance when writing for a nonspecialist, it is possible to develop a practical style suited to communicating effectively outside the pages of specialized journals.

Five Basic Guidelines

These basic guidelines may help you to handle difficulties of audience background and complex subject matter.

1. *Consider your audience. Audience* is a rhetorician's term for the people you address. Everything you say in technical and scientific writing should be filtered through an awareness of these people. What do they know already? How much more do you want them to know?

You may write for marketing staff who have no background in your field but need to have some sense of the project to begin promoting it. You'll need to deliver the information clearly and directly, with a minimum of technical detail.

You may write for a unit supervisor who is compiling a monthly report. The supervisor will want the gist of what you've done, served up neatly and specifically.

You may prepare standard operating procedures for staff that you supervise. If you are extremely familiar with the procedure, you need to incorporate details that are obvious to you but necessary for the more naive reader.

In all of these examples there is the constant effort by the writer to bridge differences in audience background by being specific and clear.

2. *Consider your objective*. The question of goal is as important as audience. Why are you writing the memo, letter, or report? List your goal(s) and think about them before you write. Thus,

I am writing this for _____(audience)_____ because
I want _____(objective)_____ .

For memos that have a broad distribution, or for a report that will be read primarily by one person, the question of objective is crucial. If, for instance, you are writing a report on the month's progress for your supervisor, you might formulate it as follows.

I am writing this for my unit manager's monthly digest of the work we've been doing because I want to stress my results and show how they fit into overall projections for the project. The procedures aren't vital.

"I only took the regular courses," Lewis Carroll says in *Alice in Wonderland*, "reeling and writhing."

Analysis of audience and objective will help a great deal to avoid "reeling and writhing." It provides a framework and a focus for writing or speaking.

3. *Develop clear, usable, everyday prose*. There is a history of fine writing in science and engineering. Despite the popular notion that "scientists aren't good writers," the literature tells another story, from the lucid accounts of Galen explaining how to lay open the muscles of the forearm to the elegant, clear prose of such modern writers as Jeremy Bernstein. Leeuwenhoek's

descriptions of protozoa are so exact that the animals can be identified today based on these descriptions. Michael Faraday was a superb writer whose clear, expository style is displayed in the 18 volumes that contain his letters, journal entries, and a series of science lectures he gave for the children of London. This writing has what Whitehead calls "the most austere of all mental qualities"—a sense for style—that which is written "simply and without waste."

The tools of fine writing are logic drawn to ends that are disinterested; precision; brevity of explication; and that virtue attributed to Newton, "extreme sobriety of statement."

4. *Be brief.* No matter what you are writing, brevity is a virtue. As Samuel Johnson commented, in his typically acerbic style, "Read over your compositions, and when you meet with a passage you think is particularly fine, strike it out."

5. *Expect to rewrite.* The most skilled writers routinely go through two or three drafts of a composition. You can't expect to do much better. From the beginning, it's wise to acknowledge that few of us manage with less than two revisions, although some people have trained themselves to use dictating machines for the first draft.

Summary

Language is a final product in scientific inquiry, and therefore an integral part of the process. Its hallmark is precision, its purpose to be a vehicle so that someone in another place, another time, can understand and replicate what one has done. This means that if you work in scientific or technical fields, you'll need to present your message directly and clearly.

Literature Cited

1. L. Thomas, *The Lives of a Cell: Notes of a Biology Watcher,* Viking, New York, 1974.

2. W. Heisenberg, *Across the Frontiers,* Allen and Unwin, London, 1958, p. 143.

3. T. H. Savory, *The Language of Science: Its Growth, Character and Usage,* Andre Deutsch, London, 1953.

4. W. Heisenberg, op. cit., p. 143.

Exercises

1. Pick a technical subject such as computer graphics, industrial robots, DNA, interferon, or the aerodynamics of the paper airplane. Find reports written on your subject at two different levels—one for a highly specialized group and the other for a more general group. For instance, if your topic is industrial robots, you might consider *Business Week* (November 24, 1980), *Industrial Engineering* (November 1980), *Time* Magazine (December 8, 1980), or other sources. Or you might choose a research report from a scientific journal such as the *New England Journal of Medicine* and a report on the same subject that appeared in a source such as *The New York Times.* Photocopy a representative portion of each report. Analyze the differences in writing style. In each case, what audience does the author address? What assumptions do you think the author has made about the audience's scientific background? Is there any use of vivid language? If so, is it effective?

2. Here are excerpts from two articles on bubble memory: the first, by Technical Director Leslie Solomon, appears in *Popular Electronics*; the other by Robert Bernard in *IEEE Spectrum*. There are differences in the writing styles of the two authors based on their objectives and the backgrounds they assume for their audiences. One writer, for instance, introduces the term *bubbles* as "magnetic domains that are moved serially in an epitaxial film of garnet," while the other introduces the term differently. Analyze and contrast the differences in the writing styles of the two authors.

> I. A NEW APPROACH TO DATA STORAGE: BUBBLE MEMORIES[1]
> A whole new approach to mass data storage is soon to become available at reasonable cost. Called "bubble memories," the new storage devices have attributes of both the RAM [random-access memory] and the ROM [read-only memory]. Like a RAM, data can be written into and read from a bubble-memory device. And, like ROM, once power is removed from the bubble memory, the data remains intact, ready to be read out when power is restored.
>
> Typical bubble-memory devices contain at least 92K bits of data-storage capacity. With an access time of 4 ms and a 50K bits/second data rate, the bubble device "looks" more like a disk

system than it does a cassette system. Note that the bubble-memory system does not make a good substitute for a RAM system—unless you have lots of time.

A bubble-memory system, which might include several 92K bubble devices and their associated interface electronics, can be mounted on a single circuit board that can be plugged into almost any bus system. Since each bubble device requires less than 700 mW of power for continuous operation, the power supply in a microcomputer will not be strained.

Formation of a Bubble A basic "bubble" begins as a magnetic domain that exists within a thin magnetic film and can assume any shape, as shown in Figure 1-1*a*. These domains form in the film in a manner that minimizes the total magnetic energy of the film.

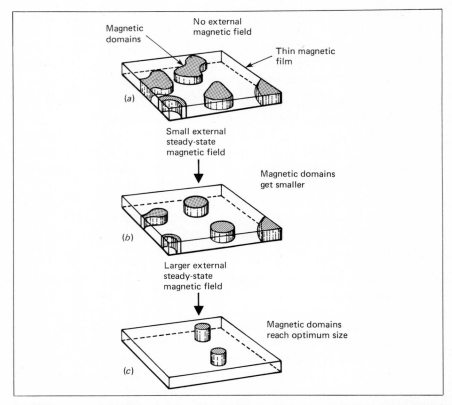

FIGURE 1-1 Small bubbles in magnetic film are shown at (*a*). With an external field applied, bubbles get smaller (*b*). They reach best size as field is increased (*c*).

Shown in Figure 1-1*a* is a typical set of domains when there is no external magnetic field applied normal (at right angles) to the film.

If a small steady-state magnetic field, such as from a permanent magnet, is applied normal to the plane, the magnetic domains tend to shrink within themselves to form smaller domains (Figure 1-1*b*). As the strength of the external magnetic field increases, the domains continue to shrink until they are between 2 and 30 microns in size (Figure 1-1*c*). If the external magnetic field's strength is increased, the bubbles essentially disappear. Experiments have revealed that the most stable bubbles are formed with an applied steady-state magnetic field of about 100 oersteds. Hence, the first hint of bubble operation is that magnetic bubbles are sensitive to applied magnetic fields.

Physical Construction The basic arrangement of a bubble-memory chip is shown in Figure 1-2. The actual bubble device (with one corner enlarged) reveals that the thin magnetic film is diffused on a nonmagnetic substrate, along with small bars that are shaped like the letters I and T.

The bubble device is mounted between two thin permanent magnets to create the tiny bubbles. Surrounding the bubble device is a pair of orthogonal coils (right angles to each other). Since we

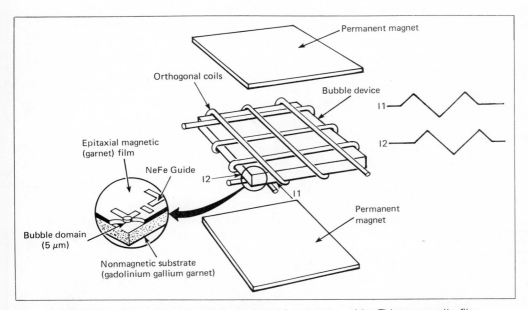

FIGURE 1-2 Basic arrangement of a bubble-memory chip. Thin magnetic film is diffused on substrate with small bars in shapes of letters I and T.

know that the magnetic bubbles are affected by magnetic fields, passing a current through the orthogonal coils, 90° apart and in-phase, will cause the bubbles to move around. Using the current flow shown in Figure 1-2, the magnetic field will rotate.

Bubble Motion   Once a bubble has been established, it must be moved around so that it can be used as a data bit. How this motion is achieved is shown in Figure 1-3. The "track" along which the bubble is to be moved is composed of a series of soft magnetic bars shaped like I's and T's that are also deposited on the nonmagnetic substrate. A "parent" bubble is located under a disk of magnetic material. Note in Figure 1-3 that another bubble is located under the first T bar and is assumed to have moved to that location during a previous cycle.

The first I bar has a tiny hairpin wire loop covering one end. When the rotating magnetic field is as shown, and when a current of about 150 mA is applied to the loop for 500 ns, a portion of the parent bubble is transferred to the vicinity of the I bar. The parent bubble is not depleted because its size is strictly a function of the local magnetic conditions. As the rotating magnetic field continues, the newly created bubble moves across to the next T bar that has the temporary magnetization shown. As the applied magnetic field continues to rotate, the slender magnetic "link" between the parent bubble and the newly formed bubble under the T bar snaps, leaving a new bubble at the T bar (first T bar in bottom row).

As the applied magnetic field continues to rotate, the right side of the T bar assumes the magnetic characteristics shown in the top row (second bubble) and further field rotation causes the bubble to move along the track, going from T bar to I bar, and so forth. Each rotation of the applied magnetic field causes a bubble to move a distance of slightly greater than 20 microns.

There are other track formations between the T and I bars. Examples are: a chevron-shaped set of bars, a Y-shaped set, and a set of contiguous disks.

Bubble Annihilation   When the bubbles reach the end of the track or when the data is no longer needed, a means must be provided for removing the unwanted bubbles. One method is to use a current pulse in a hairpin loop to disintegrate the bubble when it passes under the intense magnetic field. Another is to allow the bubble to run into a magnetic guard rail that surrounds the substrate. The bubble simply joins the magnetic field under the guard rail and vanishes. The magnetic field of the guard rail does not increase in size when this occurs. The field is a function only of the local magnetic conditions.

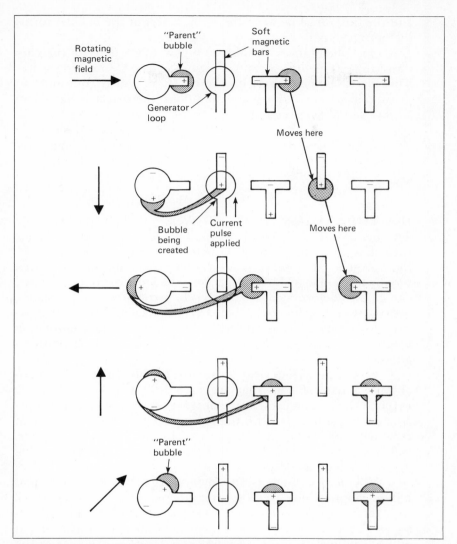

FIGURE 1-3 A bubble, once established, is moved around between soft magnetic bars by rotating magnetic field on left.

Bubble Detection   The most common way to detect the presence of a magnetic bubble is to measure the change in resistance of a magnetoresistive strip as the bubble passes over it. To reject the interference from the rotating field that drives the bubbles, a dummy detector, exposed to the magnetic field but not to the bubble, is also used. The signals from the two detectors are mixed and the difference between them (the effect of the bubble) forms the output signal.

Once the bubbles are allowed to flow to the detector (magnetoresistive) elements, the bubbles are "stretched" into wide strips. This increases their effect on the detectors and is equivalent to preamplification. Under these conditions, the detected signal can be several millivolts in amplitude.

II. BUBBLE MEMORIES: HOW THEY WORK, WHERE THEY ARE[1]

The designs of available magnetic bubble memories are minor variations on a single theme: Bubbles—representing 1s and 0s by their presence or absence—are magnetic domains that are moved serially in an epitaxial film of garnet. The bubbles are propagated along paths determined by chevron-shaped patterns of Permalloy deposited on a oxide layer that covers the garnet. When magnetized by a rotating magnetic field, the patterns have alternating magnetic polarities that attract bubbles from one chevron to another.

All commercial devices enclose the bubble-containing material with a pair of coils that are used to generate the rotating magnetic field. The presence or absence of a bubble is detected by a magnetoresistive element; the passing bubble causes a change in resistance and, thus, a change in voltage across the detector. Bubbles are created—recorded—by current pulses flowing through a generate loop.

Most bubble memories today are organized into major and minor loops, which yield shorter access times than the serial shift-register organization used in early designs. Each minor loop is a storage area of bubbles, while the major loops provide input and output circuitry. A "page" of information is stored by placing one bit in each minor loop. At playback, the bits on the desired page must rotate to the tops of the minor loops, where they are transferred—or "swapped"—to major loops.

Almost all available memories are further organized into block-replicates: Each major loop is divided into separate input and output loops, which are placed at opposite ends of the minor

---

[1]Copyright © 1980 by IEEE. Reprinted with permission from Robert Bernard, "Bubble Memories: How They Work, Where They Are," *IEEE Spectrum*, May 1980, p. 32.

loops. This clears the bottleneck that occurs in the simpler organization, where pages must be cleared from the major loop before any other operation can begin.

The most significant recent development in commercially available memories has been the 1-Mb chips. . . .

A major factor dictating the 1-Mb chip architecture is the supply voltage; the swap-gate voltage is difficult to produce from the standard 12-V supply. This problem is resolved by organizing the chip either as a 256-kb × 4 array, or 512-kb × 1.

The key factors that must be considered in selecting one architecture over another are: alignment tolerances, processing complexity, yield, and subsystem voltages. The development of wafer steppers capable of micron-resolution and quarter-micron alignment allows several of these factors to be eliminated as potential problems. The most straightforward approach of not folding the loop can be adopted with no significant penalty in drive field or yield.

These architectures lead to longer access times, but this drawback may be overcome by various block-replicating schemes and higher clock rates. Architectures must also minimize the high system-supply voltages required for large capacity chips; that voltage depends on bubble diameter, component currents, and the number of series-connected components. . . .

Bubble memories have not yet been applied widely, but enough storage units have been built and used to indicate that they are practical and reliable. The oldest and most successful applications are in the Bell telephone system and the switching networks of Nippon Telephone and Telegraph. The systems have 1 to 5 Mb, compounded from basic 64-kb units. They have generally operated at 100 MHz, with an average access time of about 3 ms and a data rate of about 750 kb/s. Error rates are reportedly one in every 10^{11} to 10^{12} read operations. Accelerated tests of a 4-Mb unit at Nippon Telephone and Telegraph reportedly showed it could operate reliably for 22 years in electronic switching networks.

A bubble memory is the heart of the TSB-1 miniprocessor, which works together with PBXs and is manufactured by the Telecommunications Service Bureau in Bensenville, Ill. It collects and analyzes call data, generates traffic reports, and stores and transmits phone messages. The memory is supplied by Texas Instruments and consists of a card containing one to six modules of 69 kilobytes each, with an access time of 50 ms and a data rate of 250 kb/s. The memory can process 2600 to 10,400 calls. In the works from TI is a new card that stores 768 kilobytes—but it costs $15,000.

Rockwell International exhibited the first 1-Mb bubble in 1977 and came out the next year with a practical 100-Mb bubble for spacecraft recorder systems. The memory is made of 1-Mb chips that are integrated by a programmable controller. A similar controller is available commercially to combine up to 16 Rockwell bubble units for memories of 256 kb to 2 megabytes. Rockwell bubbles are also used in a small computer now being manufactured by Findex in Los Angeles. . . .

Two portable terminals made by Texas Instruments use bubble memories to store data offline and transmit it at any time to host computers. The terminals have been available for a year and are installed in such retail operations as florist shops, for handling wire orders between florists; manufacturing companies, for entering and confirming orders; and insurance companies, for answering inquiries and updating policies.

3. Here is a report by B. G. Levi about Three Mile Island excerpted from *Physics Today* (June 1979, pp. 77–78). Find another treatment of the accident written at a different audience level—either simpler in approach or more sophisticated. Contract the objectives of the two articles and the authors' styles. For instance, are the types and quantity of detail different in the two articles?

WHAT WENT WRONG WITH THE THREE MILE ISLAND REACTOR?
The Three Mile Island nuclear reactor near Harrisburg, Pa. has been cooling slowly after the crisis that began there on 28 March. . . . Details of the sequence of events that led to the damage of a large fraction of the nuclear core are only gradually emerging. Some answers must wait until the core can be safely approached, and still others may never be forthcoming. . . .

The reactor—only three months old—is one of a pair of pressurized water reactors (PWR's) at Three Mile Island designed for Metropolitan Edison by Babcock and Wilcox. In a PWR the coolant in the primary loop is prevented from boiling by the pressurizer. (See Figure 1-4.) The heat is transferred to the secondary loop through two steam generators that feed a single turbine. The emergency core cooling system consists of a high-pressure injection system with three pumps and a low-pressure injection system with two pumps designed as a backup principally in the case of a loss of coolant.

The Complex Chain of Events that made up the accident began when a condensate pump stopped, and the loss of suction in turn tripped the feedwater pumps. Among the various reasons suspect-

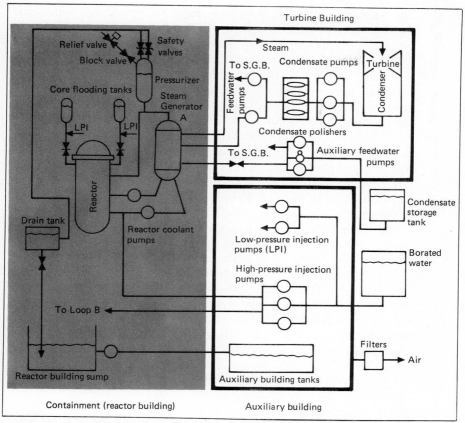

Turbine Building

Relief valve   Safety valves

Block valve

Core flooding tanks

Pressurizer

Steam Generator A

LPI   LPI

Reactor

Drain tank

Reactor

Reactor coolant pumps

To Loop B

Reactor building sump

Steam

To S.G.B.   Condensate pumps   Turbine

Feedwater pumps

Condenser

Condensate polishers

To S.G.B.   Auxiliary feedwater pumps

Condensate storage tank

Low-pressure injection pumps (LPI)

High-pressure injection pumps

Borated water

Filters

Air

Auxiliary building tanks

Containment (reactor building)   Auxiliary building

FIGURE 1-4 Pressurized-water reactor at Three Mile Island. The diagram illustrates some of the components that contributed to the accident there on 28 March. It began when condensate and feedwater pumps stopped. Auxiliary feedwater valves had been left shut; the pressurizer relief valve stuck open; the pressurizer level indicator misread; the containment building was not quickly isolated; high-pressure injectors were switched off prematurely. Thus, the core of the reactor overheated.

ed for the first pump failure are the spillage of ion-exchange resin from the demineralizer into the secondary flow, and the closing of an air-actuated valve because of moisture in the air line. . . .

The loss of the feedwater pump resulted in the shutdown of the turbine. As pressure quickly rose in the primary loop, the reactor "scrammed." Nearly simultaneously, three auxiliary feedwater pumps began to operate. The water never entered the steam generators because the two valves had been left closed after a recent maintenance check.

With the primary deprived of an adequate heat sink, its pressure rose above 2250 psi, at which point a relief valve atop the pressurizer opened. The pressure then dropped back through 2200 psi but, when the valve stuck open, the pressure continued to plummet. When the pressure declined to 1600 psi, the high-pressure injection system was automatically switched on, two minutes after the turbine tripped. One high-pressure injection pump was turned off manually two minutes later, and a second ten minutes later. Both were restored again soon after that. The reason why the operator turned them off was probably his concern that a sensor in the pressurizer was registering a high level of water. The NRC [Nuclear Regulatory Commission] staff has subsequently concluded that this level indicator was giving an erroneous reading at the time. . . .

Once the emergency core cooling system and auxiliary feed-water pumps were both back in operation, things still were under control. About one hour into the incident, an operator shut off the primary circulation pumps, apparently out of concern that they were badly vibrating, perhaps because of the bubbles in the system. Without circulation and apparently with little convection (a large temperature difference prevailed between inlet and outlet over this time), the core overheated. During the ensuing hours, the temperatures on some thermocouples on the fuel rods went above the computer-readout cutoff point of about 750° F. A large portion of the core was apparently uncovered after this point for an unknown period of time.

Bubble   When the operators restarted the circulation pumps and closed the block valve on the pressurizer, a new trouble developed. A large volume—as much as 1000 cubic feet or more—of noncondensible gas was detected in the reactor. Although no reliable measurement could be made of the composition of the gas in the reactor vessel, it was suspected to contain hydrogen. Air samples from the containment building registered concentrations of hydrogen of about 2%, and some sharp spikes in the containment building pressure—one of 28 psi—were interpreted as possible small hydrogen explosions. The hydrogen within the reactor vessel would come largely from a high-temperature oxidation reaction between the water and the zircalloy cladding. . . .

Within the containment building, the additional hydrogen in the atmosphere already present there *could* produce a flammable (at 4% hydrogen) or explosive (at 6 to 8%) mixture. These precentages could be slightly higher in the presence of water vapor. . . . To reduce this danger, two hydrogen recombiners were installed in the auxiliary building outside the containment.

The reactor continued to cool through most of the month of

April with primary pumps and one steam generator in operation. (Steam Generator B had been isolated when primary-to-secondary leaks were suspected there.) On 27 April, the primary pumps were turned off and the core left to cool by convection, with both steam generators operating. After two days, Generator B was isolated and at this writing is being equipped to run with all water and no steam. The decay-heat removal system normally employed to cool the reactor is not being used, partly because it would pump the radioactive primary coolant into the auxiliary building and might cause leakage around the seal.

Radioactivity The accident has resulted in some releases of radioactivity to the environment. With the fuel rods overheating and cracking, fission products such as iodine, xenon and krypton escaped. These elements contaminated the primary coolant while it was still flowing out of the stuck relief valve. When the seal ruptured on the quench drain tank (15 minutes into the accident), this hot liquid spilled onto the floor of the containment building. The pump sent this fluid into an auxiliary housing that is shielded and equipped with air filters. Releases occurred because the liquid volume was too large for the system to handle. The containment building was not designed to isolate automatically when the emergency core cooling system comes on. It was isolated only after five hours, when the pressure in the containment building rose above 4 psi over atmosphere.

The resulting cumulative dose equivalent from 28 March to 7 April is estimated to be from 2000 to 5000 person-rem (that is, the number of people exposed times the average dose per person) within a 50-mile radius and about half that in a 10-mile radius, according to an NRC spokesman. The average dose equivalent to a person in the smaller-radius region amounts to 10 millirem during that time, he said. This may be compared to the average dose equivalent per person per year from natural sources (in the region of Pennsylvania) of 85 to 90 millirem, according to Mark Mills of the Atomic Industrial Forum.

A massive cleanup job lies ahead to dispose of the radioactive water from the reactor core, and the estimated 400,000 gallons of liquid on the floor of the containment building. A more difficult task will be to decontaminate the inside of the building, where radioactive cesium may have been deposited.

4. The following excerpt from an article by P. Gwyne on the neutrino appeared in *Newsweek* (May 12, 1980, p. 109). Contrast this style of writing, including assumptions about audience background and knowledge, with the style of writing in two other reports on the neutrino written at different levels.

You may, for instance, want to look at *Science* (May 16, 1980) or actual proceedings in which the studies were originally reported.

THE FLIP-FLOP NEUTRINOS

The neutrino exists because theoretical physicists say it exists: they need it to make their equations come out. It is a subatomic particle whose principal function is to explain the strange disappearance of energy that occurs when a neutron ejects an electron and becomes a proton. Physicists say that neutrinos travel at about the speed of light. There are a million times as many of them as any other particle, but they are extremely hard to detect. And they have no mass, which is to say they weigh nothing.

That, at least, is what physicists thought. But last week, at the American Physical Society meeting in Washington, scientists reported experimental results that, if confirmed, will complicate the accepted picture of neutrinos and, indeed, of the universe. If we are right, said Frederick Reines of the University of California, Irvine, "there was no beginning and will be no end. The consequences are theological."

The report offered two major revelations. First, the neutrinos do seem to possess mass after all—perhaps 13,000 times less than the electron, the next lightest particle. Second, neutrinos appear to oscillate, or flip-flop, continually among at least two different forms. Reines compared the effect to seeing a dog change into a cat and then back into a dog as it walks down the street.

Vast Energy   The studies could clarify scientists' understanding of how the sun works. Physicists have long believed that the sun emits enormous numbers of neutrinos as a by-product of the nuclear fusion that produces its vast energy. But they have never been able to detect more than one-third of the neutrinos that their equations tell them should come from the sun. As a result, one of the premises of fusion theory has been called into question. If, however, the neutrinos oscillate into different forms, it could be that the detectors are identifying only one of the constantly changing types. This would reconfirm fusion theory.

5. Does it rain more by cities? Read the following clearly presented report by Stanley A. Changnon, Jr., reprinted from *Science* (vol. 205, July 27, 1979, pp. 402–404),[1] and then rewrite it for a broader audience. Specifically, in a report of no more than two pages, present the information so that it could be

---

understood by second-year undergraduates at a liberal arts college who could be assumed to have had some biology and possibly introductory chemistry or physics.

RAINFALL CHANGES IN SUMMER CAUSED BY ST. LOUIS

Climatological research results of the past 20 years have indicated that major urban areas influence clouds and precipitation. Sizable changes, > 10 percent, have been considered controversial. A major 5-year meteorological project was launched at St. Louis in 1971 to study intensively how an urban area modifies the atmosphere, how physical processes in clouds and rainfall are subsequently changed, and where any anomalous precipitation occurs. This experiment has provided a wealth of weather data and a variety of results that collectively indicated sizable (> 10 percent) localized increases in summer rainfall and storminess. It is difficult to evaluate inadvertent urban modification of rain because there is no randomization, and thus a "data analysis" approach that combines physical insight and statistical tests appears well suited.

A potentially definitive, yet simple physical-statistical test of the apparent urban-related rainfall increase at St. Louis is based on the determination of the placement and magnitude of maximum rainfall areas near St. Louis under differing wind directions. The basic hypothesis is that the low-level winds moving across the urban area define a plume of urban-altered air (aerosols, heat, and moisture) that can affect rainfall over and beyond or downwind of the city. Precipitation elements move in all directions, often not in the same direction as the low-level winds, but most precipitation elements in the St. Louis area move from westerly directions and therefore one would expect the greatest influence to be exerted essentially east of the city.

The urban plume and the precipitation elements are known to have dual and often dissimilar motions. Nevertheless, if urban influences are real, a rain increase downwind (based on the low-level wind or plume direction and not the precipitation motion) of the city should presumably occur under any low-level wind direction. Hence, a maximum should be located west of St. Louis when winds are from the east. To this end, I compared rainfall values downwind of the city, under different wind directions existing before each rain began, with those upwind and on either side of St. Louis.

Rainfall was collected at 220 recording rain gages evenly distributed within a circle 80 km in diameter centered on the city. Studies of the rainfall revealed 302 individual rainfall events in the five summers from 1971 through 1975. For each of these rain events, the low-level wind direction during the 3 hours prior to the rain was determined from available wind data at 28 stations coupled with an analysis of local synoptic weather conditions. Thus, the prevailing winds before the rain were used to provide a general estimate of the urban plume or area of influence. Whether the urban influence is related to temperature, moisture, aerosols, or all three factors is unimportant here; the plume serves only as a means of defining downwind areas of influence on the atmosphere and upwind (control) areas of no influence.

The circular network was divided into four equal-sized quadrants. The prerain winds were sorted into four directions of motion: northwest, northeast, southeast, and southwest. Then, for each direction, the quadrant rainfall was summed by the month and the summer.

The four direction patterns for June revealed that the downwind quadrant had the maximum in three of four cases (Table 1-1); in the case of southeast prestorm winds, the high was in the quadrant to the right of the city. In July the highest quadrant value occurred downwind for all four directions. In August, two of the four directions (southwest and northwest), had the maximum in the predicted downwind area. Thus, in 9 out of the 12 possible monthly cases, the maximum occurred in the downwind location. The high was always downwind of St. Louis in all months (Table 1-1) when southwest and northwest prerain winds occurred. These are also the directions of the predominate motions of individual summer rain elements. These results indicate that the urban influence was greatest when the low-level winds and storm cell motions were aligned. When northeast and southeast winds occurred and when the three monthly reversals occurred (maximum not downwind), the urban plume was moving generally in a direction opposite to the approaching storm motion, interacting with the rain well before reaching the city or downwind area, and hence being diffused and realized in the areas to the left or right of the city. . . . .

TABLE   1-1   PLACEMENT   OF   MAXIMUM QUADRANT RAINFALL WITH RESPECT TO ST. LOUIS   AND   FOR   EACH   MONTH.   THE MAXIMUM COULD BE DOWNWIND, UPWIND, LEFT, OR RIGHT OF ST. LOUIS.

Prerain wind direction	June	July	August
Northwest	Downwind	Downwind	Downwind
Southwest	Downwind	Downwind	Downwind
Southeast	Right	Downwind	Right
Northeast	Downwind	Downwind	Right

Three statistical tests were applied to the quadrant rainfall values to examine the claim that there is no urban effect on precipitation. In the first test I examined the frequency of maximum rainfall in the downwind area, in the second test the magnitude of the downwind rainfall (versus the rainfall elsewhere), and in the third test the areal distribution of the ranks achieved by the values of the four areas. The only assumption in each test was that the events tested were independent, which is highly likely when one considers that these were monthly values sorted on the basis of wind directions.

In the first test, each of the 12 monthly outcomes was viewed as an independent Bernoulli trial. The null hypothesis of the probability P being equal to one-fourth was tested; that is, the expected distribution of maximum values was one in four, versus the hypothesis that the downwind distribution was greater than one in four. Thus, if there is no urban effect or no association between prerain winds, the city, and the downwind rainfall, there is a 25 percent likelihood of having the high in the correct (downwind) position. In the sample obtained, the downwind frequency was nine maxima, which was found to be significant at $P > .0004$. Thus, the hypothesis that the wind crossing the city plays no role in the maximization of the downwind rainfall cannot be sustained. The maximum occurred downwind with sufficient frequency to be declared highly significant, if one uses the binomial test.

In the second statistical test, I evaluated the quadrant rainfall values in the 12 monthly wind-rain patterns by comparing the downwind values with those in the other quadrants. The differences, say, for downwind versus upwind, were ranked, and the one-sample Wilcoxon test was applied to these ranks. Addition of the negative ranks (upwind > downwind) for each comparison provided a number tested for its significance. The downwind versus upwind differences were significant at $P < .013$. This comparison indicated that the downwind rainfall value differed greatly from those of the three other areas around St. Louis.

In the third test I used the ranks of the quadrant rainfall values in each summer month for each wind direction. For each of the 12 patterns, ranks were assigned with the maximum quadrant given rank 1 and the minimum given rank 4. These were summed to get a summer score for each quadrant. The downwind area rank score was 16, and tests of probability reveal it to be significant at $P < .0001$. None of the rank sums for the upwind, right, and left quadrants were statistically significant.

In this analysis of the summer rainfall around St. Louis, I have considered the possible urban effect by using the prerain winds to define the probable placement of an urban-induced rain maximum. The fact that 9 out 12 possible monthly (three summer rain months and four basic wind directions) patterns and three out of four summer patterns had downwind maximums is strongly suggestive of an urban influence on precipitation over and beyond the city. Rotating the rain with the winds reveals a 22 percent rain increase in the area downwind of St. Louis.

Statistical tests dealing with both the placement of the highest quadrant rainfall and the positions of rainfall by quantity showed that the downwind values were significantly different and higher than those of surrounding areas. These results of prerain wind directions and rainfall distribution around St. Louis strongly support the concept that major urban areas lead to increased summer rainfall.

ONE

Parts of the Whole: Basic Patterns in Technical and Scientific Writing

2
Writing Definitions

Definition—The act of making clear or of bringing into sharp relief.

Precise, carefully presented definitions are essential in technical and scientific writing. Without them, the reader quickly becomes lost.

An effective definition may be as short as a one-word synonym, or as long as two or more typed pages.

The kind of definition you write depends on your audience —on how much they already know before you begin, and how much more you decide to tell them.

The classic pitfalls of definition include being circular, wordy, or too general.

1. *Circular.* A circular definition contains the name of the object defined.

    Adhesive tape dispenser: Device for dispensing adhesive tape.

2. *Wordy.* Verbiage can obscure even a relatively simple term.

Adhesive tape dispenser　A receptacle used for the containment and distribution of a rolled adhesive fastener.

Or consider this famed dictionary entry by Samuel Johnson:

Network　A network is anything reticulated or decussated, at equal distances, with interstices between the intersections.

3. *Too general.* These are definitions that lack precision.

> A spoon is used for eating.
> A banjo is a musical instrument.
> A ruler is used for measuring.

Some writers prefer alphabet soup, the familiar acronyms or abbreviations of their own group: "The CRT is an MTV-1, varied by an MRX-2." Others despair of finding a way to define terms, and solve the problem by completely omitting definitions, trusting that their readers' technical knowledge is so sophisticated and focused that no further assistance is needed. Unfortunately, this is rarely the case. Usually your reader knows *less* about the subject than you. This is true whether you write for administrators outside your particular area, for marketing people, or for people following a set of instructions. Only rarely will you have peers for an audience.

This means you'll need to explain. Definitions are crucial to these explanations, for they are the kernels out of which the reader's understanding will grow.

But the terms are too difficult, too abstract, you may exclaim. It's true that in science some terms are so abstract that one cannot do justice to all of the finer points in the definition. And some terms are so complex that the definition may take much time and thought. But with practice it is possible to define most terms you use in your working world at a level appropriate to your reader's background. The difficulty of the concepts won't vanish, but specific techniques will aid you in writing clear, comprehensible definitions.

Definition by Class and Differentiation (Logical Definition)

Definition by class and differentiation is the classic, logical definition. To use it, assign the object to a class, or genus, and then explain how the object differs from other objects within the class.

Consider the item *banjo.*

1. Assign it to a class. "Instrument" would be a bit general.

Likewise, "musical instrument" would be general. "Stringed musical instrument," however, would be adequate.

2. Then differentiate it from other stringed instruments. "The banjo is a stringed musical instrument which combines a long neck, similar to a guitar's, with a drumlike body similar to a tambourine's. There are usually four or five strings plucked with a pick or the fingers."

Term	Class	Differentiation
Banjo	Instrument	With a neck, body, and four or five strings
	Musical instrument	With a long neck and a drumlike body, and four or five strings
	Stringed musical instrument	With a long neck similar to a guitar's and a drumlike body similar to a tambourine's. There are usually four or five strings, plucked with a pick or the fingers.

Summarizing, the technique is to

1. Assign the item to a class, and then
2. Distinguish it from others in the class. What are its salient features? How is it different?

Definition by Form and Function

Definition by form and function is common in technical and scientific writing. The questions, What does it look like? How does it work? are fundamental ones. Often a form and function definition is paired with a class and differentiation definition and then followed by a figure reference. For example:

An ax is an instrument for hewing, clearing, or chopping trees. It has a squarish head fixed by a socket on a handle.

Many definitions which are logical are also functional (operational)—the banjo definition, for instance, qualifies under both categories. To define by form and function,

1. Assign the object to a category, and
2. Distinguish it from all others by asking: What does it look like? How does it work?

Definition by Etymology

This venerable technique is still popular today. To use it, give the roots of the words when the etymology will help the reader understand the new term. Then follow with a logical or functional definition.

> **Thermometer**   Derived from the Greek *therme*, "heat," and *metron*, "to measure." An instrument that measures temperature, often through the use of a confined substance such as mercury, the volume of which changes with the change in temperature.
>
> **Chromatogram**   Derived from the Greek *chroma*, "color," hence a colored compound, and *graphe*, "writing." A chromatogram is the pattern formed by zones of separated pigments and colorless substances.

Definition by Analysis

It is often useful to follow a general definition with an analysis; that is, to define the term in general, and then divide it into parts.

> **Example** (from *thermometer*, above)   Two of several basic types of thermometers:
>
> 1. *Clinical thermometers.* These are used to determine body temperature.
> 2. *Electric thermometers.* Resistance thermometers are based on the increase in resistance with increase in temperature; thermoelectric thermometers consist of two thermocouples which are connected with a potentiometer and a constant-temperature bath.

List of Properties

You may expand a general definition with a list of properties or characteristics. This example from the *McGraw-Hill Encyclopedia of Science and Technology,* for instance, defines parlor games in terms of their properties [1].

> GAME THEORY
>
> The theory of games of strategy can briefly be characterized as the application of mathematical analysis to abstract models of conflict situations. The first such models analyzed by the theory were parlor games such as chess, poker, and bridge. . . .
>
> **Games in Extensive Form**   Parlor games are specified by a list of rules. To be playable, a game must have the following properties: (1) There must be a way of starting the game. (2) There must be a well-defined list of legal (that is, permissible) moves for any

possible situation that can be reached in the game. (3) At each move, exactly one of the players must be assigned to make the choice, or else the choice is made by a chance device (such as rolling dice or a spinning pointer). (4) After a finite number of moves, the game is terminated; a winner is declared or payments are exchanged among the players, or both. Any other conflict situation that satisfies mathematical axioms similar to these rules can also be considered a game and the analysis of game theory can be applied to it.

The players of a game are called persons, and such a person may actually consist of one or more people (for instance, in bridge the pairs of partners, east-west and north-south, each make up a player in the game; it is considered a two-person game). Thus a person in a game may be considered synonymous with a team. Chance moves occur when hands are dealt from a shuffled pack, dice are rolled, or pointers are spun. One says that all chance moves are allotted to the chance player—a fiction that is useful in abstracting properties of games.

Use of Synonyms

You may have to address a general audience, and want to use a general term yet also tag the term with its technical name. In cases like this, the technical synonym is usually placed in parentheses, as shown in the following example.

During a heart attack (myocardial infarction), a coronary artery is blocked, cutting off the flow of oxygen-rich blood to the heart muscles it serves.

Expanded Definition

Expanded definitions may combine

Class and differentiation
Form and function
Etymology
Analysis
List of properties
Synonyms

Here is an example of an expanded definition which combines etymology and logical and functional information.

The term *macromolecule* is derived from the Greek *makros*, "large," and the Latin *molecula,* "particle." It is a giant molecule of very high molecular weight, usually greater than 10,000. Proteins and synthetic polymers are both examples of this type of molecule. It is built up by the repetition of many small, simple chemical units (monomers). In some cases the repetition is linear; in other cases the chains are interconnected to form three-dimensional networks.

The etymology is given first. Then there is a combination of logical and functional information. The technical synonym *monomers* is given in parentheses. The author also gives examples.

Academic Definition

Those of you writing research papers will often be called upon to define your terms in a special way—through a literature search. In this sort of writing, the author establishes the meaning of key terms based on theoretical and experimental literature in the field. Such definitions need to be exhaustive if the author intends to modify or change the term. Here is an example of a definition of the term *tolerance* [2]. The author first establishes the definition based on previous research. In the second paragraph, the subsidiary term *cross tolerance* is introduced. Finally, the author offers a definition, his own. (The dates in parentheses are the years of publication of the papers cited. All of these papers are listed in a reference section that follows the article.)

TOLERANCE

Coffin and Gardner (1972) define oxidant tolerance as a "phenomenon by which a previous exposure to a nonlethal dose of a specific toxicant will protect against a subsequent, normally lethal dose of the same chemical." They report this phenomenon for ozone (Stokinger et al., 1956; Matzen, 1957; Mendenhall and Stokinger, 1959; Henschler, 1960); for nitrogen dioxide (Mendenhall and Stokinger, 1959; Henschler et al., 1960); sulfur dioxide (Fairchild, 1962); and for mixed smoke and sulfur dioxide (Pattle and Burgess, 1957).

The phenomenon of "cross tolerance"—that is, the ability of a previous nonlethal dose of one chemical to protect against a subsequent lethal dose of another chemical—has been shown for ozone with hydrogen peroxide, ketene, nitrogen dioxide, phosgene, hydrogen sulfide, and nitrosyl chloride (Mendenhall and Stokinger, 1959; Henschler, 1962; Fairchild, 1967). Cross tolerance with single pulmonary irritants is well demonstrated against others singly or mixed; however, the various and individual cellular defense components of a "tolerant" lung are not protected against the toxic effects of ozone (Gardner et al., 1972).

Frank et al. (1970) and Alpert et al. (1971) demonstrated that the response was localized and protective. Both argue against an oversimplified view that early interstitial edema blocked subsequent edemagenic effect.

In a succinct recapitulation of the Davis, California, groups' ongoing research, Cross (1974) inferred that the close temporal relationship between the induction of "tolerance" to pulmonary irritants such as phosgene, thioureas, and oleic acid, and air pollutant oxidants; and the detection of increased activity of the hexose monophosphate shunt, the stimulation of a number of NADPH-generating enzymes, and increased levels of glutathione peroxidase; was evidence for the role of Type 2 cell proliferation in the phenomenon of "tolerance." He provided further historical evidence in the histochemical studies of Tyler and Pearse (1965) and in the more recently reported efforts of hormone administration having altered cell division, thereby increasing lung sensitivity to oxidants (Stephens et al., 1974a). . . .

We have concluded that the factors contributing to the phenomena of adaptation and tolerance constitute a spectrum, and prefer to define tolerance in terms of adaptation. Adaptation is a changed humoral or tissue state that enables a subject to return to normal function while enduring a persistent stress. Tolerance constitutes the humoral and tissue states by which adapted subjects, existing and functioning normally under persistent stress, are able to better withstand and more readily survive subsequent additional challenge.

Techniques in Definition: Contrast, Comparison, and Example

Contrast is the heart of the logical definition. One defines by showing the difference between *x* and *y*. The technique of contrast is basic to many scientific and technical definitions.

Here, for example, is the introduction to an article in *Scientific American* where the author establishes the terms *metastasis, benign tumor,* and *malignant tumor* through the technique of contrast [3].

CANCER METASTASIS
Most cancer patients are not killed by their primary tumor. They succumb instead to metastases: multiple, widespread tumor colonies established by malignant cells that detach themselves from the original tumor and travel through the body, often to distant sites.

If a primary tumor is detected early enough, it can usually be eliminated by surgery, radiation or chemotherapy or some combination of those treatments. Unfortunately the metastatic colonies are harder to detect and eliminate, and it is often impossible to manage all of them successfully. From a clinical point of view, then, metastasis can well be considered the conclusive event in the natural history of cancer. Moreover, the ability to metastasize is the property that uniquely characterizes a malignant tumor.

A tumor is initiated by the transformation of a normal cell into one that escapes the host's usual controls on growth and differentiation. The transformed cell proliferates to form a tumor, which may be benign or malignant. A tumor is generally considered benign if it remains similar in structure to the tissue from which it is derived, if it grows slowly by simple expansion and remains encapsulated by a layer of connective tissue, and if its cell nuclei divide almost normally, with few abnormal chromosomes. A malignant tumor, on the other hand, is usually atypical in tissue structure, grows rapidly and does not remain encapsulated, displays many abnormal nuclear divisions and chromosomes—and invades the surrounding normal tissue, shedding cells that have the ability to colonize new sites. Whereas distinctions between the benign and the malignant state based on rate of growth and degree of "abnormality" are not absolute, the ability to invade surrounding tissue and to colonize distant sites absolutely defines a malignant tumor or cancer. Understanding the biology of cancer metastasis is therefore of primary importance both for understanding the nature of cancer and for learning how to prolong or save the lives of cancer patients by destroying the most life-threatening metastatic tumor cells.

Comparisons and examples from daily life are often useful in definitions. Such comparisons give the reader a bridge to the new term. For instance, a new detector for inorganic and organic vapors is called "badge-sized" to evoke a picture of the device's dimensions.

Here is an example where the author uses the rustle of leaves and traffic on a busy street to illustrate different levels of sound.

Decibel: A unit used to measure the relative power of two sounds. In acoustics the lower threshold of human hearing is kept as a reference intensity in order to set up an absolute scale. The rustle of leaves in a gentle breeze is about 10 decibels; traffic on a busy street is about 68 decibels; the threshold of pain is 130 decibels.[1]

Summary

In his article on scientific terms, Wayne Biddle argues that the language of science may be "too complex to explain quickly, too abstract at its theoretical roots to clarify every nuance. Yet we make a mistake when we assume technology can't be explained" [4].

Don't make this mistake. You may not be able to do perfect justice to a term when the audience is outside your field, but you can get close.

To do so, use logical and operational definitions. Examples, contrasts, and comparisons from daily life are particularly useful in expanding a definition.

Avoid circular definitions and definitions that are too general or wordy.

Adjust your definition according to your audience. Whether management or marketing, they may know less than you about your own special territory. If so, modify your text so that it is comprehensible.

Do	**Don't**
1. Operational definitions	1. Circular definitions
2. Logical definitions	2. Wordy prose
3. Examples	3. Overly general definitions
4. Comparisons	4. Alphabet soup
5. Contrasts	

Literature Cited

1. "Game Theory," *McGraw-Hill Encyclopedia of Science and Technology*, vol. 16, McGraw-Hill, New York, 1977, p. 28.

2. R. F. Bils and B. R. Christie, "The Experimental Pathology of Oxidant and Air Pollutant Inhalation," in G. W. Richter and M. A. Epstein (eds.), *International Review of Experimental Pathology*, vol. 21, Academic Press, 1980, pp. 281–282.

3. G. L. Nicolson, "Cancer Metastasis," *Scientific American*, March 1979, pp. 66–67.

4. W. Biddle, "From Alpha to X-Ray," *Harper's*, August 1979, pp. 71–76. Reprinted by permission.

Exercises

1. Discuss the techniques used in these definitions, taken from the *McGraw-Hill Dictionary of Scientific and Technical Terms*.[1]

   Diaphragm [ANAT] The dome-shaped partition composed of muscle and connective tissue that separates the abdominal and thoracic cavities in mammals. [ELECTROMAG] *See* iris. [ENG] A thin sheet placed between parallel parts of a member of structural steel to increase its rigidity. [ENG ACOUS] A thin, flexible sheet that can be moved by sound waves, as in a microphone, or can produce sound waves when moved, as in loudspeaker. [OPTICS] Any opening in an optical system which controls the cross section of a beam of light passing through it, to control light intensity, reduce aberration, or increase depth of focus. [PHYS] 1. A separating wall or membrane, especially one which transmits some substances and forces but not others. 2. In general, any opening, sometimes adjustable in size, which is used to control the flow of a substance or radiation.

   Jetting [CIV ENG] A method of driving piles or well points into sand by using a jet of water to break the soil. [ENG] During molding of plastics, the turbulent flow of molten resin from an undersized gate or thin section into a thicker mold section, as opposed to laminar, progressive flow.

   Pour-Plate Culture [MICROBIO] A technique for pure-culture isolation of bacteria: liquid, cooled agar in a test tube is inoculated with one loopful of bacterial suspension and mixed by rolling the tube between the hands; subsequent transfers are made from this to a second test tube, and from the second to a third; contents of each tube are poured into separate petri dishes; pure cultures can be isolated from isolated colonies appearing on the plates after incubation.

   Scintillation [ELECTROMAG] 1. A rapid apparent displacement of a target indication from its mean position on a radar display; one cause is shifting of the effective reflection point on the target. Also known as target glint; target scintillation; wander. 2. Random fluctuation, in radio propagation, of the received field about its mean value, the deviations usually being relatively small. [NUCLEO] A flash of light produced in a phosphor by an ionizing particle or photon. [OPTICS] Rapid changes of brightness of stars or other distant, celestial objects caused by variations in the density of the air through which the light passes.

   [1]*McGraw-Hill Dictionary of Scientific and Technical Terms*, 2d ed., Daniel Lapedes (ed.), McGraw-Hill, New York, 1978, pp. 440, 569, 860, 1255, 1414, 1592.

Tanning [ENG] A process of preserving animal hides by chemical treatment (using vegetable tannins, metallic sulfates, and sulfurized phenol compounds, or syntans) to make them immune to bacterial attack, and subsequent treatment with fats and greases to make them pliable.

2. Define two of these terms. Then check your answers with those in a scientific dictionary such as the *McGraw-Hill Dictionary of Scientific and Technical Terms*.

universal joint
turnaround time
substrate
solar radiation
rheostat
polymer
hydration
French curve
dipstick

3. Here are Wayne Biddle's definitions of flux, bit, and extrapolation.[1] Discuss the author's techniques of definition. Does he use logical definitions? Examples? Comparison?

Flux. Flux is the volume or mass of energy flowing across a given area at a given time. For water in a garden hose, it might be measured in gallons per minute at the open end. For radiation, it might be rads per hour at a certain point of interest near the source.

Bit. In computer theory, the information content of any message is described in units called bits, which is short for "binary digits." Any properly phrased question can be answered by a single binary digit—0 or 1, yes or no. The operator of a typical IBM 370 computer system might have more than 100 million bits readily available to him. The human brain can handle around 10 trillion bits, though most are never used and there is some redundancy.

Extrapolation. Essentially a euphemism for "winging it." Mathematically, it is the extension of a relationship between two or more varying quantities beyond the range covered by knowledge. When you extrapolate, you tell what you think will happen based mostly upon a continuation of what has already happened. Engineers are expected to be clever extrapolators. Politicians and economists are generally less adept.

[1]Copyright © 1979 by Harper's Magazine. All rights reserved. Reprinted from the August 1979 issue by special permission.

4. Write expanded definitions of four of these terms (100 words). Use as many of the techniques given in the chapter as appropriate.

nucleic acid	plasma physics
absolute zero	laser spectroscopy
meltdown	gene splicing
pathogen	mutagenicity
toxin	pyrolysis
software	mean, median, and mode
integrated circuit	solar energy
lift	liquid crystal
fuel cell	isotope separation
photodiode	programmable gain amplifier
cathode ray tube	electrophoresis

5. Analyze the techniques in this extended definition.

GEYSER

A natural spring or fountain which discharges a column of water or steam into the air at more or less regular intervals. It may be regarded as a special type of spring. Perhaps the best-known area of geysers is in Yellowstone Park, Wyoming, where there are more than 100 active geysers and more than 1000 noneruptive hot springs. Other outstanding geysers are found in New Zealand and Iceland. The most famous geyser is probably Old Faithful in Yellowstone Park, which erupts about once an hour. Then for about 5 minutes the water spouts to a height of 100 to 150 feet. Other geysers are less regular, but some intermittently discharge water and steam to heights of 250 feet or more.

The eruptive action of geysers is believed to result from the existence of very hot rock, the relic of a body of magma, not far below the surface. The neck of the geyser is usually an irregularly shaped tube partly filled with water which has seeped in from the surrounding rock. Far down the pipe the water is at a temperature much above the boiling point at the surface, because of the pressure of the column of water above it. Its temperature is constantly increasing, because of the volcanic heat source below. Eventually the superheated water changes into steam, lifting the column of water out of the hole. The water may overflow gently at first but, as the column of water becomes lighter, a large quantity of hot water may flash into steam, suddenly blowing the rest of the column out of the hole in a violent eruption.[1]

[1]Albert N. Sayre and Ray K. Linsley, "Geyser," *McGraw-Hill Encyclopedia of Science and Technology*, vol. 6, McGraw-Hill, New York, 1977, p. 201. Reprinted by permission.

3

Writing a Technical Description

The formal word, precise but not pedantic.
T. S. Eliot

What does it look like?

How does it work?

When you answer these questions, you give a technical description. A technical description is an explanation of how a product or process looks or works. The ability to write clear, accurate descriptions is a basic skill in technical writing, whether you are doing quality control reports or new product releases, technical briefs or memos.

Technical descriptions often begin with and extend a definition. And like definition, technical description is based upon classic rhetorical patterns that originated in antiquity. These patterns, which include analysis by structure and analysis by process, are found today in such common formats as physical descriptions, process descriptions, and instructions.

The skills of definition, physical description, and process writing are interrelated; rarely in your work will you do a technical description that does not contain at least two of these patterns.

For clarity of presentation, however, this text will divide and distinguish between

1. Physical description

2. Process description

3. Instructions

Difference between Technical and Literary Description

What is the difference between a technical description and a literary description? Before you answer this question, consider these three descriptions of *tobacco*:

TOBACCO
Any plant of the genus *Nicotiana,* a tall annual with ample ovate or lanceolate leaves. The leaves are prepared by drying or manufacturing processes and used for smoking.

Tobacco is a dirty weed: I like it.
It satisfies no normal need: I like it.
It makes you thin, it makes you lean,
It takes the hair right off your bean;
It's the worst darn stuff I've ever seen: I like it.
G. Hemminger

A custom loathsome to the eye, hateful to the nose, harmful to the brain, dangerous to the lungs, and in the black stinking fume thereof nearest resembling the horrible Stygian smoke of the pit that is bottomless.
James I of England, *A Counterblast to Tobacco*

Literary and technical descriptions use different techniques. In technical writing, the writer's personality and opinions are hidden away, placed firmly in the background. For instance, in the first description of tobacco—the technical one—the reader has no idea whether the writer is for or against tobacco; in fact, the author's position is irrelevant to the description. In the other two excerpts on tobacco—the literary ones—the authors' opinions are fundamental to the descriptions.

In technical writing, the language tends to be very specialized; that is, many words are used which have meaning only for people who work in the particular field. For example, in the technical description of tobacco, the words *ovate* and *lanceolate* are used since they are part of the working vocabulary of those who have a technical knowledge of plants.

Literary descriptions are quite different. They appeal to the senses. They are impressionistic; that is, they try to evoke a subjective response in each reader through images.

The differences in style are related to differences in purpose. Literary writing seeks to *engage* the reader's emotions; technical writing attempts to *avoid* emotional response. Literary writing strives for the subjective, technical writing for the objective.

The classic goal of technical writing is to render full and exact descriptions so that other people in other places may replicate a product or process based upon the text. To aid in this goal, the language is deliberately impersonal.

How to Write a Technical Description—Three Examples

Answer these questions:

What is it? (definition)
What does it look like? (physical description)
How does it work? (process description)

Start with a definition—What is it?—and then give salient physical features and their functions.

Desiccator   Here is a description of a desiccator. It begins with an operational definition and a figure reference. The parts of the whole are then listed and described [1].

A *desiccator* is a container which is used to dry and store samples in a low moisture atmosphere (Figure 3-1). It consists of four parts:

1. The *body* in which a drying agent (desiccant) is placed.
2. A ground glass *lid* which *slides* onto the body to form an airtight seal.
3. A *plate* on which to place articles to be dried or maintained at low moisture levels.
3. The *desiccant,* a material which can absorb large amounts of water. It should also be easily regenerated by heating and be inexpensive.

This format is typical for describing simple devices. There is a definition, figure reference, and a list of parts. The parts of the

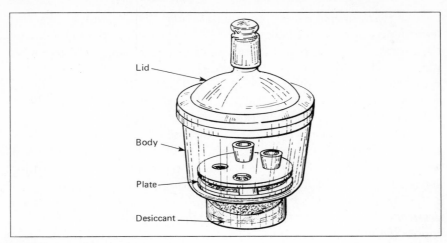

FIGURE 3-1   Desiccator

whole are listed beneath the main entry. Parts are labeled in the figure as well as text, and the reader is expected to refer from text to figure. This example adheres to an important rule in technical writing: the text and illustration complement one another. The information in the illustration is labeled so that it coordinates with and expands information in the text.

Sundial   This excerpt on the sundial is a second example of development by descriptive detail. Like the passage on the desiccator, the excerpt begins with a definition. Unlike the selection on the desiccator, however, the passage does not use a labeled parts list and accompanying figure. Instead, the information is delivered in connected, narrative discourse [2].

> An instrument for telling time by the sun. It is composed of a style that casts a shadow and a dial plate, which is the surface upon which hour lines are marked and upon which the shadow falls. The style lies parallel to earth's axis. The construction of the hour lines is based on the assumption that the apparent motion of the sun is always on the celestial equator.
>
> Sundials can be made in any form and on any surface. They may be large and stationary, or small and portable. They may be made for use in a particular place or anywhere. The most widely used form is the horizontal dial that indicates local apparent time (sun time). Other forms of the sundial indicate local mean time, and standard time.
>
> The highest form of sundial construction is found in the heliochronometer, which tells standard time with great accuracy.

Incorporated in its construction is the equation of time and the time difference in longitude between the place where it is to be used and the standard time meridian for that locality. This makes possible a sundial that can be read as a clock.

The sundial is said to be the oldest scientific instrument to come down to us unchanged. The underlying scientific principle of its construction makes it a useful device for educational purposes as well as for timekeeping.

Hamster   The following description of a hamster relies not upon illustration, but upon the building of dry, precisely stated detail [3]. It is an excellent example of the objective tone sought in careful technical description. Adjectives are used sparingly. While numbers are not used to such an extent that they make the prose impenetrable, they are used moderately to lend precision to the writing: "The burrows are not deep, rarely more than 2 ft, and consist of a large central chamber with radiating side chambers for special purposes, such as for hoarding food, for living quarters, and for excretion."

There is the liberal use of example to clarify such general terms as *large* and *small*: "The hamster uses its incisors to carry large food materials, such as carrots, while small foods, such as corn or nuts, are carried in the large cheek pouches."

Throughout the passage, the prose is used to record rather than to evoke emotion in the listener. A care for accuracy and detail is evident.

Common name for any of 14 species of rodents in family Criceti-dae. The natural range of most of the species is Asia but a few, such as the common hamster (*Cricetus cricetus*), are found in Europe.

The common hamster is a solitary, aggressive animal with interesting burrowing and hoarding habits. The burrows are not deep, rarely more than 2 ft, and consist of a large central chamber with radiating side chambers for special purposes, such as for hoarding food, for living quarters, and for excretion. Hamsters are clean animals and avoid soiling their living quarters. A so-called summer chamber is used for breeding. A single animal may hoard as much as 200 lb of roots, seeds, nuts, and various tubers, and each type of food is stored in a separate chamber. The hamster goes into his burrow in the autumn, closes off the entrance, and goes to sleep. It does not hibernate deeply and wakes up from time to time to eat.

The hamster uses its incisors to carry large food materials, such as carrots, while small foods, such as corn or nuts, are carried in the large cheek pouches. Foraging is always nocturnal. This animal also hunts lizards, birds, mice, insects, and snakes. The hamster has 16 teeth and the dental formula is I 1/1 C 0/0 Pm 0/0 M 3/3.

This rodent has scent glands on each flank, and by rubbing any structure with its flanks, it marks a territory as a warning to other hamsters. When mating, the male invades the territory of the female after first mixing his scent with hers. After mating, the female drives the male away and raises the young herself.

Describing a Process

The third question in technical descriptions—How does it work?—is a complicated one. When you answer it, you describe a process—an orderly series of steps resulting in a state or product.

A process is a kind of narrative: in a sense, you are telling a story. But the plot is not the series of casual links that make up a story, but the series of causal links that make up the process.

It is tricky to write a clear, straightforward description of a process. Beginning writers often have trouble because they plunge into too much detail without giving an overview, that is, without preparing the reader.

Five Examples of Analysis by Process

Acid Rain   Here is a description of a process [4].

Acid rain is the end product of a series of complicated chemical reactions that begins when sulfur dioxide and nitrogen oxides are spewed into the atmosphere from coal-, oil-, and gas-burning power plants, iron and copper smelters, automobile exhausts, and from such natural sources as volcanoes and wetlands. Each year the United States pumps out some 30 million tons of sulfur dioxide and 25 million tons of nitrogen oxides, most of which are man-made. Often carried aloft by the tall smokestacks that ironically were built to reduce local pollution, these gases enter the atmosphere, undergo further changes, and eventually react with moisture to form sulfuric and nitric acids. Prevailing winds can carry the pollutants for . . . thousands of miles, often across national boundaries. Half to two-thirds of the pollution falls as acid rain or snow; some of the remainder is deposited as sulfate or nitrate particles that combine with dew and mist.

The passage follows chronological order: There are four steps in the process that ends in acid rain, and the author has given each in the proper sequence. The information is presented in a narrative form. It might also have been presented as a listing:

1. The chemical reactions begin when sulfur dioxide and nitrogen oxides are spewed into the atmosphere.
2. Carried aloft by tall smokestacks, the gases enter the atmosphere and eventually react with moisture to form sulfuric and nitric acids.
3. After prevailing winds have carried pollutants thousands of miles, they fall as acid rain or snow, or are deposited as sulfate or nitrate particles that combine with dew and mist.

The information could also have been conveyed in a diagram showing the stages of the process. (See Figure 3-2.)

Regardless of the method—narrative prose, listing format, or diagram—chronological order is necessary.

Fireworks   This passage on fireworks also follows a pattern of chronological order. Note the use of descriptive adjectives such as *gritty*, and direct, visual verbs such as *burst* [5].

> Unlike most other forms of combustion, pyrotechnic displays need no oxygen from the atmosphere to burn. The chemicals themselves provide a substance to supply oxygen—usually potassium chlorate —and one to provide color and special effects—a metallic salt. The metallic salts produce the colors as they burn: strontium burns red, barium green, sodium yellow, and copper blue; magnesium provides brilliancy. After the chemicals are mixed, water is added to make a gritty black dough, which is then pressed and cut into square fragments called "stars" because they burst across the sky in colored streaks as they fly from the center of the exploding shell.

The Lure of a Cave   This process description integrates definitions of terms such as *speleotherms* directly into the text. Detail is introduced gradually, and the author uses three paragraphs to complete the description [6].

> Formed by the slow movement of water over millions of years, limestone caves are carved from calcium carbonate, or calcite, deposited on the floors of ancient seas by the gentle rain of skeletal remains of microscopic marine organisms.
>
> Once these sea floors are thrust up by the natural forces that

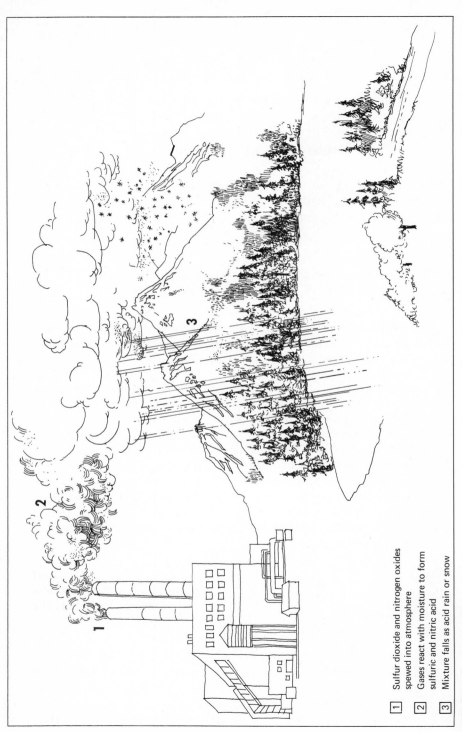

1 Sulfur dioxide and nitrogen oxides spewed into atmosphere

2 Gases react with moisture to form sulfuric and nitric acid

3 Mixture falls as acid rain or snow

FIGURE 3-2 Acid rain cycle

create mountains, the sculpting process begins. Rainwater percolating through decaying plants in the soil picks up carbon dioxide, which becomes a dilute carbonic acid solution. Seeping into rock pores and fractures, the acidic water dissolves the calcite. Following paths of least resistance, it slowly hollows out the limestone, enlarging passages as it flows toward outlet springs.

When the water drains from the cave, either because the earth is uplifted or because the water table is lowered, and the cave is opened to air, speleotherms, those breath-taking forms of cave architecture, begin to grow. Water dripping from the roof of a cave releases dissolved calcite, forming tiny stalactite structures. Sometimes the delicate tubes fill in and water flowing off the cave ceiling creeps down the outside of the deposits, broadening and lengthening them to stone icicles called stalactites. The growth rate is extremely slow, about four-thousandths of an inch a year. Drippings from the lengthening stalactites splat on the cave floor, and form up-pointed stalagmites that sometimes join with stalactites overhead to create continuous columns.

Laser Method Gives One-Pulse IR Spectrum This longer example is typical of industrial process writing; it describes a new laser method.[1]

A new laser technique . . . makes it possible to record a complete infrared spectrum with one laser pulse of about five nanoseconds' duration.

Developed . . . by IBM, the technique will be useful as an aid to understand what is happening in fast-acting chemical reactions such as combustion. . . .

The technique consists of two steps. The first is a method of generating a flash of infrared light having a broad, uniform range of frequencies. The second is what IBM scientists term an "upconversion process."

The source of light for the infrared beam is an organic dye cell pumped by the third harmonic of a high-power, solid-state neodymium/yttrium aluminum garnet laser. Part of the output from the dye cell is converted into a very uniform broadband infrared beam in a potassium vapor cell by the conventional technique, stimulated electronic Raman scattering. However, the IBM scientists achieve a frequency range about a hundred times larger by eliminating the mirrors normally used for a laser.

Infrared light that has passed through the sample is focused into a second potassium vapor cell. A beam of blue light from a

[1]Reprinted with permission of the copyright owner, The American Chemical Society, from the June 19, 1979, issue of *Chemical and Engineering News* [7].

second organic dye laser, precisely tuned to a narrow frequency range, is focused on the cell simultaneously.

In the up-conversion process, the second beam acts to raise the potassium atoms to an intermediate energy level from which they can absorb the infrared photons coming from the sample beam. As the atoms return to the ground state, they emit light with energy that is the sum of the infrared energy and the energy of the intermediate level of the potassium atoms.

As a result of this up-conversion process, the light emitted is virtually an exact replica of the infrared spectrum. But its energy is shifted into the visible region where the spectrum can be recorded on a photographic plate in a conventional spectrometer.

The infrared spectral region of greatest interest for identifying molecular species is 2 to 20 micrometers. So far, the IBM scientists have covered the region from about 2.5 to 3.7 micrometers.

There are several valuable techniques in this description:

1. *There is an overview.* The author began with a two-paragraph introduction in which he defined the technique operationally:

   A new laser technique makes it possible to record a complete infrared spectrum with one laser pulse. . . . [It] will be useful in understanding fast-acting chemical reactions such as combustion.

2. *There are lead sentences clearly indicating the pattern of organization.* The author divided the process into two steps and then announced the two steps *before* describing them.

   The technique consists of two steps. The first is a method of generating a flash of infrared light having a broad, uniform range of frequencies. The second is what IBM scientists term an "up-conversion" process.

3. *Detail is introduced within the pattern.* Having clearly stated the two steps, the author then described the first step. Only here did he introduce detail:

   The source of light for the infrared beam is an organic dye cell pumped by the third harmonic of a high-power, solid-state neodymium/yttrium aluminum garnet laser.

Summarizing, the subject is introduced clearly by definition, form, and function. Then there is a general statement of the categories that will be covered. Then each category is dealt with separately. The organization is clearly labeled by lead sentences so that the reader follows the author's direction.

Badges Monitor Worker Exposure to Gases   Here is an article which combines physical description with a technical process.[1]

> Two new types of badge-size devices for monitoring worker exposure to hazardous gases now are being produced by Du Pont's applied technology division. One type provides quick colorimetric analysis for inorganic vapors. The second type can detect as many as 140 organic vapors when coupled with gas chromatography.
>
> Both types of detectors are passive and are worn on the clothing as small badges. Although the basic purpose of the monitors is to measure individual exposure to hazardous vapors, they also may be used as stationary detectors.
>
> At present, sulfur dioxide, ammonia, and nitrogen oxide detectors are available. Additional detectors for other vapors are being developed.
>
> The inorganic vapor detectors operate by diffusion of the contaminant through a polymeric envelope and subsequent absorption in an appropriate solvent. The polymeric envelope contains the reagents for analysis of the trapped gases in compartments that are separated by breakable seals.
>
> The badges are activated by removing them from a protective outer envelope. After real or suspected exposure, the reagent seals are broken in the proper sequence, and the contents of the envelope mixed thoroughly. The intensity of the color produced is measured quantitatively in a small dedicated colorimeter that reads out the contaminant exposure level on a digital screen. The entire analysis takes place within the envelope and requires no special skill. The time required is several minutes.
>
> The exposure range of the ammonia badge, for example, is from 50 to 600 ppm-hours, which corresponds to the range from 0.125 to 1.5, the threshold limit value (TLV) assigned for that contaminant by the American Conference of Government Industrial Hygienists or by the Occupational Health & Safety Administration. The exposure range for the sulfur dioxide and nitrogen dioxide badges is from 10 to 100 ppm-hours, corresponding to a TLV of 0.25 to 2.5.
>
> According to Elbert V. Kring, staff chemist in Du Pont's applied technology division and one of the developers of the badges, the only significant ambient influences on the rate of uptake of contaminants by the badges are concentration and

[1]Reprinted with permission of the copyright owner, The American Chemical Society, from the July 9, 1979, issue of *Chemical and Engineering News* [8].

temperature. The temperature effect is small, and a correction is supplied with each badge.

The chemistry for the analyses of the inorganic contaminants has been well known for some time, Kring notes. The biggest developmental problem was in designing materials for the envelopes. Extensive laboratory and field testing has established that the detectors meet or exceed OSHA requirements for reliability, he adds.

The organic vapor monitoring system is designed around a small strip (300 mg) of activated charcoal contained in a rectangular envelope perforated with a known number of accurately sized pores. After activating the badge by removing impervious covers from the pores, the contaminant(s) diffuse through the pores and are adsorbed on the charcoal. The badge can be deactivated by replacing the impervious strips. Two sampling rates, 50 cc per minute and 100 cc per minute, can be selected by using one or both sides of the badge. Each side has an impervious cover over the porous badge.

To analyze for contaminants, the charcoal strip is removed and placed in a vial containing a set amount of solvent. The solvent desorbs the contaminants from the charcoal strip, and analysis is by conventional gas chromatography.

Ambient air velocity has little effect on the sampling effectiveness of the badge, Kring says. Only when air velocity drops below 15 feet per minute does a stagnation effect deplete the available contaminant. Similarly, the angle of incidence of wind on the surface of the badge has no detectable effect. The badge is virtually independent of pressure effects and is only slightly affected by temperature.

Depending on the organic contaminant adsorbed by the charcoal, the sampling range varies between 0.2 ppm-hour and 4000 ppm-hours. An even greater range is possible if a pumped system is employed. The desorption efficiency for common vapors, such as benzene, toluene, and carbon tetrachloride, is between 95 and 100%. Larger molecules, such as acrylonitrile, show smaller desorption efficiencies, but they are well within National Institute for Occupational Safety & Health requirements and give reproducible results.

As with the inorganic vapor detectors, the analytical procedures for the organic badges are well established. Again the main developmental problem was one of materials engineering.

Diffusion coefficients of various vapors through the pores of the organic badges virtually duplicate the accepted literature values for those vapors, Kring says. The passage of vapors through the pores is controlled strictly by molecular diffusion.

The easy availability of inexpensive and accurate pollution-monitoring badges may present a problem if improperly used,

Kring cautions. Self-appointed "analysts" may arouse public opinion needlessly, relying on information gathered with the new devices, he warns. However, he has no doubts that the badges will reflect accurately their exposure to contaminants.

The article may be divided into two parts. The introduction is in the first three paragraphs. It answers the basic questions— What is it? What does it do?—immediately and in plain, direct language. There are two types of devices for monitoring hazardous gases. One type is for organic vapors, the other for inorganic vapors.

These three paragraphs follow the guidelines for writing a technical description. The author has defined the mechanism immediately, giving the function in as few words as possible. Necessary physical detail is given using comparisons that help the reader imagine the object. In this case, the devices are called "badge-size" to give the reader a sense of how small they are. This is more effective than stating the dimensions, for the comparison with lapels gives the reader an immediate notion of the dimensions involved.

The more complicated question—How does it work?—is saved for after the first three paragraphs. Then the two different processes are introduced by lead sentences:

1. "The *inorganic* vapor detectors operate by . . . " followed by five paragraphs of detail;
2. "The *organic* vapor monitoring system . . . " followed by five paragraphs of detail.

Three Techniques in Process Writing

Use Transitional Words and Phrases *Transitional words* are those that take the reader from one idea to the next. You make use of transitions when you connect parts of a report with such expressions as *first, second, therefore,* and *in conclusion.*

There are two types of transitional words that are particularly useful in describing processes: spatial transitional words and time transitional words.

Spatial words are those that help the reader follow an extended physical description. Examples include *on the left, on the right, above, below, connected to, farther, extending along the perimeter, next.*

Time-order words are those that help the reader follow a chronological description. These include *first, second, soon, then, afterward, later.*

If you write a description of a process in narrative form—in paragraphs where you take the reader from one stage to the next—you will find the systematic use of transitional words invaluable.

Consider, for example, this excerpt from *Science 80* on the process of producing synthetic oil [9].

> The process involves draining the muskeg swamp and removing vegetation and soil covering from the tar sands. Then the deposits are mined with a bucketwheel excavator and carried to the extraction plant on conveyer belts, the longest of which is more than eight miles. At the plant, the material is mixed with hot alkaline water, rendering the tar less dense so that it separates from the sand and floats to the surface. The sand is allowed to settle out. The tar is then fed to a refinery where the large, organic molecules are broken down, and the resulting mixture distilled to make kerosene and other petroleum "fractions." After treating to remove sulfur, some components are blended to make a synthetic crude oil that is piped to conventional refineries further south; other components are burned to generate power from the mining operation.

The author has deliberately used a series of transitional words to connect the stages in the process (emphasis has been added). The word *then* introduces the second sentence, the phrase *at the plant* introduces the third sentence. Words indicating time order—such as *first, then, later, afterward*—are used throughout the description to aid the reader in following the process.

> The process involves draining the muskeg swamp and removing vegetation and soil covering from the tar sands. **Then** the deposits are mined with a bucketwheel excavator and carried to the extraction plant on conveyer belts, the longest of which is more than eight miles. **At the plant**, the material is mixed with hot alkaline water, rendering the tar less dense so that it separates from the sand and floats to the surface. The sand is allowed to settle out. The tar is **then** fed to a refinery **where** the large, organic molecules are broken down, and the resulting mixture distilled to make kerosene and other petroleum "fractions." **After** treating to remove sulfur, some components are blended to make a synthetic crude oil that is piped to conventional refineries **further** south; other components are burned to generate power for the mining operation.

Emphasize Cause and Effect   When you describe a process, you essentially describe a chain of causes and effects. Underscore this relationship by the use of words that make the causes and their effects clear to the reader. Use such phrases as *consequently, thus, as a result, therefore, because of this, for this reason*. They will help direct reader attention to the important links in the causal chain you are describing.

Use a Sequence of Captioned Pictures Use illustrations and caption them so that stages in the process are shown. Use an orderly scheme in the illustrations. If you use a simple callout, coordinate references in the text so that prose and illustrations agree. (See Chapter 11, "Effective Illustration," for further detail.)

Guidelines for Describing a Process

1. *Begin with an overview.* Use the opening paragraph or paragraphs to define essential terms and to establish a general description of form and function.
2. *Maintain chronological order.* You may use either narrative prose, listing format, or flowcharts and diagrams.
3. *For longer descriptions, use lead sentences that clearly indicate your pattern of organization.* For instance, divide a process into three parts. Write a lead sentence saying, "This process had three steps: step *a*, step *b*, and step *c*."
4. *Introduce details within this pattern.* Once you have indicated your scheme of organization, you can introduce detail within it. You may need two paragraphs for step *a*, and three paragraphs for step *b*. Your reader will be able to follow you because you have established a framework from the beginning.

This is an effective way to describe a complicated process. Instead of losing your readers in a welter of detail, you introduce them gradually and logically to the subject.

This technique brings to mind the story of a minister who was often interviewed on the secret of his success as a public speaker.

"I tell them what I am going to tell them," he said. "Then I tell them," he added. "And then," he concluded, "I tell them what I've told them."

Summary

Here are general guidelines for writing a technical description.

1. *Definition.* Define the object, mechanism, product, or process immediately.

2. *Form and function.* Give necessary physical details, using spare, accurate language that will help the reader picture what you are describing. When appropriate, use illustrations and caption them so that they complement the text.
3. *Definition + form + function = overview.* A combination of definition, form, and function should give readers an overview or general introduction to the object, product, or process. In this way you will introduce them to the unfamiliar in a direct and orderly manner.

Literature Cited

1. R. L. Pecsok and K. Chapman (eds.), *Modern Chemical Technology*, vol. 1, American Chemical Society, Washington, D.C., 1971, p. 96.

2. Robert N. Mayall, "Sundial," *McGraw-Hill Encyclopedia of Science and Technology*, vol. 13, McGraw-Hill, New York, 1977, p. 297.

3. Charles B. Curtin, "Hamster," in ibid., vol. 6, p. 379.

4. "Rain of Troubles," *Science 80*, July/August 1980, p. 75.

5. "Stars and Snakes Forever," in ibid., p. 80.

6. "The Lure of the Cave," in ibid., p. 87.

7. "Laser Method Gives One-Plus IR Spectrum," *Chemical and Engineering News*, June 19, 1979, p. 46.

8. "Badges Monitor Worker Exposure to Gases," *Chemical and Engineering News*, July 9, 1979, p. 21.

9. "Synfuels," *Science 80*, July/August 1980, p. 50. Reprinted by permission.

Exercises

1. Describe a clinical thermometer. First give a definition. Then describe parts. Then tell how it works.
2. Write a short technical description (200 to 400 words) of one of the following devices:
   (a) a felt-tipped pen
   (b) a soldering gun
   (c) pliers
   (d) a syringe

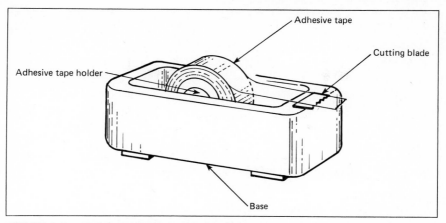

FIGURE 3-3   Adhesive tape dispenser

3. Here are two versions of a technical description of a desk-top tape dispenser. Edit them. That is, make corrections in the text that will make the writing more effective.

Adhesive Tape Dispenser

An adhesive tape dispenser is a divice that permits the user to obtain the desired length of adhesive tape easily with one hand.

The adhesive tape dispenser consists of three main parts: the base, the adhesive tape holder, and the cutting blade. (See Figure 3-3.)

The Base

The base serves as the mounting surface for the adhesive tape holder and cutting blade. The base is made out of plastic. It is formed by a process which involves the injection of hot molten plastic into a mold where the plastic is left to harden through cooling. The base has a heavy bottom to prevent the dispenser from tipping over or sliding forward. The bottom is covered with rubber to further help prevent the dispenser from sliding. The base has grooves molded inside for the adhesive tape holder. (See Figure 3-4.)

The grooves prevent the adhesive tape from being detached from the base when pulled forward. But the grooves allow the tape to roll freely. The base is shaped like an ellipse when viewed from the top. The top part of the base is hollow, and that space permits the adhesive tape to be placed there.

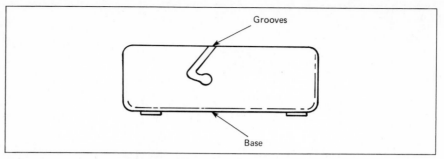

FIGURE 3-4   Dispenser cut in half to show grooves

The Adhesive Tape Holder

The adhesive tape holder holds the tape and attaches it to the base. The holder is made out of plastic using the same construction method for the base. The holder is round with a rod molded through its center rotation axis. See Figure 3-5. Its outer diameter is the same as the inner diameter of the tape and its width is also the same as the width of the tape. These dimensions allow the tape holder to fit tightly into the hole of the adhesive tape. The tips of the rod fit into the grooves in the base. This allows the tape to roll freely around its rotation axis and to unreel the wound tape.

The Cutting Blade

The cutting blade is a cutting edge that permits the user to trim the tape to the desired length. The cutting blade is made out of steel. It is shaped like a saw, Figure 3-6; this shape permits faster cutting of the tape and an edge that will not dull easily. The cutting blade is fastened to the base by a rivet. The cutting blade also serves as a surface for holding the edge of the adhesive tape.

The adhesive tape dispenser provides the ease of unreeling

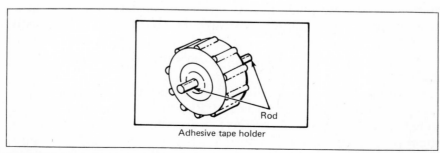

Adhesive tape holder

FIGURE 3-5   Adhesive tape holder

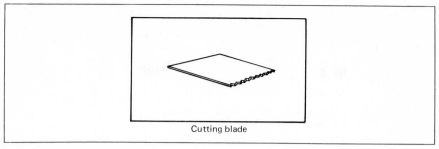

Cutting blade

FIGURE 3-6   Cutting blade

and cutting of an adhesive tape which make it a very useful office tool.

The Tape Dispenser

The tape dispenser has two functions:

(a) It holds the roll of tape firmly, and
(b) It may be used to remove tape neatly from the roll.

The dispenser holds the roll on a spindle so that it may be rotated about the axis as it is pulled.

As tape is pulled from the roll in the direction indicated by Figure 3-7, the roll rotates freely on the spindle. When the desired amount of tape has been pulled off, it may be separated using the serrated metal edge. The free end of the roll remains attached to the cutting edge so that the roll of tape is ready for the next time it is needed.

4. The following article, reprinted from *Chemical and Engineer-*

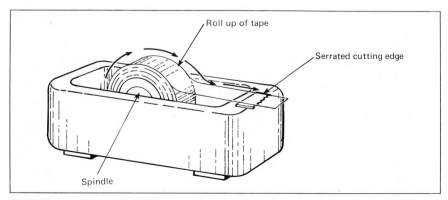

FIGURE 3-7   Tape dispenser

ing News, is a new product release on a flue gas scrubber. The first paragraph gives a brief, clear definition. The description of the process is introduced in the third paragraph. As in many other examples given in this chapter, it is clear that a process is best presented after definitions and basic overview of form and function have been provided. Using this article as a model, write a new product release on a desk stapler.

NEW FLUE GAS SCRUBBER USES DRY ABSORBENT[1]

A new flue gas scrubber requiring no water and yielding stable, nonsoluble by-products is being marketed by Energy & Pollution Controls Inc. (EPC), a subsidiary of Flick-Reedy Corp., Bensenville, Ill. The EPC dry reactor, when used in conjunction with a commercial cartridge bag filter unit, can remove up to 80% of the sulfur dioxide and virtually all of the particulate matter issuing from most commercial boilers fired with coal.

Key element in the EPC dry scrubber is a conical reactor for contacting and reacting suitable absorbents with flue gas. Lime, limestone, and soda ash have been used successfully as absorbents.

Flue gas enters the reactor through a diverging nozzle. A rapidly rotating disk in the throat of the nozzle distributes the finely divided absorbent throughout the flue gas. Intimate contact is maintained long enough, through recirculation and high turbulence, to permit absorption and reaction. The disk is driven by a hydraulic motor, which is internally pressurized to eliminate bearing contamination by hot gases or particulates. Hydraulic drive fluid also cools and lubricates the motor.

Reactive absorbent can be recycled several times before being exhausted. Fly ash and other particulates pass on to be trapped in the cartridge bag filter. The only products other than the cleaned gas are spent absorbent, usually gypsum anhydrite, and the fly ash from the bag house. Both are fine dry powders. The absence of water virtually has eliminated corrosion problems in the system, even in the case of mild steel materials.

According to Grant T. Hollett Jr., vice president of EPC, the total pressure drop over the system is less than 6 inches of water. The reactor is available in several sizes up to 25,000-cfm capacity. Larger flows are handled by parallel multiples and the largest installation now being offered will treat 250,000 cfm.

The systems are intended for operators of small and medium-size industrial boilers who must treat exhaust in compliance with regulatory requirements. In most cases the boilers are fired with locally purchased coal. The immediate market, says

[1]Reprinted with permission of the copyright owner, The American Chemical Society, from *Chemical and Engineering News*.

Hollett, includes those Illinois operators who want to use high-sulfur Illinois coal.

The alternative to using Illinois coal is to import low-sulfur western coal. An EPC analysis of comparative economics indicates that the dry scrubber will permit the use of Illinois coal, satisfy the pollution regulations, and still yield a savings as much as $4.00 per ton over imported western coal. This is not claimed to be typical of experience elsewhere but the economics are still attractive.

5. Write a one- to two-page (typed) process description on one of the following subjects:
   (a) How an earthquake develops
   (b) How a volcano erupts
   (c) How lichen forms on tree bark
   (d) The crumbling of concrete roadways after the rigors of winter
   (e) Life in airplanes
   (f) A biological process

6. This physical description by Peter Freuchen describes the igloo used by polar Eskimos.[1] Analyze Freuchen's technique. How has he organized the description? That is, what pattern is used to lead the reader through the igloo? What is the tone? Are there occasional literary touches in the otherwise spare language? Notice the description of the Eskimo lamp. Is it well executed? Why or why not?

> You enter the winter house through an entrance tunnel, usually about fifteen feet long so as to provide both ventilation and protection against the outside cold. Since the house usually faces the sea, it is on a hill which the horizontal tunnel cuts into. The floor of the tunnel is laid with flat stones, the walls are piled-up stones, and the ceiling is made of flat stones covered with peat or turf. It is low, so that you have to crawl in on your hands and knees. . . .
>
> The entrance tunnel ends up just inside the front wall of the house itself, and you find yourself a couple of feet below the level of the floor, which you then step onto. Now you are in a room, rarely more than fifteen feet in diameter and roughly circular, inasmuch as the wide front wall, the converging side walls, and the narrower back wall of the house are curved evenly into each other. It is about nine feet high from floor to ceiling, but the roof slants

[1] P. Freuchen, *Book of the Eskimos*, World Publishing, Cleveland, 1961, pp. 40–46. Copyright © 1961 by Dagmar Freuchen. Reprinted by permission of the Harold Matson Company, Inc.

toward the back wall. Besides, the whole back half of the room is filled from wall to wall by a big platform about three feet high. Since the house is sunk a little into the earth to give it extra protection against the gales, the platform usually represents the level of the ground outside. It is laid with flat stones which are extended along the front edge so as to create an overhang, under which there is storage space. On the sides, they extend into two side platforms that rest on stone supports, but also have storage space under them. What is left of the floor, which is also laid with flat stones, is then only a space about seven feet square in the front center part of the house. It serves well when game or frozen meat has to be brought in for the family meal.

The walls of the house are double, two layers of stones with peat or earth filled in between them. The roof is made of flat stones, deftly built up and overlapping each other, at last reaching so far toward the center that a main stone slab can rest on them, their outer ends being weighed down with boulders for stability. The size of a house largely depends upon how many large flat stone slabs can be found for this purpose. Only when an extra large house is wanted will the Eskimos solve the problem by building pillars up from the platform to support the ceiling. . . .

The platform in the house is the family's sleeping bunk. Here they sleep in a neat row with their feet toward the back wall. Against the back wall are usually piled extra clothes and skins so that it isn't too cold. The bunk is covered with a thick layer of dried grass, upon which skins of musk ox and caribou are spread. The family and its eventual guests sleep under blankets made of fox, hare, caribou, and eider duck skins. The natural colors of these animals' feathers and fur are used to make beautiful patterns.

Only when it is overcrowded are the side bunks used for sleeping, but they are less desirable because they are colder. Otherwise, the blubber lamps are placed on the side bunks. One of them may be used to place a piece of meat or game on for everybody to nibble on. Then there is a bucket or sealskin basin for ice to thaw in for drinking water.

On the other side bunk, there would then be knives, trays, and other household gear. The storage space under the bunks is used for skins and other property. On the walls may be pegs of caribou ribs or antler for hanging things on. Under the ceiling is suspended a framework of wood or bones. As it is for drying clothes on, it is directly above one of the blubber lamps. It is very important especially for the kamiks and stockings. . . .

The house has one window, which is in the front wall above the entrance. The windowpane is made out of the intestines of the big bearded seal, which are split and dried and sewn together, then framed with sealskin, and the whole thing is put in the wall opening and fastened to the sides. One cannot see through such a window, but it lets quite a good light through. At one side there is a little peephole to look out of. More important, the ventilation of the house is provided through another and larger opening in the upper corner of the windowpane. Fresh air comes in through the entrance tunnel and is often regulated by a skin covering the entrance hole. This skin, when weighed down with a couple of stones, will also keep the dogs out of the house when the family is asleep. The dogs are rarely allowed in the house, anyway, but in very rough weather they may be resting in the entrance tunnel.

The flow of air out through the hole in the windowpane is regulated by a whisk of hay stuck in it. It is easy to see when the air is getting close because the flame in the blubber lamp starts to burn low. And although no draft is ever felt, the house is always well ventilated. . . .

The Eskimo lamp is cut out of soapstone. It has a deep depression in the middle, at one side of which a whisk of long-burning moss is placed. Lumps of blubber are put in the lamp, and as the moss burns, the blubber melts and is sucked up in the moss to be consumed. By placing the lamp on three stones or on a tripod, and slanting it at the right angle, one can regulate the flow of blubber to the side where the moss-wick is. A stick serves to open or close the wick, making it narrow or wide according to whether a large or a small flame is wanted. This demands great practice, and only Eskimo women know this art to perfection. The lamp is kept burning at all times; only when the house goes to sleep the flame is made very narrow, and the lamp is filled up with fresh blubber. If it is properly regulated it burns easily through the period of sleep.

There are two types of lamps. One is oval, with a slanting bottom to help the regular flow of the blubber; the other is kind of shell-shaped, with a row of little knobs along the long curved side. This latter is a prototype of the Thule Culture, and is the one used by the Polar Eskimos.

This is rather significant, for there are few household possessions that play as big a part in Eskimo domestic life as the lamp. The wife has to tend the lamp, and it belongs under her jurisdiction. The more lamps she can take care of the cleverer she is, and many lamps are a sign of wealth and prestige. Since there rarely is any permanent place called home, the lamps become the symbol of the home.

7. Describe the room in which you are studying technical writing (one to two pages, typed).
8. Write a physical description of a place that you can observe closely. Some possibilities are a physics or chemistry laboratory, the computer room, a supermarket, the courtyard or central area in front of the main building in your school or

place of business, the cafeteria or one of the eating rooms in your school or place of business. Use illustrations if necessary, and caption them so that they complement the text. The written description should be two to three pages (typed). First reread the excerpt by Freuchen (Exercise 6), which may prove useful as a model.

9. Write a short description (400 to 600 words) of one of the following:

    (a) the face of a clock radio

    (b) the dashboard of an automobile

    (c) a control panel of your choice

10. Write a description of two to three pages (typed) about one of the following:

    (a) a glider

    (b) a three-speed bicycle

    (c) the spinal column

    (d) a solar water heater

    (e) an elevator

4

Writing Instructions

When all else fails, read the instructions.
— Sign in a laboratory

Instructions are a type of process writing. Rather than use narrative form, however, the writer presents a series of steps directly to the reader.

Here is a paragraph taken from the article you read earlier on gas detectors. In this first example it is written in narrative form.

> The badges are activated by removing them from a protective outer envelope. After real or suspected exposure, the reagent seals are broken in the proper sequence, and the contents of the envelope mixed thoroughly.

This same information could have been presented as a set of instructions:

HOW TO ACTIVATE BADGE

1. Remove the badge from its outer envelope.

2. Break the reagent seals in proper sequence and mix contents of envelope.

The content is the same, but the rhetorical stance—the position of the writer in relation to the audience—has shifted. In instructions, the writer addresses the reader *directly* rather than indirectly. Further, it is assumed that the reader will actually enact the instructions. If you are writing a murder mystery and omit an element in the plot, the most damage you're likely to do is to the nerves of the reader who likes neat endings; but if you are writing a testing procedure and omit an element, the experiment may be invalidated by the government agency spot-checking your experimental protocols.

The test of any set of written instructions is its comprehensibility. The trick is to write in such a way that the reader can follow what is written. If you have ever opened the package for an unassembled object and sat down with the "14 Easy Steps to Assembly," only to discover that steps 4, 7, and 9 were unaccountably missing, you've learned that instructions are the one type of writing where the *reader* is completely at the mercy of the *writer*. Clarity, accuracy, and completeness are of the utmost importance.

Unfortunately, it is easy to accidentally omit steps in instructions. Typically the writer is an expert at the job being described, and anyone who is extremely familiar with a procedure may assume that the person following the instructions shares an ability to read between the lines. This is rarely true. The procedure may be obvious to the writer, but it is likely to be unfamiliar to the user, who will depend upon the printed word for specific guidance.

Your audience will vary. You may write instructions for technicians assisting in a laboratory, or for staff who will execute testing procedures. You may write protocols that state formally the standard instructions or standard operating procedures (SOPs) for a particular routine. In the drug industry, for instance, there are voluminous SOPs—detailed procedural codes for each step in the development, testing, and manufacture of drugs— required by the federal agencies that monitor each step in a drug's development. If you write this sort of SOP, your audience will be not only people who execute the procedures but also government officials who will read the text and decide whether the company is complying with government guidelines.

Writing Instructions for Tying a Necktie

Since you will often write instructions for jobs that are familiar to you, but unfamiliar to your reader, we'll start with an example within that context. The instructions are for tying a necktie—a mundane act that is probably perfectly familiar to you, the doer. The procedure is second nature to most men, and newly fashionable for women. Neither group, though, is likely to have attempted to place words to the act.

Before you read the sample instructions here, try your own hand at writing instructions for tying a necktie. Assume that your reader is a newcomer to the job—perhaps the son of this newspaper columnist [1].

> My son called the other afternoon from Florida. He was on his way to some puberty rite at which he would be required to make a speech on mathematics. He was wearing a suit. He needed to complete his suit with a tie. He had forgotten how to tie a tie. Imagine, if you can, trying to explain how to tie a tie on the telephone. I went to get a tie so that I could attach words to the manipulations necessary to achieve the noose. His sister held the phone on his end to leave both his hands free. I found that I couldn't knot my tie because I had wrapped it around the telephone cord. We were not serious people.

Remember that the bottom line in instructions is comprehensibility. Therefore, test your own instructions by reading them aloud and having someone else follow them—*someone who does not already know how to tie a tie*. If you are using this book in a classroom, there are probably two or three naive subjects in the room. Choose one of them to act out your instructions.

Here is a sample set of instructions.

THE NECKTIE
Tie should be placed around neck in such a way that both ends hang down in front of the body. Put the wider side on your left. Pull the wider side down so that it's twice as long as the thinner side. Cross the two ends so that the wider side goes over the thinner side. Grasp the wider side about 3 inches from the crossing point and push the tie toward the left. Continue rotating the wider side and stop when the wider side is in back of the narrower side. Bring the wider side over the top and down the front, passing it underneath the loop you created in the first turn.

Hear are some criticisms of this piece of writing.

1. The title is not focused. Retitle it "How to Tie a Necktie."
2. There is no opening statement giving the reader an overview. Something simple but direct, such as "Follow these five steps to tie a necktie. Reverse directions if you are left-handed," would have provided a simple introduction.
3. A listing format would improve the layout.
4. Each step in the instructions should begin with a verb. Each verb should be in command or imperative form. As the passage stands, many of the verbs—the information the reader needs first and foremost—are buried. "Place tie around neck" is preferable to the passive "Tie should be placed around neck." Beginning each step with an imperative makes it easier for the reader, who is swiveling from instructions to object, to keep an eye on the verb.
5. Instructions should be tested on a naive subject for comprehensibility. These, for instance, aren't explicit. If we try to do what the writer says and "place the tie around the neck," we'll end up with a noose instead of a necktie. The writer must have meant, "under the collar." And even if we place the tie under the collar, we'll soon find that the tie is inside-out unless the writer tells us to keep the side with the seam next to the chest.
6. What about simple illustrations? They would be helpful in describing how to tie the knot.

Here are two sets of instructions for tying a necktie. Read them, correct them for accuracy and comprehensibility, and compare them with the ones you've written.

HOW TO TIE A NECKTIE
There are seven steps to tying a necktie. They are as follows:

1. Place necktie around your neck with the broad end to the right and the seam turned in. (See Figure 4-1.)
2. Adjust the necktie so that the length of the broad end is twice that of the narrow end.
3. Place the broad end over the short end as shown in Figure 4-2.
4. Using the broader end make two complete revolutions around

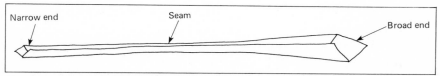

FIGURE 4-1　Principal parts of necktie

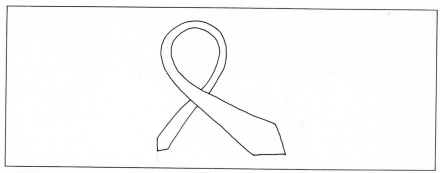

FIGURE 4-2   Broad over narrow

the narrow end. There is now one loop formed. This is shown in Figure 4-3.

5. Make half a revolution around the short end with the broad end. There are now two loops formed.
6. Carry the broad end through the V shape and between the two loops formed in steps 4 and 5 as shown in Figure 4-4.
7. Pull the broad end until the joint formed is firm. This is shown in Figure 4-5. The operation is now complete.

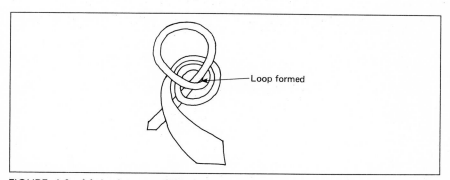

FIGURE 4-3   Make two revolutions

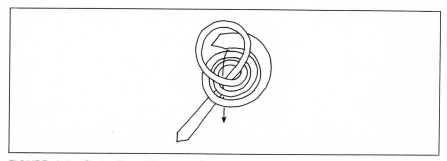

FIGURE 4-4   Carry through

FIGURE 4-5   Completed knot

HOW TO TIE A NECKTIE

The following steps will instruct the reader on how to tie a necktie:

1. Put on shirt, button the collar button, and turn up the collar.
2. Place the tie around your collar, with the seam toward you, and let it lie in front of you. Put the wider side on your left side. Pull the wider side down so that it's twice as long as the thinner side.
3. Cross the wider side over the thinner side. See Figure 4-6. Switch hands so that your right hand is now holding the wider end.

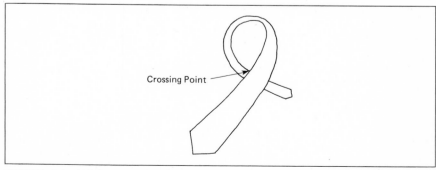

FIGURE 4-6   Wider over thinner side

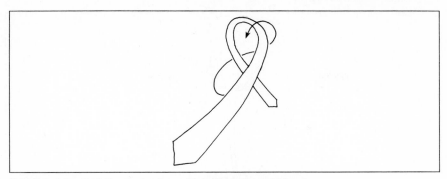

FIGURE 4-7   Pull tie around and into hole above knot.

4. While holding the crossing point with your left index finger and thumb, grasp the wider side about 3 inches from the crossing point and push the tie toward the left under the crossing point. Take your right hand over the point, grab the wider side, and push it totally through the hole above the point. See Figure 4-7. Take your left fingers out of the knot just made.

5. Now while holding the tie knot with your right index finger and thumb, hold the wider side about 4 inches from the knot and pull it across the knot and into the space above the knot. (See Figure 4-8.)

6. With your right index finger open the gap between the part of the tie over the knot, and the knot itself. Tuck the wider piece totally through the gap. (See Figure 4-9.)

7. Hold the sides of the tie knot with your right index finger and thumb and adjust the tie by pulling the narrower end until the tie lies snugly against the collar. Pull down the collar. (See Figure 4-10.)

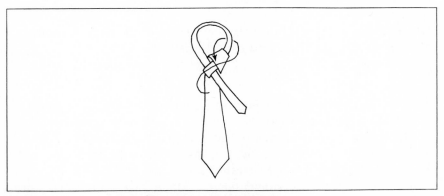

FIGURE 4-8   Across the knot and into open space

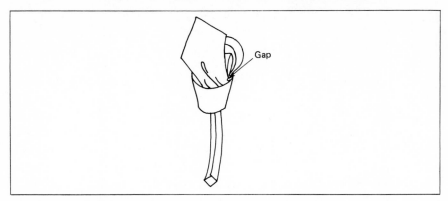

FIGURE 4-9   Pulling the wider piece through the gap

FIGURE 4-10   Finished tie

Use of Illustration in Technical Instructions

Illustrations are useful in technical instructions; they may replace a great deal of writing, and do a better job.

If you use illustrations, be sure to remember the following steps:

1. *Caption all illustrations.* Beginning writers often think a picture speaks a thousand words. It won't unless you give the reader the proper cues beneath the picture. Your captions should identify and elaborate on the visual information. (For a detailed discussion of illustration see Chapter 11.)
2. *Coordinate the captions with the test.* Make sure your illustrations actually illustrate the points you want to make. Beginning writers tend to add illustrations that have no logical connection

to the text. The puzzled reader plods along, expecting to find some relationship between the illustrations and the text, but no such relationship materializes.

Example: Dry Column Chromatography   Here is a set of instructions for dry column chromatography [2]. Dry column chromatography is a technique used to separate mixtures into components which can then be identified. The person puts the sample in the column and adds a solvent. As the mixture and solvent move down the column, the components of the mixture move at different rates, separating into layers. When the process is finished, the separated zones can be identified.

Analyze these instructions. Are there ways that the writing could be improved? What are strengths and weaknesses of the language, the layout, and the use of pictures and captions?

HOW TO USE DRY COLUMN CHROMATOGRAPHY
1. Prepare the nylon column by tying the tubing at one end and inserting a small pad of cotton or glass wool.
2. Punch several holes in bottom of tubing to allow trapped air to escape.
3. Fill the nylon tubing with adsorbent using a funnel. Make certain that the adsorbent is compacted. This can be achieved by

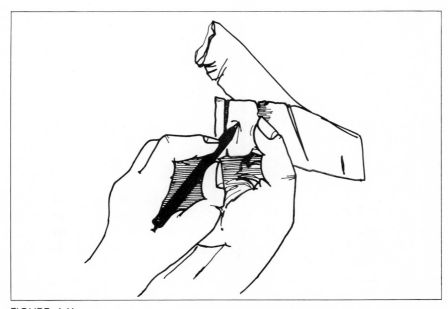

FIGURE 4-11

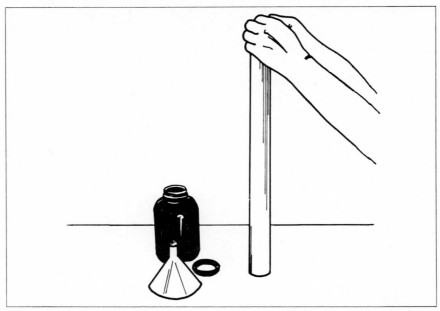

FIGURE 4-12

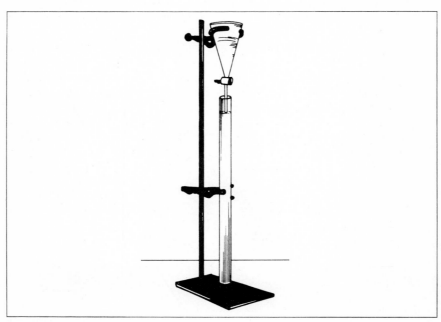

FIGURE 4-13

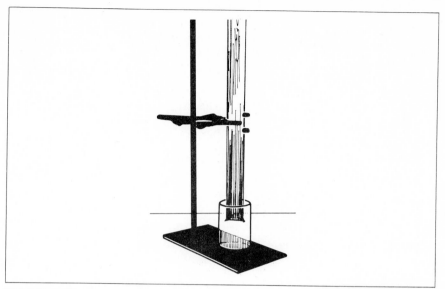

FIGURE 4-14

shaking or tapping the column. A properly compacted column can be held upright using a ring stand and tube clamp.

4. Add the sample to be separated to the top of the column either as a concentrate or adsorbate.

5. Add the appropriate solvent to the column. Maintain a 1–2 cm head. (Do not let the column run "dry.") The solvent moves down the column by capillary action and separates the mixture. When the solvent reaches the bottom of the column the separation is complete.

6. There is no elution taking place. For visible chromophores the separated zones are easily identified and the column is marked and cut with a razor or knife for isolating the zones. With U.V. absorbers use a 254 energy lamp (low pressure Hg) to identify the zones, mark and cut for isolation.

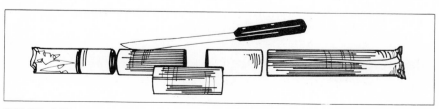

FIGURE 4-15

Summary

Here are guidelines that will help you write clear instructions.

1. *Stance.* Who are readers? How much do they know already? What do you want them to know?
2. *Title.* Does your title focus on the specific subject of the instructions?
3. *Lead.* Do you have a brief, introductory statement to guide the reader? If you are going to present five steps, say so. Begin, "Follow these five steps in assembling this equipment. Don't let the reader stumble gradually onto the secret of what you intend to say. State the topic at the beginning.
4. *Order.* Maintain strict chronological order in instructions. If someone is following a process that you are detailing, sequence is essential. If there are preliminary steps that must be taken before the main steps, say so. Use a subheading, "Before You Begin," and explain any prior activities that must be undertaken before the actual procedure. If there are materials that must be on hand before beginning the procedure, list them *before* the instructions.
5. *Style.* Use imperatives when possible. Say "Wear safety goggles" instead of "Safety goggles must be worn." Imperatives speak directly to the reader. They are easier to understand than passive instructions. The important part of the information— the verb—is right at the front. It makes following the instructions much simpler.
6. *Pattern.* Use subheads to help you organize the information. If it is complicated, introduce steps with clear statements such as "Follow these five steps:"; list the five steps below.
7. *Illustrations.* Caption all illustrations so that the information complements the text. A picture is worth 1000 words only if it has a caption that connects it clearly and unambiguously to the text.
8. *Trial run.* Test the content for accuracy, clarity, and correct order of presentation. Remember that the test of good instructions is someone else's ability to execute them.

Literature Cited

1. J. Leonard, "Private Lives," *The New York Times*, May 29, 1980. Copyright © 1979/80 by The New York Times Company. Reprinted by permission.

2. "Dry Column Chromatography." Reprinted by permission of ICN Pharmaceuticals, Inc., Cleveland, Ohio 44128.

Exercises

1. Here is a set of rules for safety in a polymer laboratory. Please edit the rules so that the language is more direct.

Polymer Laboratory Safety

Most chemical reagents used in polymer synthesis and processing are highly toxic, flammable, and even explosive. Particularly insidious are the common solvents such as benzene, which cause chronic poisoning on prolonged exposure. Many reagents, such as metal-organic catalysts and peroxide initiators, either ignite spontaneously in contact with air or moisture, or are actually explosive. These liquids or their vapors can be ignited not only by open flames, but by sparks in electrical contacts. Since polymerization reactions are inherently dangerous, laboratory safety precautions are required.

The following rules will be adhered to at all times:

1. Safety goggles must be worn during all chemical experiments.
2. No smoking and eating are permitted in the laboratory.
3. One should familiarize oneself with the safety materials, such as fire extinguishers, fire blankets and eye wash, etc., and their location.
4. All hazardous reagents should be used in a well-ventilated hood.
5. Any flammable reagent should be kept away from motors, ovens or any hot area.
6. Waste hazardous reagents should never be poured into a sink; they must be collected in a waste can.
7. Reaction vessels should be protected by wrapping them in metal screen or wire mesh.

2. Figure 4-16 shows a set of instructions. Which techniques has the writer used? Are the instructions effective?
3. Here are two versions on instructions for doing string art. Both were written by Robert DePrisco. What are the differences

extra strength

efferdent

- Removes stubborn stains between teeth in minutes
- Works fast
- Leaves dentures fresh-tasting and odor free
- Whitens and brightens
- Fights plaque on dentures

Directions for daily use:

1 Drop one tablet into enough very warm water to cover denture.

2 Place denture, bridge, or orthodontic appliance into effervescing blue solution.

3 When the blue clears (10-12 minutes) denture is cleaned, odor free.

4 Remove and rinse denture thoroughly. It's fresh-tasting, ready to use.

For best results use at least one a day.

Your dentures may be safely soaked in Efferdent overnight.

See Your dentist regularly.

CAUTION: KEEP OUT OF REACH OF CHILDREN. AS WITH ANY EFFECTIVE CLEANSER, DO NOT PLACE TABLETS IN MOUTH.

FIGURE 4-16

between the first and second versions? Is the second version more effective? Why or why not?

Equipment
1. Thin string comparable to sewing thread (slightly glossy).
2. Three hundred $\frac{1}{2}$ inch nails with a small, flat head.
3. Small hammer.
4. Small pair of pliers.

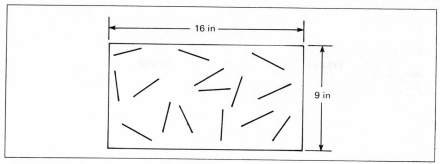

FIGURE 4-17

5. Piece of wood, approximately 9 × 16 inches which will take a decent stain or paint (ask woodworker). The wood should be at least $\frac{1}{2}$ inch thick.
6. Paint or stain.

Procedure

Stain or paint the wood whatever color you desire. The darker the color the better. Draw lightly 15 straight lines $2\frac{1}{2}$ inches long on the board wherever you like. Try to cover the entire board. See Figure 4-17.

Hammer the nails along these lines $\frac{1}{8}$ inch apart (leave $\frac{1}{4}$ inch of the nail out of the board), and use the pliers to make the nails stand up straight. Once all of the lines are completed you are ready to begin stringing.

First choose two lines, making sure that the extensions of either line do not cross the other line. See Figure 4-18. In addition, avoid other rows of nails which interfere with the design.

Tie the string around any one of the four corner nails and run the string diagonally across to the opposite line. The strings may be placed at either the top or the bottom of the nails as you prefer. See Figure 4-19.

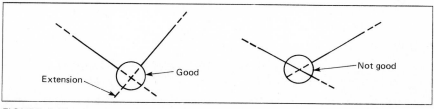

FIGURE 4-18

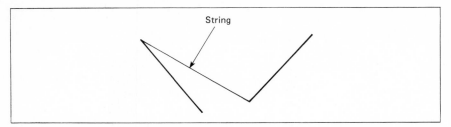

FIGURE 4-19

Wrap the string around the nail and the adjacent nail as is shown in Figure 4-20. Now run the string back diagonally across to the opposite line next to the nail where you began. Wrap the string once again in the same manner as before, following the example in Figure 4-20.

Repeat this procedure until you reach the nail on the opposite line and at the opposite corner from where you began. Tie the string around the last nail leaving as little hanging as possible.

You may now choose any other two lines keeping in mind the precautions given before. Any line may be used as many times as you wish. Try to overlap the individual patterns to add to the beautiful effects. See Figure 4-21.

String Art is Easy, Attractive, and Very Enjoyable

If you like to spend your free time relaxing, while making something beautiful, then follow these instructions. Your string art will take only a few days to make but will last a lifetime.

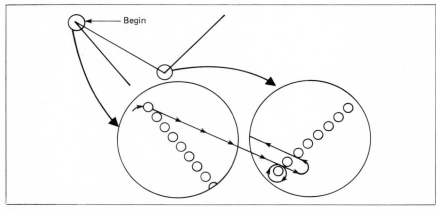

FIGURE 4-20

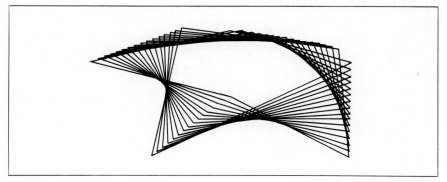

FIGURE 4-21

Equipment

1. Thin string, preferably slightly glossy. Sewing thread is fine.
2. Three hundred $\frac{1}{2}$ inch nails with a small flat head.
3. Hammer.
4. Pair of pliers.
5. Piece of wood at least $\frac{1}{2}$ inch thick, approximately 9 × 16 inches.
6. $\frac{1}{2}$ pint of a dark color paint or stain.

Procedure

Stain or paint the wood. Draw lightly 15 straight lines $2\frac{1}{2}$ inches long on the board wherever you like. Try to cover the entire board. (See Figure 4-22.)

Hammer the nails along these lines $\frac{1}{8}$ inch apart (leave $\frac{1}{4}$ inch of the nail out of the board), and use the pliers to straighten the nails. It is important that the heads of the nails are in a straight

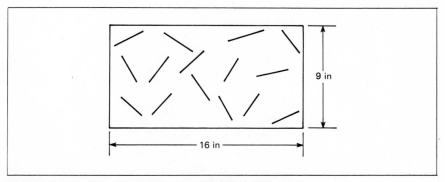

FIGURE 4-22   Board after staining with lines penciled in

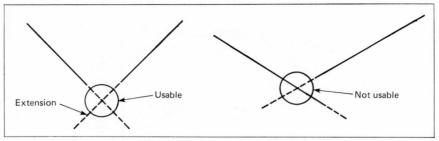

FIGURE 4-23   Illustration showing which lines may be used

line. Once all of the lines are completed you are ready to begin stringing.

First choose two lines, making sure that the extensions (imaginary lines) of either line do not cross the other actual line. (See Figure 4-23.) In addition, avoid other rows of nails which may interfere with the design.

Tie the string around any one of the four corner nails and run the string diagonally across to the opposite line. (See Figure 4-24*a*.) The strings may be placed at either the top or the bottom of the nails as you prefer. Now wrap the string around the end nail and the adjacent nail as is shown in Figure 4-24*b*.

Once the first and second steps are completed, run the string back diagonally across to the opposite line where you began. The next step is essentially the same as is shown in Figure 4-24*b* except now you skip the end nail where you began and follow the same pattern shown in Figure 4-24*b*. Repeat this same step each time, alternating lines until you reach the last nail on the opposite line from where you began. Tie the string around the last nail leaving as little hanging as possible.

You may now choose any other two lines keeping in mind the precautions given before. Try to overlap the individual patterns to add to the effect. (See Figure 4-25.)

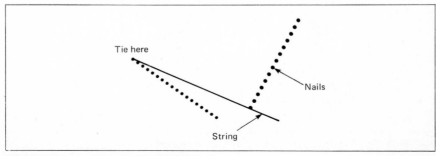

FIGURE 4-24*a*   First step in stringing

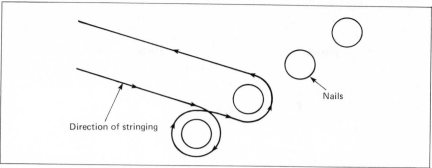

FIGURE 4-24*b*   Second step in stringing

FIGURE 4-25   Illustration showing the better effects achieved (*a*) with overlapping compared with (*b*) without overlapping.

4. Write a set of instructions of two to three pages (typed) on one of the following topics:

   (a) How to measure output voltage at no load
   (b) How to separate toluene and methanol using simple distillation
   (c) How to use a strain gauge
   (d) How to use an ammeter
   (e) How to use a surveyor's transit
   (f) How to use a centrifuge
   (g) How to use a soldering iron
   (h) How to change the stylus on a record player
   (i) How to tune a guitar or violin
   (j) How to do a basic football tackle
   (k) How to install a universal joint
   (l) How to execute a procedure used in a biology laboratory

5. Write a description of a mousetrap. Include a physical description, a process description explaining how it works, and instructions for baiting the trap. Figure 4-26 is a drawing you may find useful as a beginning. If you wish, follow up with sketches to accompany each step in the operation, that is, for *ready, release,* and *closed* positions. Write appropriate captions.

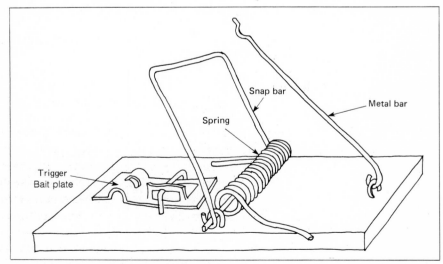

FIGURE 4-26   Elements of the mousetrap

5

Basic Rhetorical Patterns: The Art of Arrangement

Begin at the beginning, and go on till you come to the end: then stop.
Lewis Carroll

Rhetoric is the classic art of arranging what you have to say clearly and forcefully. It is the art of using words to influence that part of the mind that makes reasoned decisions.

In ancient Greece the term referred exclusively to speaking, for rhetoric was originally an oral art; in fact, Cicero once apologized to a correspondent for delaying a letter because he'd had a sore throat.

Today the term refers to either spoken or written communication. And although the content in scientific and technical writing changes with developments in knowledge, the basic rhetorical patterns developed in antiquity remain today the backbone of written scientific and technical discourse. Three of these rhetorical patterns—definition, analysis by structure (physical descriptions, e.g., desiccator), and analysis by function (process description, e.g., acid rain)—are so important to scientific writing that separate sections have been devoted to them in Chapters 2 and 3.

There are also other patterns in expository writing you will find particularly useful when you do technical and scientific reports. These patterns include

Analogy
Comparison and contrast
Problem-solution
Cause and effect
Inductive/deductive order
Enumeration and classification

This chapter will discuss each of these patterns, citing examples from the literature of science and technology. All discussion of the techniques is based on the assumption that to make a point—to be telling—the *arrangement* of the argument is as important as choice of language.

Analogy

In logic, analogy is a form of inference in which it is reasoned that if two things agree with one another in one or more respects, they will probably agree in other respects.

Analogy is a useful rhetorical device in science writing; it allows you to explain the unfamiliar through something that is more familiar to the reader.

One of the most famous analogies in the literature of science writing occurs in Sir James Jeans's explanation of why the sky looks blue. In it he draws an analogy between waves striking against a pier and light colliding with molecules [1].

WHY THE SKY LOOKS BLUE

Imagine that we stand on an ordinary seaside pier, and watch the waves rolling in and striking against the iron columns of the pier. Large waves pay very little attention to the columns—they divide right and left and reunite after passing each column, much as a regiment of soldiers would if a tree stood in their road; it is almost as though the columns had not been there. But the short waves and ripples find the columns of the pier a much more formidable obstacle. When the short waves impinge on the columns, they are reflected back and spread as new ripples in all directions. To use the technical term, they are "scattered." The obstacle provided by the iron columns hardly affects the long waves at all, but scatters the short ripples.

We have been watching a sort of working model of the way in

which sunlight struggles through the earth's atmosphere. Between us on earth and outer space the atmosphere interposes innumerable obstacles in the form of molecules of air, tiny droplets of water, and small particles of dust. These are represented by the columns of the pier.

The waves of the sea represent the sunlight. We know that sunlight is a blend of many colors—as we can prove for ourselves by passing it through a prism, or even through a jug of water, or as nature demonstrates to us when she passes it through the raindrops of a summer shower and produces a rainbow. We also know that light consists of waves, and that the different colors of light are produced by waves of different lengths, red light by long waves and blue light by short waves. The mixture of waves which constitutes sunlight has to struggle past the columns of the pier. And these obstacles treat the light waves much as the columns of the pier treat the sea-waves. The long waves which constitute red lights are hardly affected but the short waves which constitute blue light are scattered in all directions.

Thus the different constituents of sunlight are treated in different ways as they struggle through the earth's atmosphere. A wave of blue light may be scattered by a dust particle, and turned out of its course. After a time a second dust particle again turns it out of its course, and so on, until finally it enters our eyes by a path as zigzag as that of a flash of lightning. Consequently the blue waves of the sunlight enter our eyes from all directions. And that is why the sky looks blue.

Comparison and Contrast: Two Examples

Writers use comparison to demonstrate similarity of ideas, and contrast to argue difference in ideas.

The rhetorical technique may be the basis for single paragraphs, for a series of paragraphs, or for extensive arguments.

Stalactites and Stalagmites   Here is an example of comparison and contrast. The author begins with a definition and follows with a description of stalactites. He then describes stalagmites, contrasting them with stalactites [2].

Stalactites, stalagmites, dripstone, and flowstone are travertine deposits in limestone caverns (see Figure 5–1), formed by the evaporation of waters bearing calcium carbonate. Stalactites grow down from the roofs of caves and tend to be long and thin, with hollow cores. The water moves down the core and precipitates at

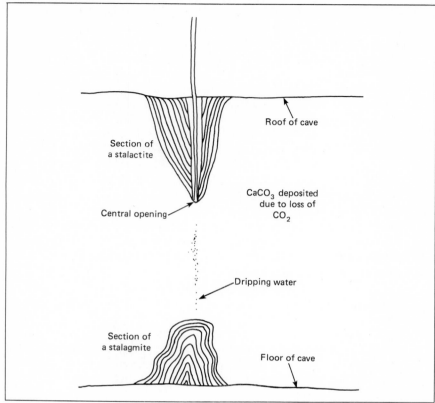

FIGURE 5-1   Stalactite and stalagmite deposits

the bottom, slowly extending the length while keeping the core open for more water to move down. Stalactites are banded concentrically to the center.

Stalagmites grow from the floor up and are commonly found beneath stalactites; they are formed from the evaporation of the same drip of water that forms the stalactite. Stalagmites are thicker and shorter than stalactites and have no central hollow core. The banding of stalagmites is parallel to the surface at the time of deposition of each band.

There are many ways you can arrange comparison and contrast.

1. *Sentence by sentence.* Develop the contrast or comparison by first stating a point about subject *x*, and then immediately comparing or contrasting it in the next sentence with subject *y*. If, for example, the article on stalactites and stalagmites were rewrit-

ten this way, one sentence would give a property of stalactites. The next sentence would contrast or compare this same property in stalagmites.

> Stalactites grow down from the roofs of caves and tend to be long and thin, with hollow cores. Stalagmites, in contrast, grow from the floor up, and are thicker and shorter, with no central hollow core.

2. *Paragraph by paragraph.* In this method, the first paragraph is about subject x and the second paragraph is about subject y. This is the pattern followed in the article on stalactites and stalagmites. In addition, the author uses a sentence-length contrast in the second paragraph: "Stalagmites are thicker and shorter than stalactites and have no central hollow core."

Glioma   Here is a second example of comparison and contrast. The author is concerned with describing glioma, a malignant form of brain cancer. He states all the information on subject x—meningioma—in the first paragraph, then uses the succeeding three paragraphs for subject y—glioma.[1]

> Glioma is the malignant form of brain cancer; the benign form is called meningioma. Meningiomas originate in the meninges, the lining cells that separate the brain from the skull, and usually grow enclosed in a capsule. If discovered in time, a meningioma can be removed by a neurosurgeon, and that, usually, is the end of the tumor. If ignored, a meningioma can kill simply by occupying so much space in the skull that the brain dies. Moreover, some meningiomas grow in parts of the brain which a neurosurgeon cannot reach, or which he dares not penetrate for fear of damaging healthy tissue. These meningiomas kill.
>
> Unlike meningiomas, gliomas originate within the brain itself. The brain consists of two types of cells, neurons and glial cells. The chemical and electrical interactions of neurons permit thought, speech, sight and movement. Once the brain reaches maturity, neurons no longer divide and multiply like other cells. Since cancer is a wild proliferation of cells, tumors do not normally originate in neurons. It is the glial cells, the essential structural units of the brain which surround the neurons, that produce gliomas. Glial cells do divide and multiply. A glioma is born when they do so without restraint.
>
> Unchecked, gliomas grow without pause and send metastases to every part of the brain. Gliomas first cripple and then kill by

[1] Copyright © 1979/80 by The New York Times Company [3]. Reprinted by permission.

successively destroying the different brain centers that direct the many functions of the body. At first a patient may have difficulty speaking and understanding speech; then his right arm and right leg may become partially or totally paralyzed; he may begin to lose his sight, and later go completely blind. As the destruction of the brain progresses, the patient may lapse into a coma. Finally, the tumor disrupts an essential function such as breathing; the patient dies unless he is hooked up to a mechanical apparatus that can continue to perform that function.

Precisely because a glioma can originate in any part of the brain, its initial symptoms vary, and the tumor may go undiagnosed for months. Often the first signs are an unaccustomed tiredness and lack of energy or a drastic change in personality. Severe and frequent headaches are sometimes a symptom of brain tumors, though the overwhelming majority of headaches have nothing to do with glioma. An epileptic fit in an adult who has never had one before is an ominous sign requiring thorough investigation.

Problem Solution: Two Examples

If you are using a problem-solution format, you proceed typically as follows:

1. State the problem in the opening paragraph or paragraphs.
2. Then, if the problem has been solved, state the solution. Continue by developing details of the solution.
3. If the problem hasn't been solved, state the problem and then state possible solutions, with advantages and disadvantages for each alternative. Conclude if appropriate with a recommendation.

Here is an example of problem-solution writing. The subject is liver cancer in China.

Chinese Liver Cancer[1]
Liver cancer occurs with remarkably high frequency in certain parts of China, notably along the north shore of the Yangtze River, at its mouth. Identification of the disease's cause could help to combat it elsewhere.

The results of a survey reported by Su DeLong in the November issue of the Chinese medical journal of Shanghai First

[1] Copyright © 1979/80 by The New York Times Company [4]. Reprinted by permission.

Medical College point to the drinking of stagnant, highly polluted ditch water as a likely cause. The disease was found to be relatively rare in communities using well water, whereas among those drinking the polluted water the mortality rate sometimes exceeds 40 per 100,000 people.

It has been suggested that a history of hepatitis might predispose inhabitants of the region to liver cancer or that mold derivatives, such as aflatoxin, might be to blame, but neither hypothesis is supported by the study. The report notes that the Chinese commonly eat fermented bean curd and other moldy foods, yet the liver cancer incidence seems unrelated to such eating habits.

Instead, the report casts suspicion on toxic substances washed from the fields, such as pesticides or fertilizers. "The beginning of the unprecedented increase in liver cancer," says the author, coincides with the local introduction of organo-chlorine pesticides such as DDT and their effect "should not be lightly excluded." No attempt, however, has yet been made to narrow down the cause.

The first paragraph states the problem, the second paragraph the likely solution. The author then develops the point by contrast.

Here is a second example in the problem-solution format.

Blackest Black[2]

Scientists and manufacturers have long sought a way to make the surface of objects pure black, because a pure black coating or paint would absorb all light, including the energy in it. Such a coating would make solar collectors much more efficient and would improve scientific devices used in radiation and heat measurements.

The National Bureau of Standards reports that one of its scientists, Christian E. Johnson, has discovered a way to enable the surface of an object to absorb 99.5 percent of the light that strikes it. Objects with such surfaces are the blackest ever produced by man. If an object could absorb 100 percent of all light striking it, the object would be invisible, except in silhouette against a lighted background.

Coatings and paints ordinarily derive their colors, including black (which is the absence of color), through the use of fine particles known as pigments. But Dr. Johnson's discovery yields a blackness caused by the microscopic structure of the surface, not by pigments. The coating is prepared from nickel in which phosphorus has been dissolved. When treated with nitric acid, its silvery surface is partly etched in such a way as to leave a microscopic pattern looking like steep mountain peaks. They are much too small to be seen with the naked eye, and a surface covered with them looks and feels smooth. When light strikes the surface it is trapped in the valleys between these peaks in a way that allows very little of it to escape. The effect is an uncanny blackness.

Dr. Johnson cautioned that it will be some time before his discovery can be put to practical use, because the tiny mountain peaks covering the nickel surface are very fragile. Rubbing the surface with an ordinary eraser quickly destroys the blackness, leaving the original metallic shine. For applications in which the black surface would be subject to wear, a coating must be found that would protect the fragile structure without making it reflective.

In the first paragraph, the author states the problem; in the second paragraph, the solution. The third paragraph develops the point through contrast and through descriptive detail. Note the use of analogy: "When treated with nitric acid, its silvery surface is partly etched in such a way as to leave a microscopic pattern looking like steep mountain peaks. They are much too small to be seen with the naked eye, and a surface covered with them looks and feels smooth. When light strikes the surface it is trapped in the valleys between these peaks in a way that allows very little of it to escape. The effect is an uncanny blackness."

Nestorian Order   If you are giving a number of solutions, it's possible to weigh your presentation. You can either start with the solution that you prefer, giving it the prominence of first place, or conclude with the solution you favor. The latter pattern is called Nestorian order; here the most important point is presented *last*. You need a certain amount of writing skill to use this technique since you may easily lose readers while you are wending your way toward the point.

Here is an example of how you might use Nestorian order: the problem that concerns you is the disposal of waste from nuclear power plants. Your report discusses three possible solutions: (1) use of ceramic materials to seal radioactive wastes; (2) use of ordinary glass materials; and (3) use of a new, high-silica glass. The last solution is the one you think most promising, and you plan on describing it in some detail.

If you are following Nestorian order, begin with the problem: some 4000 tons of radioactive waste have accumulated, with more to follow. Then state and discuss the first two methods for disposal. In each case, define the process and state the advantages and the drawbacks. You'll need at least one paragraph, and possibly two or three, for each of the first two methods. Finally, state the case for the new high-silica porous glass, placing and developing this solution *last*.

Cause and Effect: Two Examples

A typical rhetorical device is the use of cause and effect, which can be presented in one of two ways:

1. Start with the effect. Then list the cause or causes. Then develop each cause.
2. Start with the cause. Then list effects. Then develop each effect.

Here is an example in which the effect is followed by a list of causes.[1]

> In the past, malignant brain tumors received relatively little attention from cancer researchers. Even today, out of $1 billion devoted to cancer research every year, only a few million dollars are spent on the study of glioma.
>
> One reason for this is the brain's uniqueness. A vastly complex organ contained entirely within the skull, the brain until recently has been closed to early inspection or examination. Until recent years, ordinary X-rays revealed very little to specialists. It is only with the development of the computerized axial tomography (CAT) scanner that a wealth of information about the brain has become available. The CAT scanner uses a battery of X-rays to take a cross-sectional picture—a tomogram—of the patient's brain. Then computers put the millions of bits of information together in a clear picture on a computer screen. This picture usually answers the question of whether someone has a tumor.
>
> Another reason for the limited research on brain cancer is that official statistics underestimate the number of such deaths each year. According to some epidemiologists, many people die of this disease who are never properly diagnosed. They believe the correct number—if all brain tumors were discovered either before or after death—could be two or three times larger than the

published figure of 8,000 annual deaths. In addition, 50,000 deaths a year are caused by metastatic tumors to the brain, mostly from lung cancer, breast cancer, malignant melanoma, lymphoma and leukemia.

A third reason is that few famous people have died of glioma in the last 50 years. While other forms of cancer have stricken such prominent people as Edward R. Murrow, John Foster Dulles, Stewart Alsop and John Wayne, the most famous victim of brain cancer was the composer George Gershwin, who died in 1937. The other prominent casualty was John Gunther, Jr., who died in 1947. John Gunther's classic, "Death Be Not Proud," the story of his son's losing struggle against glioma, is perhaps the best-known account of a brain tumor case.

Here is a more complicated format: the cause is acid rain. The author first defines the terms and gives a detailed process description. He then lists the effects, and subsequently develops each one.[1]

Acid rain has developed into one of the most serious, worldwide environmental problems of the coming decades. . . . Although many aspects of the physical and chemical actions that occur in the formation of acid rain are not known, scientific research has pinpointed the major events that take place. Acid rain is formed when the gases of nitrogen oxide and sulfur oxide are emitted into the atmosphere and, as they are carried along by wind current, they combine with water vapor molecules and are transformed over a period of hours or days into microscopic drops of nitric and sulfuric acids. They are returned to earth when they encounter rain or snow-producing clouds, sometimes hundreds or thousands of miles from their original point of emission. . . .

The effects of acid rains include the decimation or malformation of fish, particularly trout and salmon, in acidified streams and lakes in North America and Europe. It has been estimated that some 50,000 lakes in the Adirondacks and Canada have become acidified to the point that the fish population has declined or been destroyed. . . .

Acid rains can cause the leaching of essential plant nutrients from the soil and can reduce nitrogen fixation by microorganisms, causing the soil to be less fertile. Further, above-normal amounts of acids in the lakes and streams tend to cause the extraction from the bottom sediments of toxic metals such as cadmium, lead and aluminum. These, like sulfuric acids, can destroy fish and contaminate drinking water.

Inductive Order: Specific to General

In developing a theme by induction, begin with specific instances. Then lead the reader to the idea that the instances suggest. Then explain the idea.

Here is a brief example, taken from Haldane's "On Being the Right Size"[8]:

> You can drop a mouse down a thousand-yard mine shaft; and, on arriving at the bottom, it gets a slight shock and walks away. A rat would probably be killed, although it can fall safely from the eleventh floor of a building; a man is killed, a horse splashes. . . . Divide an animal's length, breadth, and height each by ten; its weight is reduced to a thousandth, but its surface only to a hundredth. So the resistance to falling in the case of a small animal is relatively ten times greater than the driving force.

Here is another example of inductive order.[1]

> It can start in just one of the body's billions of cells, triggered by a stray bit of radiation, a trace of toxic chemical, perhaps a virus or a random error in the transcription of the cell's genetic message. It can lie dormant for decades before striking, or it can suddenly attack. Once on the move, it divides to form other abnormal cells, outlaws that violate normal genetic restraints. The body's immune system, normally alert to the presence of alien cells, fails to respond properly; its usually formidable defense units refrain from moving in and destroying the intruders. Unlike healthy cells, which stop reproducing after repairing damage or contributing to normal growth, the aberrant cells respect few limits or boundaries. They continue to proliferate wildly, forming a growing mass or tumor that expands into healthy tissue and competes with normal cells for nutrition. Not content with wreaking local damage, the burgeoning tumor sends out groups of malevolent cells, like amphibious invasion forces, into the bloodstream, which carries them all over the body. Some perish on their mission. But here and there, many of these mobile cells establish beachheads on healthy tissue and begin dividing, forming new tumors. Eventually the marauding

---

[1] Reprinted by permission from *Time,* The Weekly Newsmagazine [9]. Copyright © 1980 by Time, Inc.

cells infiltrate, starve and destroy vital organs, incapacitating and usually bringing death to their unwilling host. Cancer has claimed another victim.

Inductive order offers a certain amount of suspense or tension, provided one handles the topic carefully. The reader is led to the solution in a kind of puzzle order in which all of the pieces are presented, and then assembled.

It is, however, a difficult pattern to handle and is usually combined with a deductive pattern.

Deductive Order: General to Specific

Deductive order is the preferred format for paragraphs, series of paragraphs, and general arguments in expository prose. In the pattern, one states a generalization and then supports it with particulars. In scientific papers, one starts with a statement of the findings and then follows this statement with supporting evidence.

In the following example, "Long-term recognition of father's song by female zebra finches," the author states his findings at the close of the first paragraph: "I report here that adult female finches can recognize the song of their own father after a period of early exposure followed by more than 2 months of separation while attaining sexual maturity." He then follows with supporting evidence. [10]

LONG-TERM RECOGNITION OF FATHER'S SONG BY FEMALE ZEBRA FINCHES

Recently, attention has been directed at the question of how sexual imprinting, or the development of mating preferences, affects assortative mating within polymorphic species and regulates the extent of inbreeding and outbreeding in a population. It may be selectively advantageous for a young organism to learn individual characteristics of parents and/or siblings to avoid subsequent mating with kin as well as to avoid hybridisation by not mating with individuals that differ greatly from rearing partners. I report here that adult female zebra finches (*Taeniopygia guttata*) can recognise the song of their own father after a period of early exposure followed by more than 2 months of separation while attaining sexual maturity.

The zebra finch is an Australian grassfinch (family Estrildidae), the young of which are totally dependent on parental care on hatching. Hatchlings are fed by both parents and do not leave the nest until about the third week. Between days 30 and 40, the young leave (or are driven off by) the parents and form mixed flocks with other young finches. Sexual maturity is reached by 90 d. Thus, in early development (that is, before 40 d of age), females are exposed to the song of their father, and thereafter to the developing songs of male siblings that typically bear some resemblance to the father's song. Adult male zebra finch song is highly variable between individuals in acoustic structure but relatively stable within an individual, thus providing a possible basis for individual recognition.

Females were hatched in rooms containing 12-21 breeding cages (82.0 cm long, 39.0 cm high, 30.0 cm deep) with one adult zebra finch pair per cage. (No other species were housed in these rooms.) At 35 ± 3 d after hatching, females were separated from their parents and housed in a soundproof room with other young female zebra finches in $82.0\times39.0\times30.0$-cm cages, each containing three females. At day 100 ± 3, each female was given a single 30-min simultaneous auditory choice test involving the song of her father and either the song of another adult male zebra finch that differed considerably from her father's song in acoustic structure, or the song of another adult male zebra finch that was similar to her father's song in acoustic structure. All male zebra finch songs used in the playback tests were recorded when the male was singing to his mate. No sounds other than the male's song were on the test tapes. The purpose of the first type of test (father's song compared with dissimilar song) was to assess the general capability of a female to recognise and show a preference for her father's song over that of a randomly chosen conspecific male that was not a close relative. The second type of test (father's song compared with similar song) assessed the specificity with which a female could distinguish her father's song from one that was similar. (Because song structure can differ considerably among individual males, a song similar to that of the father could be obtained only by recording either the female's uncle and/or male siblings, as related males tend to have similar songs due to early vocal learning.) Each female was tested only once in either the first or second test.

The rectangular test apparatus, housed in an anechoic chamber, was divided into two approach zones at opposite ends separated by a neutral zone, each zone being 70.5 cm long. Two loudspeakers were located outside the apparatus adjacent to each approach zone. Behavioural measures recorded were (1) latency of approach from a centrally located start box in the neutral zone to each approach zone, and (2) total time spent in each approach zone. A preference was recorded when a bird spent twice as much time in one approach zone as in the other.

The results are [that] female zebra finches recognised and significantly preferred the song of their own father to the dissimilar song of another male zebra finch. When confronted with the perceptually more difficult test of the father's song compared with a similar song, females still recognised their father's song. Although the tendency of females actually to prefer their father's song in the latter test was not statistically significant, those females that did prefer their own father's song had significantly longer duration scores than those preferring the similar song.

Thus, female zebra finches can recognise their father's song as a function of early exposure followed by a relatively long period of isolation from male song. These tests of approach behaviour do not necessarily reflect sexual motivation on the part of the female and therefore do not represent a demonstration of sexual imprinting as such. Rather, they demonstrate the extent to which females can recognise and discriminate their father's song from that of another conspecific male. Indeed, as females presumably do not mate with their fathers in nature, I would have predicted the outcome of these tests to be quite different had they been assessing sexual behaviour. Nevertheless, this study may have important ramifications regarding the study of sexual imprinting in general. The learning of both supra-individual (species) and individual characteristics during early exposure may, at the time of sexual maturity, influence an animal to (1) mate with its own species—a direct effect of learning supra-individual features—and at the same time (2) avoid mating with close kin—a direct effect of individual recognition. However, many studies have shown that, in several species, individuals can identify conspecifics in advance of exposure to them and that embryonic and postnatal self-stimulation probably plays an important part in these and other instances of "instinctive" preferences for species-typical stimuli. Thus, it is conceivable that the role of imprinting in mate selection in nature may be of greater relevance to the learning of individual rather than supra-individual characteristics. . . .

Lister's paper "On the Antiseptic Principle in the Practice of Surgery" (see Chapter 9) also provides a good example of the deductive pattern in writing. In this case, Lister takes two paragraphs to give the historical context of the problem and concludes with a statement, "decomposition can be avoided by applying as a dressing material capable of destroying the life of the floating particles," which the remainder of the paper develops.

Enumeration and Classification

To analyze is to divide a whole into parts. In expository writing, you may analyze in many ways—by process, by physical description, and by causes, among others. The method of analysis depends on the logic dictated by the subject material. For instance, a logical way to analyze information about stalactites is by process; a logical way to analyze information about a desiccator is by a description of the whole and its parts.

In addition to analyzing by process, structure, and cause, there is analysis by classification, whereby you take a general subject and divide it into categories or classes, and by enumeration, where you simply list items that you have grouped together.

In this article on solar heating and electricity, enumeration is used throughout to develop the thesis [11].

> Other alternative pricing schemes would better serve to influence solar users and provide equitable charges. A utility might petition its regulator for such rate structures as:
>
> *Rate Inversion*   Under this plan, the first kilowatt-hours purchased by any user are cheapest, and prices increase with additional consumption. The effect would be to encourage solar heating systems and conservation, but there would be no incentive to shift demand.
>
> *Peak-Load (Time-of-Day) Pricing*   High rates are charged during peak-demand hours, lower rates during off-peak hours. The effect would be to level peaks, since consumers would seek low rates. The impact on solar heating depends on the availability of low-cost storage.

Here are excerpts from an article on musical instruments. The author has chosen the pattern of classification, grouping the information on instruments "in a general way for the kinds of sounds they produce, even though woodwind instruments are not necessarily made of wood, nor are brass instruments always made of metal." Particular instruments are then enumerated within each classification [12].

> Instruments for producing musical sounds have long been classified as woodwinds, brass, percussion, or strings: to these must be added electrical and electronic instruments. In a sense, all these instruments implement and extend the capability of the original musical instrument, the singing voice. The classes mentioned are useful in grouping instruments in a general way for the kinds of sounds they produce, even though woodwind instruments are not necessarily made of wood, nor are brass instruments always made of metal. . . .
>
> *Woodwind Instruments*   Woodwind instruments are distinguished primarily by the fact that the effective length of the vibrating air column is shortened by opening lateral side holes in succession. Two distinctly different means of generating the sound are em-

ployed. For the flute, and its half-size version the piccolo, the player blows across the embouchure hole near one end in such a way as to cause periodic puffs of air to enter the tube; after a turbulent turning these puffs excite the air column longitudinally. This method of excitation leaves the tube acoustically open in the sense that the contained air vibrates much as it does in a simple tube with both ends open to the atmosphere. . . .

For the double-reed oboe or bassoon, the player holds between his lips a pair of thin reeds (pieces of cane appropriately thinned, shaped, and bound together) that beat against each other to change the player's breath to puffs of air. For clarinets and saxophones, a single reed attached to a mouthpiece by a ligature functions in a similar way. The portion of the mouthpiece (the lay) against which the reed beats must be appropriately curved; the character of the sound is modified somewhat by the volume of the mouthpiece as well as by the shape and material of the reed.

For both the single- and double-reed instruments, the reeds vibrate under the influence of sound waves reflected back from the distant end of the air column and allow the puffs of air to enter when the sound pressure within the instrument is large. . . . The lateral side holes in woodwinds necessitate relatively simple geometric shapes: The flute and clarinet are nearly cylindrical, whereas the oboe, saxophone, and bassoon are approximately conical but of different tapers. . . .

Brass Instruments   In brass instruments the puffs of air are introduced via the vibrating lips of the player that are stretched across the cup-shaped mouthpiece. Again the action is like that in the clarinet, by which the end is nearly closed acoustically. The length of the air column is increased by tubing switched in by the use of valves, either piston or rotary: a common arrangement is such that the first valve lowers the intonation by two semitones, the second by one semitone, and the third by three semitones. For a given length of tubing, different tones are produced by tensioning the lips to excite different modes of vibration. . . .

Percussion Instruments   Instruments such as the timpani (kettledrums) and xylophone are called percussion instruments because the sound is initiated by a blow. Two kinds of sound producers are involved: a membrane under tension, associated with a cavity that can influence the frequency of vibration, as in the case of the timpani; and a rigid bar or plate vibrating transversely, whose frequency is little affected by any resonator that may be attached. Some percussion instruments give a well-defined sound that excites a sensation of definite pitch, such as does a church bell; others, such as drums, cymbals, and triangles, are useful primarily for rhythm effects.

Stringed Instruments   For the harp and guitar, strings are set into vibration by plucking. A resonator or soundboard of some kind is attached to help radiate sound to the surrounding air, but the frequency of vibration is primarily established by the length, tension, and mass per unit length of the string. . . .

Keyboard Instruments   Instruments such as the celesta, pipe organ, accordion, and piano are usually put in a group called keyboard instruments, because the respective vibrating bars, pipes, reeds, and strings in these instruments are selected by use of keys in a keyboard. The celesta and piano could also be described as percussion instruments, because hammers strike the bars and strings; the pipe organ and the accordion, with its wind-driven free reeds, are wind instruments. By its multiple keyboards (and pedal board) the pipe organ puts under the control of a single player thousands of sources whose distinctive sounds can be reproduced on command.

Electrical and Electronic Types   Musical instruments of the kinds already described become quasi-electrical instruments by the addition of a microphone to pick up the airborne sound, an amplifier, and a loudspeaker. Alternately, a vibration pickup can be used to generate an electrical signal directly from the vibration of a string; this is the case in the electric guitar and electric piano. The signal can be modified electrically before being radiated as sound from a loudspeaker. Since the resonance box or sounding board is not needed for these electrical stringed instruments, the damping is very slight and the vibration can last for a long time so that relatively sustained sounds can be obtained if desired.

Summary

"Work from a suitable design," E. B. White advises in *The Elements of Style.* "Design informs even the simplest structure, whether of brick and steel or of prose."

You may design by problem and solution, by comparison and contrast, by classification and enumeration. You may choose to arrange your argument by starting with the general and leading to examples, or by starting with examples and leading to the general.

When you write by such plans, you use rhetorical patterns. Why use them? For the same reason authors of technical papers favor spare, unadorned language: to help make their points quickly and clearly. A sharply drawn contrast, a series of apt examples, a telling analogy—all may prove useful when you want to write effective expository prose.

Literature Cited

1. Sir James Jeans, "Why the Sky Looks Blue," from *The Stars in Their Courses*, Cambridge University Press, Cambridge, 1931. Reprinted by permission.

2. Raymond Siever, "Stalactites and Stalagmites," *McGraw-Hill Encyclopedia of Science and Technology*, vol. 13, McGraw-Hill, New York, 1977, pp. 35–36. Reprinted by permission.

3. H. Schwartz, "Stretching Their Lease on Life," *The New York Times*, April 13, 1980.

4. "Chinese Liver Cancer," *The New York Times*, January 13, 1980.

5. "Blackest Black," *The New York Times*, January 13, 1980.

6. H. Schwartz, op. cit.

7. B. Webster, "Acid Rain," *The New York Times*, November 6, 1979.

8. J. B. S. Haldane, "On Being the Right Size," from *Possible Worlds*, Harper & Row, New York, 1928.

9. "The Big IF in Cancer," *Time*, March 31, 1980, p. 60.

10. D. B. Miller, "Long-term Recognition of Father's Song by Female Zebra Finches," *Nature*, August 2, 1979, p. 398.

11. M. A. Maidique and B. Woo, "Solar Heating and Electric Utilities," *Technology Review*, May 1980, p. 28. Reprinted by permission.

12. "Musical Instruments," *McGraw-Hill Encyclopedia of Science and Technology*, vol. 8, McGraw-Hill, New York, 1977, pp. 771–773. Reprinted by permission.

Exercises

1. Here is the introduction to an article on heat transfer. What method or pattern of organization will the author follow?

   Heat, a form of kinetic energy, is transferred in three ways: conduction, convection, and radiation. Heat can be transferred only if a temperature difference exists, and then only in the direction of decreasing temperature. Beyond this, the mechanisms and laws governing each of these ways are quite different. This article gives introductory information on the three types of heat

[1] *McGraw-Hill Encyclopedia of Science and Technology*, vol. 6, McGraw-Hill, New York, 1977, p. 423. Reprinted by permission.

transfer (also called thermal transfer) and on important industrial devices called heat exchangers.[1]

2. Describe collisions of gas molecules, using billiard balls as an analogy (three to five paragraphs).
3. Explain chemical bonds, using springs as an analogy (three to four paragraphs).
4. Explain electricity, using the flow of water as an analogy (two to three paragraphs).
5. Explain the parts of a computer, using the human brain as the analogy (three to four paragraphs).
6. Compare the circulatory system of the body to a hydraulic system (four to five paragraphs).
7. Explain the thrust of a jet engine, using comparison and contrast to develop the argument (one to two pages).
8. Write a description of how to play an electronic game such as Space Invaders. Use comparison and contrast in developing the explanation (one to two pages).
9. Write a description of two devices (such as a T-shaped corkscrew and an air-pressure corkscrew) using comparison and contrast to develop the description (four to five paragraphs).
10. Find an example of comparison and contrast in, for instance, the *McGraw-Hill Encyclopedia of Science and Technology*. Analyze its effectiveness.
11. Find an example of classification and enumeration in, for instance, *Van Nostrand's Scientific Encyclopedia*. Analyze it.
12. Choose an example of deductive order from *Science, Science 80*, or another magazine of science. Rewrite it so that it is inductive.
13. Describe how to throw a curve ball. Use comparison and contrast in developing the description (three to four paragraphs).
14. Write a problem-solution technical brief of three to six paragraphs in which the problem is: "sulphur oxides result when coal is used as a fuel." Give three solutions and develop each. Use Nestorian order if you wish.
15. Write a problem-solution brief on a subject of your choice. First state the problem. Then state and develop three possible solutions. Use Nestorian order if you wish (two pages).
16. Write a cause-effect technical brief on acid rain. Acid rain is the cause. State and then develop at least two effects (three to five paragraphs).
17. Write a cause-effect technical brief on a subject of your choice (one to two pages).

TWO
Preparatory Work: Stages in the Process

6

The Writing Process

. . . a raid on the inarticulate with shabby machinery, always deteriorating.

T. S. Eliot

Writing is a difficult job. "I do not like to write," Gloria Steinem once said, "but I like to have written."

She was not alone in this sentiment. For most people, writing is a thorny job from start to finish, and its pleasures lie in contemplating the completed manuscript, not in creating it.

The writing process becomes even harder if you think of it as a mysterious, creative act over which you have no control. This results in situations such as sitting in front of the typewriter for an hour waiting for inspiration, failing to write a word, and finally quitting because you decide you "can't write."

It helps a lot if you think of writing instead as a process—a series of steps that can be analyzed and accomplished in an orderly way.

This will not solve all the problems, but there are ways to break the writing job into small, manageable tasks, as well as pragmatic techniques you can use to fend off inertia.

Accordingly, this chapter will present an overview of technical writing from the beginning to the end as a process which can be organized and handled in an efficient way. The process is broken into four stages: entering the data, beginnings, first and second drafts, and final copy.

Entering the Data: First Assemble, Then Assimilate

For any complex writing job, the first step is a literature search. It may begin informally in conversations with colleagues, or formally with an on-line computerized search. At the same time that the information is assembled, there is another step: many scientists use the word *percolate* to describe it. They look through offprints (a separately printed excerpt, usually a journal article) or the latest review volumes, and then set the reading aside for a time and let what they've read percolate. They may talk with workers in their groups, discussing ideas or questions. They then start to write. These two steps may be described as (1) first assemble, and (2) then assimilate.

First Assemble   The literature of science is complex—so complicated, in fact, that E. Bright Wilson once commented that for the beginning researcher it sometimes seems easier to rediscover facts than to look them up.

To keep up with the deluge of primary sources, a variety of indexing, abstracting, and table-of-contents services has evolved. (See Chapter 7 for a detailed discussion of such services.) Through the use of these services, you will soon be availed of news magazines, abstracts, citations, and review articles.

How can you avoid being swamped by this information as it starts to pile up? People in the field have developed a number of ingenious systems for coping.

1. *Subject files.* One chemist whose topic is organometallic chemistry decided that "the key to the game is to pick two to three variables and then go to work." He keeps his 3×5 card files in two categories: the first is "metallic elements." He may have 15 cards on aluminum, including articles, books, and review articles. His other dimension is "type of reaction." These cards are indexed by such categories as oxidation, reduction, and hydrolysis. In this way, he has some duplication, but the amount is tolerable, and he is able to keep up with the literature.

2. *Offprints, files.* A good labeling system is essential; otherwise you won't find the article when you need it. Many people also notate articles as they read them. These marginal comments are often valuable on returning to a paper, sparking remembrance of an insight long forgotten.

   Offprints are available through table-of-contents journals for a fee. Computerized services also supply entire documents, although the citation alone is more common. You may also write directly to the author, but be forewarned that many avoid responding. Be prepared to write two or three times.

3. *Original journals.* Most working scientists subscribe to three to four journals within their fields which they then store in the office for ready reference. Many also subscribe to an annual review volume in their field—a book or special number of a journal which prints a roundup of the year's progress and extensive citations that provide a good starting point for a literature search.

4. *Model formats.* Keep a folder with models or examples of formats you find difficult. For instance, if you have trouble writing opening statements, look through materials you read for effective openings. Analyze them according to standard types—question, anecdote, example, topic statement, contrast—and file the openings you like. Later, if you've trouble getting started, you can read your favorites and perhaps be inspired to adapt one of the formats to your own material.

   One engineer accumulates successful proposals and looks them over whenever she gets to a particular section in her own proposals that baffles her. What is an "articulated management plan by objective" suddenly required in the latest government subsection? A successful proposal may give some idea of how the writer coped with the "governmentese."

   In summary, your background materials will vary according to the task, from research data to models of successful formats. Some people use 3 × 5 cards; others combine cards with offprints, annotated journals, and review volumes. All are following an essential first step—they are accumulating the information before they begin to write. The next step is to digest it.

   Then Assimilate   People who try to write before they assimilate the data describe an inefficient and frustrating process. They start to write, stop to read about an item, return to their notes, and discover their writing veering off in a new direction, sparked by the latest piece of reading. This inefficient process happens when there's not enough time to absorb the information.

If you have ever been caught in this process, then you know it is far better to read first and allow time for the information to settle. You will still have to go back to consult your material, but it will be to find a particular quote, to locate a specific citation.

A common expression is "to write off the top of one's head." Few people actually do this successfully, and then only for the simplest of tasks. The first step in writing is to read and talk about the information, the second to give it a little time to take root.

If you are going to write on a subject the next day, look over your notes or comments. Let the information percolate overnight if you have time. Some psychologists suggest that one should reread information just before going to sleep to improve retention. The technique won't improve retention if you have never studied the material before, but if you've made a first pass at it, a second perusal of this sort is effective.

To summarize, the first step in writing is to assemble the background information you need; then allow time to assimilate it. There is a Latin expression for this process. *Ex nihilo nihil venit*, or, "Out of nothing comes nothing." Computer people have their own aphorism for this same process: "Garbage in, garbage out."

Assemble, then assimilate. These are the first two steps in any writing job.

Beginnings

When I was in high school, my English teacher told me I couldn't use an A in an outline unless I also used a B. There were rules, also, for Roman numerals and indentations. Under these circumstances, I did the same thing as my classmates. First I wrote the paper, and then I went *back* and wrote the outline. In that way, I got the form right—the A's and B's, the ranks of indentation. I also took care of the far trickier problem—did the outline match what I had finally ended up writing?

A great deal of nonsense has been taught in the name of outlining. Students are shown the traditional format: Roman numerals for main topics, capital letters for second-level headings, Arabic numerals for third-level headings, and lowercase letters for fourth-level headings, as follows:

I.
   A.
      1.
         a.
         b.
      2.
   B.
II.

A variation on this is decimal format:

1.
   1.1
   1.2
   1.3
2.
   2.1
   2.2
      2.21
      2.22
      2.23

There is nothing wrong with either of these outline formats; they may prove useful for the person preparing a complicated proposal, report, or review article. The writer's stress, however, should be on the *function* of the outline, not on its form, for thinking of outlines as formal, detailed skeletons that must be followed rigidly makes them less useful. The outlines that are more practical are the informal, scratch outlines that launch a project and, once it's in motion, help keep the author on track.

Thus, you may want to build an outline initially as a simple list of words or phrases under your objective. Then move the words, phrases, or sentences around until you're satisfied with the coherence and completeness of the skeleton. In playing with the various divisions and subdivisions, the organization and development of your subject will probably become clearer. As you manipulate your scratch outline, remember that the outline is a guide for you, the writer—not a formal contract. You are not bound to follow it exactly as written; indeed you will usually find that your outline changes as you write.

Here, for instance, is an example of a scratch outline prepared by a statistician who works for a food processing firm. He had been asked to visit a plant where there were problems in the bottling of an oil/vinegar compound (product 12Q). As you can see, the outline went through several versions before the author was satisfied.

OBJECTIVE

Trip report on visit to plant in Westport.
They are having a problem with 12Q. Aqueous
phase underfilled because of problem with
foaming at surface.

Report on trip to Westport. 12Q's total volume
is below stated volume. This is happening
because of a shortfill in the aqueous phase
caused by foaming at the surface.

Trip report to Westport plant. Problem—12Q's
total volume is low because of shortfill in
the aqueous phase.

I Intro (problem)
Date, time, production period
Total weights under target
Detailed background

II Adjustment procedure
First steps taken
Results of two trials
A Trial 1. Results
B Trial 2. Results

III Recommendations
A. Modify procedure in trial 2
B. Reasons to use trial 2

A modified scratch outline has many advantages:

1. *It overcomes inertia.* A scratch outline is an excellent way to get started, to set forth categories, to help crystallize thought.

2. *It puts the argument in its starkest form.* It's common to become bogged down in detail once a paper is under way. An outline of major points will help you avoid this. If you've enumerated your arguments in advance, you can refer to your list when working. In this way, you're less likely to stray from the point or to omit a basic argument.

3. *It is a simple way to spot imbalance.* As you write, you may discover that you have nine of one sort of argument, and only one of another. The simplicity of the outline form will help you see where you are supplying too much or too little.

4. *It acts as an organizer and as a guide to major points.* If the writer concentrates on the function rather than the form, the outline is a useful device, reducing the amount of time necessary for the actual writing job.

First Draft

There are four steps that will help you in doing the first draft.

1. Break the writing job into small, manageable tasks.
2. Do the writing a section at a time.
3. Do the easier sections first.
4. Watch out for data poisoning.

Break the Writing Job into Small, Manageable Tasks   For instance, many people are stopped cold by the notion of writing a proposal, classically a long and complicated piece of writing. Yet people who start with an outline for the proposal can generate a fairly detailed plan that breaks the proposal into smaller and smaller parts. The proposal doesn't write itself—that would be too good to be true—but the task changes from a backbreaking chore to one that can be tackled step by step.

Write a Section at a Time   Pick a section from your scratch outline and go to work on it. Try to get through the entire section in one sitting.

It's a mistake to write and rewrite particular sentences for style in a first draft. Instead, concentrate on completing an entire section with the time available. If necessary, use very broad strokes to do the job. Omit words, skip quotes, and then fill them in later. One scientist comments this way on his writing: "I always try to go straight through a particular section. If I can't think of a word, I just put it in parentheses and go back later to clean it up. Otherwise, I may get bogged down. And if I stop halfway through and then return the next day, I find I have to repeat a lot of the work. I lose the focus of the section."

Another scientist, Marshall Beringer, author of more than 60 papers, comments, "When I wrote my first scientific paper, I spent all morning on the first three sentences. Then I realized that if I continued that way, I'd be retired before I finished it. Now I use an outline, so as not to start wandering, and then try to do the first draft—or a piece of it—all in one sitting. Of course, I'll go back for two or three revisions later. But I try to go straight through the first time around."

Do the Easier Sections First   *In Alice in Wonderland*, the King of Hearts gives this advice: "Begin at the beginning, and go on till you come to the end: then stop." That is certainly the traditional way to go about writing a report. But beginnings are notoriously difficult: they have a way of expanding to fill all the available time.

Many writers get around this problem by beginning in the middle with a quick, manageable task. Then they write the more difficult parts, a section at a time. They postpone handling the introductory historical material because it is often unwieldy. The writer has to decide how much will interest the reader, how much should be available for reference. Consequently, it is sometimes more efficient to do straightforward sections such as the report of the results or the procedure and leave the more difficult parts for later, especially if you are working under time constraints.

Watch Out for Data Poisoning   This disease is endemic to technical writing. It begins with the essential job of accumulating citations and articles in one's area of interest. One is soon possessed of folders with clippings, offprints, 3×5 cards, sheaves of computer printouts, review volumes, annual indexes, and lists of abstracts.

At a certain point, what skilled writers refer to as "data poisoning" occurs. You'll know you're in danger if any of the following things occur:

1. You find yourself quoting at length when there's no need.
2. You find yourself including background information from your research folders that is not essential.
3. You decide you are not doing justice to your sources, and include many citations that are not essential to the argument.
4. You find yourself going off on tangents, interesting avenues that open up with each new piece of background information you decide to include.
5. Instead of using references to check a point, you find yourself reading in new areas and then including information from these sections. While the new information is interesting, it is not essential.
6. You feel overwhelmed by your background information, decide it is far too comprehensive to include within one piece of written work, and quit.

Data poisoning is the point at which the background information becomes unwieldy. A certain amount of information is essential, but then, at a point that varies for each person, the scales shift and you have too much information. Instead of assimilating material first, you find yourself constantly reading as you write. You return to your sources, and then find yourself pushed in directions you had not intended to go, forced there by the sheer mass and pressure of data.

If you find yourself constantly consulting your sources, quoting at length, or going off into interesting new avenues, you have probably gathered more information than you can assimilate. Cut back your references, digest the basic information, and then write without consulting your sources except when you need to verify or expand a point.

Summary   The first draft that you write is the one in which your major ideas are set forth and elaborated.

If you have time, put this draft away for a night or two. Then take it out again. Ask yourself, Have I covered my major points? Go back to your outline and make sure you have actually developed all of your major arguments. It is easy to leave essential information out. Do you need more tables? spectra? Do you have a conclusion? Or did you leave it to your reader to infer the conclusion from the data?

Second Draft: Persuasiveness

Once you have a first draft and are satisfied that it covers the basic arguments, you will want to go back and check for the persuasiveness of your arguments.

"I check for logic, coherence, and flow at this point," William Litchman, a physical chemist in nuclear magnetic resonance spectroscopy with more than 26 publications, says. "I want the person reading me to follow and come to the same conclusions I've reached. This is crucial for a writer," he adds. "If you can explain your point on paper, cover all the bases, lead your reader to the only reasonable explanation, then you've done the job. If there are two or three alternative explanations, each of them equally good, then your paper is not worth publishing."

Marshall Beringer comments similarly. "Once I have a first draft, I often find it doesn't have its emphasis in the places that I want.

"I write to persuade," he continues, "whether it's a memo, a report, or a paper. I establish a frame of reference, a view of the universe. And then, by weighing my facts, by ranking them and presenting them in a particular order of importance, I try to lead my reader *inescapably* to my conclusion."

Looking over your first draft, satisfied that you've included most of the raw material you need, you may find that you have failed to do that essential thing, "lead the reader inescapably to your conclusions."

Move, Insert, Expand At this point, you may need to do some moving, insertion, and expanding of points. Many experienced writers find that felt-tipped pens, scissors, and paste pots are their most valuable writing tools at this point. They dismember parts of the copy and rearrange them so the writing is more persuasive. It is more a matter of rearranging than rewriting.

"In the real world," Beringer comments, "everything is connected to everything else. It is a seamless web. But in writing one tries to make a path, an arbitrary channel with one site leading naturally, inevitably to the next. Sometimes one fails and has to go back several times before one is satisfied that the path has been made."

The second draft is often referred to as the "cut and paste" version in which one rearranges, moves, inserts, and expands until one is satisfied that the reader has been properly conducted along the path.

Third Draft: Mechanics

Once you are satisfied that your arguments are persuasive, you need to go over what you've written for more prosaic, mechanical considerations. Is the text accurate? Have you checked every figure reference? every citation? Do text references match figure references? Have numbers been accidentally transposed? Did you use the dictionary to check the meanings of words when you weren't sure of their usage? At this point, meticulous attention to detail is essential. If anything in the paper looks questionable—from the spelling of a word to a figure citation—check and verify.

Transitions and Topic Sentences   You should also check to make sure you've included transitions, the words that lead readers from one argument to the next, and topic sentences, the opening sentences of paragraphs or sections which state the points you then develop.

Beginning writers often underestimate the importance of transitions, those clear, unmistakable signposts of a writer's arguments. When you are in the middle of writing a report, the internal logic of the paper may be quite obvious to you. However, it may not be so apparent to your reader, who does not have your familiarity with the subject—or your outline—to follow.

Transitional words and phrases can function as an outline.

Experienced writers simply insert these words and phrases after they have finished writing. They use such standbys as *first, second,* and *third* to prefix their main points. They add *in conclusion* before the conclusion. When they are enumerating, they add *in addition* or *furthermore* so that the reader will realize the points are related to each other as part of a list. They use these words as markers to make the progression of their ideas clear to the reader.

The use of transitional words and phrases and of topic sentences will help the reader to follow your arguments.

Headings   There is a second device that many writers include at this stage. Heads and subheads are effective signposts for readers and good organizing aids for writers. The traditional heads of "Introduction," "Procedure," "Results," and "Conclusions," used in laboratory reports, can often be adapted for technical papers and reports. Many people use these headings as part of their outlines; others add headings as part of a later draft.

Wringing the Water Out   The order, coherence, and clarity of one's arguments are fundamental in good writing. It is also important to make these arguments with a minimum of repetition: economy of statement is a virtue in scientific writing.

In your final draft, check for passives, unnecessary repetition, and qualifiers. Favor unadorned, direct statements of your points.

Summary

A productive scientist or engineer easily averages 1000 pages a year. After the literature search or laboratory work, there is the report, proprietary document or patent application, the memos and briefs, the commercial applications. If the document is a research report, it enjoys an afterlife through computerized indexing and abstracting services and through inclusion in review articles.

The process begins with data assembly, scratch outline, first draft, and goes on through the stages described in this chapter. (See Figures 6-1 to 6-5.) Writing is not a tidy act. It would be a simple, straightforward matter if there were a one-for-one correspondence between what one thinks and what one puts down on paper. This is not so. One's ideas change as one writes.

That's what makes writing exciting. If it were simply transferring to paper ideas one already had, moving from one medium to another, that would be one thing. But that is not what happens. Instead, one's grasp of the subject changes as one develops one's understanding. By page 4 you have an idea you didn't have on page 1.

The writing process is not programmable, for awareness of the subject grows as one writes. But there are procedures which can be used to make the process more manageable.

Literature Cited

1. E. Bright Wilson, Jr., *An Introduction to Scientific Research,* McGraw-Hill, New York, 1952, p. 10.
2. Ellis Mount, *Guide to Basic Information Sources in Engineering,* Wiley, New York, 1976.

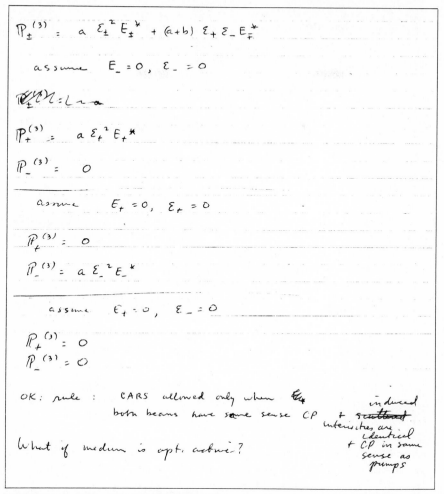

FIGURE 6-1   This series of illustrations (Figures 6-1 to 6-5) shows successive drafts of an actual research proposal. The author began with a set of equations which led him to ask the question, "What if the medium is optically active?"

Exercises

If you are studying in a group, take an inventory of your writing habits and report to each other on these questions:

1. How do you keep up in your field? What publications do you read? How do you keep track of citations? Do you use offprints or index cards? How? Do you notate journals? How?

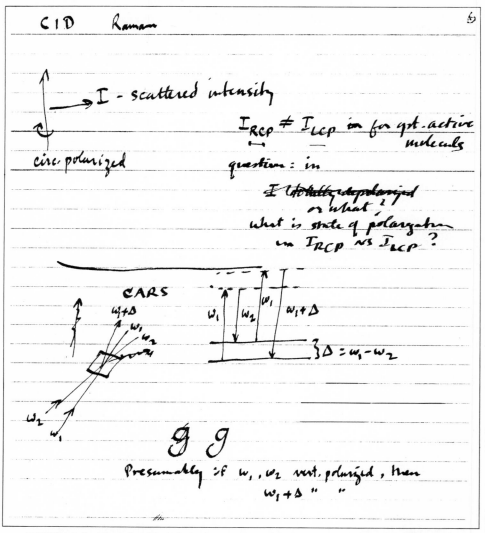

FIGURE 6-2   Then he began jotting down drawings and ideas for an experiment as he imagined it might take place.

2. How do you handle these classic pitfalls: Quoting unnecessarily? Going off on interesting but inessential tangents? Becoming overwhelmed by sources and abandoning the paper?
3. How many drafts of a paper do you write? Do you have a goal for the first draft? for the second draft?
4. Beringer says, "I write to persuade, whether it's a memo, a

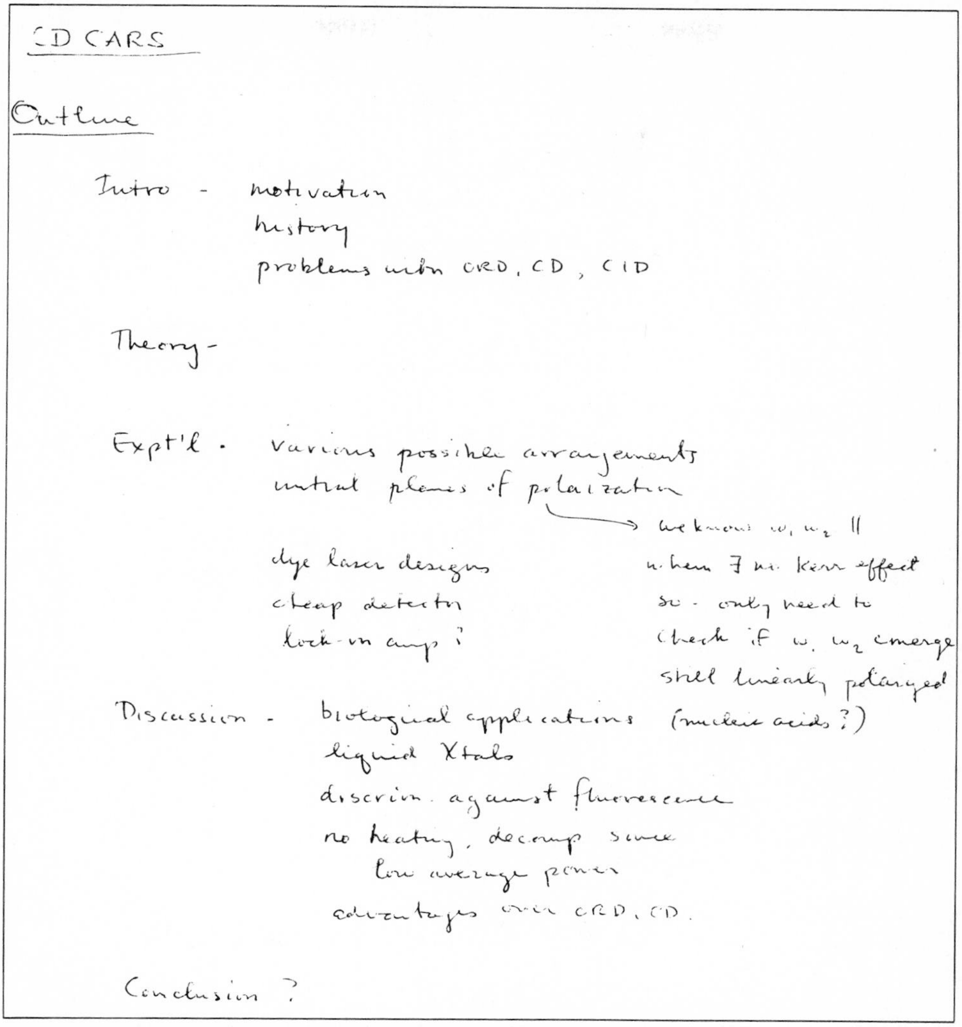

CD CARS

Outline

    Intro - motivation
              history
              problems with ORD, CD, CID

    Theory -

    Expt'l . various possible arrangements
              central planes of polarization
                       → we know ω_1, ω_2 ‖
          dye laser designs   when $\exists$ no Kerr effect
          cheap detector   so - only need to
          lock-on amps ?   check if $\omega_1 \omega_2$ emerge
                                still linearly polarized

    Discussion - biological applications (nucleic acids ?)
                liquid Xtals
                discrim. against fluorescence
                no heating, decomp since
                    low average power
                advantages over ORD, CD.

    Conclusion ?

FIGURE 6-3   At this point, he did an outline for the topic—a technique for using two lasers and polarization optics to study particular properties of molecules.

report, or a paper. I establish a frame of reference, a view of the universe. And then, by weighing my facts, by ranking them and presenting them in a particular order of importance, I try to lead my reader *inescapably* to my conclusion." Do you agree with this tactic? Discuss,

5. Do you use headings? When? Why? Do you use transitions? When? Why?

CIRCULAR DIFFERENTIAL CARS

A Research Proposal

Introduction

~~It is~~ Only within the last decade [~~we have become aware~~] *It has been observed*
that Raman scattered intensities from optically active molecules
are different for incident right and left circularly polarized
(RCP and LCP) ~~radiation~~ *light*. Circular differential Raman is a recent
development in Raman spectroscopy and [~~promises~~ to become] a *has gives expectations of becoming* *is likely*
powerful tool in the determination of absolute configurations of
chiral groups in large molecules. The method presently suffers
from the same problems which [plague] conventional Raman spectro- *too strong* *afflict*
scopy: weak signals, the ~~need for~~ a large ~~spectrometer~~, and the *monochromator* *necessity of*
heating of samples due to high input powers. Parallel~~ing the~~ *to the* *double t?*
development of CD Raman has been the utilization of high peak
power, low average power, tunable dye lasers to produce coherent
anti-Stokes Raman signals. The CARS technique, although requiring
tunable lasers, dispenses with the ~~need for~~ a spectrometer, since
the CARS signal is in the form of a collimated, laser-like beam
which is spatially separated from the two exciting laser beams, thus
eliminating ~~the [problem of]~~ Rayleigh-scattered background. Because *interference from the*
the signals are collimated and intense (10 x the conversion
efficiency of conventional Raman), ~~the need for~~ expensive, sensitive
photon-counting equipment is ~~eliminated~~. Since the anti-Stokes *unnecessary*

FIGURE 6-4   In the second draft he edited for persuasiveness, used a synonym dictionary for questionable choices, and began weeding out unnecessary words.

RESEARCH CORPORATION
A Foundation for the Advancement of Science

(Please confine responses to this form, using one side only; attach as additional pages only those requested on Page 3)

PRINCIPAL INVESTIGATOR

ADADEMIC RANK AND DEPARTMENT

INSTITUTION AND ADDRESS

EDUCATION AND EXPERIENCE (Degrees, postdoctoral appointments, principal previous employment—when and where)

SHORT TITLE OF PROPOSED RESEARCH

CIRCULAR DIFFERENTIAL COHERENT ANTI-STOKES RAMAN SPECTROSCOPY (CD CARS)

SIGNIFICANCE OF PROPOSED RESEARCH (State succinctly the importance of the problem, the originality of this approach and the contribution it will make if successful)

The conformation and configuration of amino acids, peptides and proteins have been the subject of much spectroscopic study, owing to their importance to the understanding of biological activity at the molecular level. The routine determination of absolute configuration in chiral molecules remains an elusive goal for physical chemists. Anomalous x-ray scattering, the most direct technique, requires the crystallization of the sample, which is often not possible. Optical rotatory dispersion and circular dichroism, which probe the electronic optical activity, provide an unfocussed view of the nuclear structure, and are limited to the study of asymmetric centers in the vicinity of the active chromophore. Vibrational optical activity offers a more direct probe of the structural chirality, and some inroads have been made in this direction: vibrational circular dichroism[1] and circular differential Raman spectroscopy.[2] However, transition dipoles in the infrared are often extremely small, leaving Raman as the most sensitive method at present. I propose a significant improvement in sensitivity by applying coherent anti-Stokes Raman spectroscopy[3] (CARS) to the study of vibrational optical activity. CD CARS should permit the investigation of a wide range of molecules of biological interest, which are inaccessible by conventional CD Raman, owing to large fluorescence cross sections, heating effects, or their availability only in dilute solutions.

PLAN OF PROCEDURE (Experimental plan of what is to be done and its relation to above statement; point out innovative features and annotate literature references which are particularly pertinent)

In optically active media, scattered Raman intensities are different for incident exciting light which is right or left circularly polarized (RCP and LCP).[4] The important parameter is the circular intensity differential (CID) defined by $(I_{RCP} - I_{LCP})/(I_{RCP} + I_{LCP})$. Its magnitude is a measure of the chiral character of the particular vibrational mode under observation, while its sign is related to the absolute configuration of the particular chiral group; the CID changes sign when the compound is replaced by its enantiomer.

In CD CARS, an analogous CID is expected for the coherent anti-Stokes beam, which is generated by the nonlinear interaction in the sample of the two input laser beams at the central and Stokes frequencies. The planned experimental arrangement utilizes a pulsed nitrogen laser, which pumps two tunable dye lasers, whose outputs are focussed into the sample at the appropriate phase-matching angle. The resulting anti-Stokes beam is isolated using a spatial aperture, and further discrimination against scattered light and fluorescence can be made with an interference filter. The CARS signal is detected with a conventional silicon PIN photodiode.

PLEASE OBSERVE MARGIN

FIGURE 6-5   Here is a sample from the proposal itself.

7

Using the Library: Keeping up in Science and Engineering

Six hours in the library may save six months in the laboratory.
E. Bright Wilson, Jr.

Part of a technical report is created in the laboratory and part at the typewriter. But a significant portion of most reports evolves in a third location—at the library or at a computer terminal.

The library and computerized search services are necessary for accurate surveys of literature in particular fields; such surveys are essential to avoid both repetition and error.

E. Bright Wilson writes perceptively about literature searches [1]:

> Six hours in the library may save six months in the laboratory. Sometimes, however, the investigator is tempted to believe that the opposite is true; that the scientific literature is so complex and confused that it is easier to rediscover facts than to look them up.

The literature *is* complex, and it is common to be daunted by the volume of information. The assortment of primary sources—periodicals, technical reports, patent literature, books, and serials —is vast, and it continues to grow. Originally there were only three scientific periodicals: *The Philosophical Transactions of the Royal Society of London* and the *Journal des Scavans* (later the *Journal des Savants*) both published in 1665, and the *Acta Eruditorum*, published in Germany in 1682. Since then, the number of periodicals has multiplied at an astonishing rate: more than 60,000 scientific periodicals were published between 1900 and 1960 alone.

How does a scientist or engineer keep up? Working scientists and engineers derive some of their information informally—through correspondence with colleagues and through conversations with others in their field. Some of the information comes across the desk through the two or three journals one is likely to receive as part of a professional membership, plus a news magazine or newsletter within one's field.

Many people also subscribe to *Current Contents*, a weekly service that reproduces tables of contents for the journals in a field, allowing one either to seek the journals in the library or to write either the author or a related service, OATS (Original Article Tear Sheet), for reprints.

There is also an array of indexing and abstracting services that enables researchers to sort through the primary sources—journals, reports, and patents—in an efficient way. Abstracts give descriptive or informative summaries, and indexes give bibliographic citations with title, author, subject, and related information.

Indexing services abound: the 1976 *A Guide to the World's Abstracting and Indexing Services in Science and Technology* lists 2300 such services. Most of these indexing and abstracting services are printed and placed in the library so that the user can do a manual search. Today, there are also computerized retrieval systems with many data bases to search the literature of chemistry, physics, engineering, the life sciences, geology, astronomy, and other fields. Both types of services, manual and computerized, cover periodicals—the mainstay of scientific literature. The services also cover new books, government reports, proceedings, films, and patents. Several services deal exclusively with technical reports, which are often difficult to locate if the report is issued by a private company or is done by a researcher as part of a government contract. The enormous patent literature is well served by both manual and computerized systems. A relatively new addition to the literature is the citation index; this useful service lists citations or references to particular papers.

Use of the literature is essential for most technical and scientific writing. This chapter provides a general introduction to the resources available for a literature search. The citations are not exhaustive but should suggest a range of useful sources for the beginner.

General Sources

If you've no background at all in the subject, the first step is an overview of the sort provided by an encyclopedia. Handbooks, too, are traditional sources for general information. Third, there may be textbooks in the field with extensive reference lists. While the information may not be current, the references will provide an adequate beginning for background reading.

Encyclopedias   These will be useful if you are embarking on a new topic, for they provide general introductions. There are also many situations in which one needs to place the subject in a larger framework. For instance, one may have assistants on a project who understand the particular experiment but not the history of the inquiry. General encyclopedias, such as *Encyclopaedia Britannica* and *Encyclopedia Americana*, have a place here.

There are also three outstanding general encyclopedias in science:

Harper Encyclopedia of Science, rev. ed., James R. Newman (ed.), Harper & Row, New York, 1967.

McGraw-Hill Encyclopedia of Science and Technology, 4th ed., McGraw-Hill, New York, 1971.

Van Nostrand's Scientific Encyclopedia, 4th ed., Van Nostrand Reinhold, New York, 1968.

These three encyclopedias are found in most reference sections of large libraries. *The McGraw-Hill Encyclopedia* is supplemented by an annual *Yearbook of Science and Technology*. The illustrations in both Van Nostrand's and Harper's are excellent.

While these encyclopedias may be too general for the specialist, they are ideal for a beginner who wants an overview for both the articles themselves and the citations that follow.

There is also an abundance of specialized encyclopedias:

Astronomy

Larousse Encyclopedia of Astronomy, Prometheus, New York, 1959.

Biology

The Cambridge Natural History, Macmillan, New York, 1895–1909.

Encyclopedia of the Biological Sciences, 2d ed., Peter Gray (ed.), Van Nostrand
   Reinhold, New York, 1970.

Encyclopedia of the Life Sciences, Doubleday, New York, 1964–1965.

Hall, E. Raymond, *Mammals of North America,* Ronald, New York, 1959.

Chemical Engineering and Chemistry

Chemical and Process Technology Encyclopedia, D. Considine (ed.), McGraw-Hill,
   New York, 1974.

Encyclopedia of the Chemical Elements, Clifford A. Hampel (ed.), Van Nostrand
   Reinhold, New York, 1968.

Encyclopedia of Chemical Process Equipment, William J. Mead (ed.), Van Nostrand
   Reinhold, New York, 1964.

Encyclopedia of Chemical Technology, 3d ed., R. E. Kirk and D. F. Othmer (eds.),
   Wiley, New York, 1980.

Encyclopedia of Chemistry, 3d ed., Clifford Hampel and G. G. Hawley (eds.), Van
   Nostrand Reinhold, New York, 1973.

Encyclopedia of Polymer Science and Technology: Plastics, Resins, Rubbers, Fibers,
   Herman F. Mark and Norman G. Gaylord (eds.), Wiley, New York,
   1964–1972.

Kingzett's Chemical Encyclopedia: A Digest of Chemistry and Its Industrial Applications,
   9th ed., D. H. Hey (ed.), Van Nostrand Reinhold, New York, 1967.

Modern Plastics Encyclopedia, McGraw-Hill, New York, 1941–.

Engineering

Encyclopedia of Engineering Materials and Processes, H. R. Clauser et al. (eds.), Van
   Nostrand Reinhold, New York, 1963.

McGraw-Hill Encyclopedia of Environmental Science, McGraw-Hill, New York, 1974.

Materials Handbook: An Encyclopedia for Purchasing Agents, Engineers, Executives,
   and Foremen, 10th ed., George Stuart Brady (ed.), McGraw-Hill, New York,
   1971.

Newnes' Concise Encyclopedia of Nuclear Energy, D. E. Barnes (ed.), Newnes,
   London, 1961.

Geology

Larousse Encyclopedia of the Earth, Prometheus, New York, 1961.

Mathematics

Universal Encyclopedia of Mathematics, Allen and Unwin, London, 1964.

Medicine

U.S. Pharmacopoeia and National Formulary, U.S. Pharmacopial Convention, Rockville, Md., 1982.

Physics

Encyclopaedic Dictionary of Physics, J. Thewlis (ed.), Pergamon, Elmsford, N.Y., 1961–.

Encyclopedia of Physics, 2d ed., Robert M. Besancon (ed.), Van Nostrand Reinhold, New York, 1974.

Handbooks and Texts   There are many handbooks within each field. Most reference desks have several for each specialization. Working engineers and scientists use them as desk-top references—especially for the sort of information that is not superseded quickly.

Like encyclopedias, handbooks are not timely—even with frequent updates they cannot keep up with newly generated data. Nonetheless, they serve as a useful starting point.

They are too numerous to list. CRC Press, Inc., a foremost handbook publisher in engineering and science, offers 50 handbooks, among them the classic *CRC Handbook of Tables for Applied Engineering Science,* edited by Ray E. Bolz. McGraw-Hill offers more than 100 handbooks; their titles include *Chemical Engineers' Handbook, Standard Handbook of Civil Engineers, Concrete Construction Handbook, Standard Handbook for Electrical Engineers,* and *Electronic Engineers' Handbook.* Van Nostrand Reinhold publishes many handbooks, as does Wiley. Among Wiley's classic volumes is *Handbook of Engineering Fundamentals,* edited by Mott Souders. There are also excellent handbooks that are updated yearly, among them *Kempe's Engineers Year-Book,* published by Morgan-Grampian in West Wickham, Kent, England.

Textbooks can also prove useful at the beginning of a search—particularly if they have good reference lists. Although textbooks generally were not ordered by libraries prior to 1960, they are usually available now.

Guides to the Literature   There are guides to the literature of mathematics, of physics, and of chemistry, biology, astronomy, medicine, and geology.

The quality of literature guides varies: in general, it is best to choose one that is annotated, since a long list of references will probably mean little to the beginner without some descriptive comments.

A well-annotated literature guide is invaluable for lists of basic references, outstanding journals, useful reviewing and abstracting services, and miscellaneous sources of information.

Three outstanding ones include:

Malinowsky, H. Robert, *Science and Engineering Reference Sources*, 2d ed., Libraries Unlimited, Littleton, Colo., 1976.

Mount, Eli, *Guide to Basic Information Sources in Engineering*, Norton, New York, 1976.

Woodburn, Henry M., *Using the Chemical Literature*, Marcel Dekker, New York, 1974.

Secondary Sources

Abstracting and indexing services are invaluable for working scientists and engineers, enabling them to remain current in their fields and to conduct efficient literature searches.

Computerized Search Systems These allow researchers to request citations on a topic—for instance, patents on heat exchanger fins, 1971 to the present. The researcher may ask for the information at a computer terminal or ask a librarian or information officer to help. Within minutes, most systems will deliver a printout of test citations.

There are many data bases in science, technology, engineering, business, and economics used in these machine searches. In science, technology, and engineering, for instance, a single company, Lockheed Information Systems, offers searches of a vast literature of patents, journals, and reports.

To use a service such as Lockheed's, researchers write in their own words what they are seeking, by (1) defining terms with special meanings, (2) giving years to be covered, (3) listing approximate number of citations expected, and (4) specifying the language or languages.

Then the researcher writes out two examples of the type of citations expected. The library information officer institutes the search, which takes about two minutes. Since on-line time is expensive, it is customary to simply print out a sample. If citations similar to the test ones appear in the sample, then the search is on the right track and a printout of the citations can be mailed to the researcher within the week.

There are two drawbacks to the system: (1) Most of the data bases commence at 1969 to 1970; therefore, for information printed earlier a manual search is necessary. (2) The user is charged for the service. 1980 Lockheed rates are given in the accompanying table. These rates are typical, ranging from $25 per hour to $150 per hour. A typical search takes two minutes.

Several off-line print services are available. Most people request references in bibliographic form, and it is cheaper to have these delivered off-line than to have the citation list printed on-line. Some people request abstracts and even entire documents from files.

Here are two examples of the use of on-line search services:

Results by Mail A graduate student is interested in the literature since 1970 of reactions in which molecular nitrogen becomes attached to the metal of an organometallic compound—not in nature, but in the laboratory. The head of her research group, a professor, is writing a proposal on this subject, and she is assigned the "Related Literature" section.

She has approval to spend $25 on the search. She contacts the information officer at the library. Together they decide the key words for the search are *nitrogen, fixation,* and *synthetic.* The researcher writes in her own words what she is seeking, defining terms and giving the years of the search, the approximate number of citations expected (100), and the language. Afterward she writes out two examples that should be automatically retrieved if the search is accurate.

The information officer does the search. The key words are correct and produce the test citations. The 100 bibliographic citations requested by the researcher are delivered later by mail.

Results Printed Off-Line A researcher is using a citation index. That is, he is using an earlier article (Francis Crick's 1971 article in volume 234 of *Nature* on chromosomes of higher organisms) to find more recent publications on the premise that current publications in the subject will of necessity cite Crick. He gives the information officer the author, publication in which the article appeared, year, and volume.

The information officer enters the file, expands the reference, and promptly retrieves 148 current publications citing Crick's article. (See Figures 7-1 and 7-2). The items are printed. The search takes less than two minutes and costs $16.20.

TOPIC: Find all publications which cite Francis Crick's 1971 article in volume 234 of *Nature* on chromosomes of higher organisms (pp. 25-27)

This search involves using a cited reference (Crick's article) to retrieve current publications. It will use the Cited Reference (CR=) index.

①   Enter File 34, SCISEARCH

②   EXPAND cited reference name and year to obtain exact form used; note that journal name is not necessary.

③   SELECT both forms of reference to the article; E4 shows a specific reference to the second page of Crick's article. 148 current publications citing Crick's article are retrieved.

④   PRINT the 148 items offline.

⑤   Search completed, requiring less than 2 minutes.

FIGURE 7-1   Example of procedure librarian uses to trace references to the Crick article, SCISEARCH is the data base used. (*Courtesy ISI.*)

```
①    ? BEGIN 34
              8jul77 11:25:02 User316
      $0.08  0.003 Hrs File1
              File34:SCISEARCH 74-77/WK18
              Set Items Description (+=OR;*=AND;-=NOT)
              --- ----- ----------------------------
②    ? EXPAND CR=CRICK F, 1971?
      Ref  Index-term              Type Items RT
      E1   CR=CRICK F, 1971--------       1
      E2   CR=CRICK F, 1971, P429--       1
      E3   CR=CRICK F, 1971, V234,
              P25-----------------       147
      E4   CR=CRICK F, 1971, V234,
              P26-----------------         1
      E5   CR=CRICK F, 1971, V25,
              P429----------------         5
      E6  -CR=CRICK F, 1971?--------
③    ? SELECT E3, E4
              1    148 E3, E4
                        E6: CR=CRICK F, 1971?
④    ? PRINT 1/2/1-148
      Printed1/2/1-148
⑤    ? LOGOFF
              8jul77 11:26:14 User316
        $1.40  0.020 Hrs File34 2 Descriptors
       $14.80  148 Prints
       $16.20  Estimated Total Cost
      LOGOFF 11:26:20
```

FIGURE 7-2   Sample of printout for the Crick citation search. (*Courtesy ISI.*)

Here is a list of some of the computerized data bases available. Most begin in 1969 or 1970, although MEDLARS (National Library of Medicine) begins in 1964, and METADEX (American Society for Metals) in 1966.

LIST OF CURRENT DATA BASES AND COSTS THROUGH LOCKHEED INFORMATION SYSTEMS

File No.	Data Base (Supplier)	On-Line Connect Rate, $/Hour	Off-Line Print Rate Per Full Record, ¢
1	ERIC (Educational Resources Information Center)	25	10
2	CA CONDENSATES 1970–1971 (American Chemical Society)	35	8
3	CA CONDENSATES/CASIA 1973–1976 (American Chemical Society)	45	16
4	CA CONDENSATES/CASIA 1977–present (American Chemical Society)	45	16
5	BIOSIS PREVIEWS 1972–present (Biological Abstracts, Inc.)	45	10
6	NTIS (National Technical Info. Service, U.S. Dept. of Commerce)	35	10
7	SOCIAL SCISEARCH® (Institute for Scientific Information)	70	10
8	COMPENDEX (Engineering Index, Inc.)	65	10
9	AIM/ARM (Center for Vocational Education)	25	10
10	AGRICOLA (Natl. Agricultural Library, U.S. Dept. of Ag.)	25	5
11	PSYCHOLOGICAL ABSTRACTS (American Psychological Assoc.)	50	10
12	INSPEC 1969–1977 (Institution of Electrical Engineers)	45	10
13	INSPEC 1978–present (Institution of Electrical Engineers)	45	10
14	ISMEC (Data Courier, Inc.)	65	12
15	ABI/INFORM (Data Courier, Inc.)	65	10
16	PTS PROMT (Predicasts, Inc.)*	90	20
17	PTS WEEKLY (Predicasts, Inc.)	90	20
18	PTS F&S INDEXES (Predicasts, Inc.)*	90	20
19	CHEMICAL INDUSTRY NOTES (American Chemical Society)	90	20
20	PTS FEDERAL INDEX (Predicasts, Inc.)	90	20
21	PTS FEDERAL INDEX WEEKLY (Predicasts, Inc.)	90	20
22	EIS INDUSTRIAL PLANTS (Economic Information Systems, Inc.)	90	50
23	CLAIMS™/CHEM 1950–1976 (IFI/Plenum Data Company)	150	10
24	CLAIMS™/CHEM 1977–present (IFI/Plenum Data Company)	150	10
25	CLAIMS™/CLASS (IFI/Plenum Data Company)	90	10
26	FOUNDATION DIRECTORY (The Foundation Center)	60	30
27	FOUNDATION GRANTS (The Foundation Center)	60	30
28	OCEANIC ABSTRACTS (Data Courier, Inc.)	55	10
29	METEOROLOGICAL ABS. (Am. Meteorological Soc. and NOAA)	50	10

LIST OF CURRENT DATA BASES AND COSTS THROUGH LOCKHEED INFORMATION SYSTEMS (Continued)

File No.	Data Base (Supplier)	On-Line Connect Time Rate, $/Hour	Off-Line Print Rate Per Full Record, ¢
31	CHEMNAME™	60	12
32	METADEX (American Society for Metals)	80	12
33	WORLD ALUMINUM ABSTRACTS (American Society for Metals)	60	10
34	SCISEARCH® 1978–present (Institute for Scientific Information)	70	10
35	COMPREHENSIVE DISSERTATION ABS. (Xerox U. Microfilms)	55	12
36	LANGUAGE & LANGUAGE BEHAVIOR ABS. (Sociological Abs., Inc.)	55	15
37	SOCIOLOGICAL ABSTRACTS (Sociological Abstracts, Inc.)	55	15
38	AMERICA: HISTORY & LIFE (ABC-Clio, Inc.)	65	15
39	HISTORICAL ABSTRACTS (ABC-Cilo, Inc.)	65	15
40	ENVIROLINE® (Environment Information Center, Inc.)	90	20
41	POLLUTION ABSTRACTS (Data Courier, Inc.)	65	15
42	PHARMACEUTICAL NEWS INDEX (Data Courier, Inc.)	65	15
43	CA PATENT CONCORDANCE (American Chemical Society)	45	8
44	AQUATIC SCIENCE & FISHERIES ABSTRACTS (NOAA)	35	10
45	APTIC (Air Pollution Tech. Info. Ctr. and The Franklin Institute)	35	10
46	NICEM (National Information Center for Educational Media)	70	20
47	MAGAZINE INDEX (Information Access Corp.)	45	10
48	PIRA (Research Assoc. for Paper & Board, Printing & Packaging Industry)	55	15
49	PAIS INTERNATIONAL (Public Affairs Information Service, Inc.)	60	15
50	COMMONWEALTH AGRICULTURAL BUREAUX ABSTRACTS (Commonwealth Agricultural Bureaux)	65	15

AGRICOLA is the cataloging and indexing data base of the National Agricultural Library. This file provides coverage of journal and monographic literature on agriculture and related subjects. (1970–present)

BIOSIS PREVIEWS contains citations from both *Biological Abstracts* and *Bioresearch Index*, the major publications of BioSciences Information Service of *Biological Abstracts*. Nearly 8000 primary journals as well as symposia, reviews, preliminary reports, semipopular journals, selected institutional and government reports, research communications, and other secondary sources provide citations. (1969–present)

CA CONDENSATES is the computer-readable file corresponding to the printed *Chemical Abstracts*. Coverage includes journal articles, patent specifications, reviews, technical reports, monographs, conference proceedings, symposia, dissertations, and books. (1970–1971)

CA CONDENSATES/CASIA is an expanded data base which was produced by the merger of two files: the CA CONDENSATES file, which contains the basic bibliographic information appearing in the printed *Chemical Abstracts* (CA), and the CASIA file, which contains CA General Subject Headings from a controlled vocabulary and the CAS (Chemical Abstracts Service) Registry Numbers, a number assigned to each specific chemical compound. (1972–present)

CA-PATENT CONCORDANCE correlates patents issued by different countries for the same basic invention. For any given invention, an abstract is published in CA for the first patent received and covered by the CAS. Subsequent patents covering the same basic invention are not abstracted in CA but rather are entered in CA PATENT CONCORDANCE. (1972–present)

COMPENDEX is the machine-readable version of the *Engineering Index* (*Ei, Monthly/Annual*). The *Ei* data base provides coverage of approximately 3500 journals, publications of engineering societies and organizations, papers from the proceedings of conferences, and selected government reports and books. (1970–present)

ENERGYLINE is the machine-readable version of *Energy Information Abstracts* and also includes 8000 energy and environmental records dating back to 1971 from *The Energy Index*. Coverage includes journals, books, congressional committee reprints, conference proceedings, speeches, and statistics. (1971–present)

ENVIROLINE provides indexing and abstracting coverage of more than 5000 international primary and secondary source publications reporting on aspects of the environment. (1971–present)

EXCERPTA MEDICA is one of the two principal sources for searching the biomedical literature. It consists of abstracts and citations of articles from over 3500 biomedical journals published throughout the world. It is used by libraries, hospitals, medical schools, health organizations, and chemical and pharmaceutical companies. (1975–present)

GEOARCHIVE indexes more than 100,000 references each year in the geological sciences, including 5000 serials, books, conferences, doctoral dissertations, and technical reports. (1969–present)

INSPEC is a file corresponding to the printed *Physics Abstracts, Electrical and Electronics Abstracts*, and *Computer and Control Abstracts*. Published by The Institution of Electrical Engineers (London), it forms the largest English-language data base in the fields of physics, electrotechnology, computers, and control. Foreign-language material is included but abstracted and indexed in English.

ISMEC (Information Service in Mechanical Engineering) indexes articles in mechanical engineering, production engineering, and engineering management from approximately 250 journals published throughout the world. In addition, books, reports, and conference proceedings are indexed. (1973–present)

METADEX (*Metals Abstracts/Alloys Index*) produced by the American Society for Metals and the Metals Society (London), provides coverage of international literature on the science and practice of metallurgy. Included in this data base are *Review of Metal Literature* (1966–1967), *Metals Abstracts* (1968–present), and since 1974, *Alloys Index*. (1966–present)

NTIS (National Technical Information Service, U.S. Department of Commerce, Springfield, Virginia): This data base consists of government-sponsored research, development, and engineering plus analyses prepared by federal agencies, their contractors, or grantees. Unclassified reports from such agencies as the National Aeronautics and Space Administration (NASA), Department of Health and Human Services, and the Department of Housing and Urban Development (HUD) as well as some 240 other units are available through the service. State and local government agencies are now beginning to contribute their reports to the file. (1964–present)

POLLUTION ABSTRACTS lists references to environmentally related literature on pollution. (1970–present)

SCISEARCH, a general index to the literature of science and technology prepared by the Institute for Scientific Information, contains all the records published in *Science Citation Index* (SCI) and additional records from the *Current Contents* series of publications not included in the printed version of SCI. Articles, reports of meetings, letters, editorials, and other items from about 2600 scientific and technical journals are indexed. (1974–present)

On-Shelf Abstracting and Indexing Services   While computerized search services offer an edge in fields where the flow of information is prodigious, traditional indexing and abstracting services also have advantages—among them accessibility, low cost, and more extensive historical coverage.

Engineering Index (*Ei*), for instance, the most recent portion of which is now available on-line as COMPENDEX, begins in 1884. It includes periodicals, serials, symposia, books, and reports; is regarded as the outstanding index to engineering news; and is on the shelves of most university libraries.

As with many other indexes, *Ei* has alphabetically arranged main subject headings and subheadings. It also has an alphabetically arranged author index, done both monthly and in the cumulative volumes.

Figure 7-3 is an illustration from the *Author* index of *Ei*. The author is Y. T. Shah. The numbers following Shah's name are the *Ei Monthly* abstract number. A copy of the abstract itself appears in Figure 7-4.

Abstracts in the *Monthly* index are placed in alphabetical order by main subject headings and published as the *Annual*.

AUTHOR INDEX

SHAH, S.R., 085266
SHAH, Y.T., 083061
SHAH, YATISH T., 079250

FIGURE 7-3   Sample from the author index to *Engineering Index*. The numbers following Shah's name are the *Ei Monthly* abstract number. (*Courtesy Engineering Index.*)

Beginning in 1973, abstracts in the *Annual* are listed as well by abstract number.

Copies of the text of most articles in the *Monthly* can be requested for a fee from Engineering Societies Library, 345 East 47 Street, New York, N.Y. 10017.

The hardbound volumes of *Ei* are issued annually just after the close of the calendar year.

Here is a list of on-shelf abstracting and indexing aids that are available in most technical libraries. The list is not complete, but should serve as an introduction to services available.

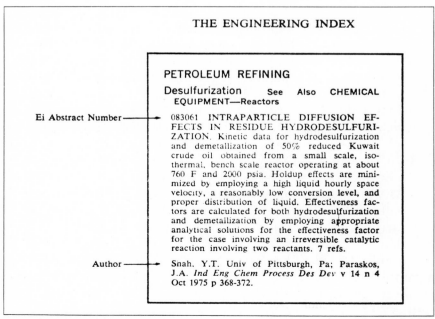

THE ENGINEERING INDEX

PETROLEUM REFINING

Desulfurization   See Also   CHEMICAL EQUIPMENT—Reactors

Ei Abstract Number —— 083061 INTRAPARTICLE DIFFUSION EFFECTS IN RESIDUE HYDRODESULFURIZATION. Kinetic data for hydrodesulfurization and demetallization of 50% reduced Kuwait crude oil obtained from a small scale, isothermal, bench scale reactor operating at about 760 F and 2000 psia. Holdup effects are minimized by employing a high liquid hourly space velocity, a reasonably low conversion level, and proper distribution of liquid. Effectiveness factors are calculated for both hydrodesulfurization and demetallization by employing appropriate analytical solutions for the effectiveness factor for the case involving an irreversible catalytic reaction involving two reactants. 7 refs.

Author —— Snah. Y.T. Univ of Pittsburgh, Pa; Paraskos, J.A. *Ind Eng Chem Process Des Dev* v 14 n 4 Oct 1975 p 368-372.

FIGURE 7-4   The abstract of Shah's article as it appears in *Engineering Index*. (*Courtesy Engineering Index.*)

Manual Indexing and Abstracting Services

Air Pollution Abstracts, U.S. Environmental Protection Agency, 1970–present.

Applied Mechanics Reviews, American Society of Mechanical Engineers, New York, 1948–present.

Applied Science and Technology Index, Wilson, New York, 1913–present. (Only English literature is covered. No author's index or abstracts.)

ASCE Publications Abstracts, American Society of Civil Engineers, New York, 1966–present. (Abstracts of all papers appearing in all the ASCE journals and in *Civil Engineering*.)

Biological Abstracts, BioSciences Information Service of Biological Abstracts, Philadelphia, 1927–present. (Abstracts of periodicals in zoology, botany, biochemistry, physiology. Available on-line.)

Chemical Abstracts, American Chemical Society, Columbus, Ohio, 1907–present. (Considered the foremost technical and scientific abstracting service. Available on-line, it covers new books, journals, patents, conference proceedings, and technical reports.)

Computer and Control Abstracts, Institution of Electrical Engineers, London, 1966–present. (Covers periodical literature. Part C of *Science Abstracts*, it is available on-line.)

Computing Reviews, Association for Computing Machinery, New York, 1960–present.

Engineering Index, Engineering Index, Inc., New York, 1884–present. (Includes periodicals, serials, symposia, books, and reports; regarded as the outstanding general index to engineering literature. Available as COMPENDEX.)

Electrical and Electronics Abstracts, Institution of Electrical Engineers, London, 1898–present. (Part B of *Science Abstracts*; covers all areas of electrical engineering.)

Energy Index, Environment Information Center, New York, 1973–present.

Environment Index, Environment Information Center, New York, 1971–present.

Government Reports Announcement and Index, U.S. National Technical Information Service, Springfield, Va., 1946–present. (For technical reports, indexed by author, agency, report number, contract number, and subject. Reports done on behalf of most government agencies available. On-line service.)

INIS Atomindex, International Atomic Energy Agency, Vienna, 1970–present. (Nuclear energy: books, patents, technical reports.)

International Aerospace Abstracts, American Institute of Aeronautics and Astronautics, New York, 1961–present. [Aeronautics; space science. A companion volume to Scientific and Technical Aerospace Reports (STAR).]

Mathematical Reviews, American Mathematical Society, Providence, R.I., 1940–present.

Metals Abstracts, Institute of Metals, London, 1968–present. (Comprehensive abstracting service. Available on-line.)

Monthly Catalog of United States Government Publications, Superintendent of Documents, 1895–present. (For technical reports by government agencies.)

Physics Abstracts, Institution of Electrical Engineers, London, 1898–present. (Part A of *Science Abstracts*. Outstanding coverage of physics and astronomy. Available on-line.)

Science Citation Index, Institute for Scientific Information, Philadelphia, Pa. 1961–present. (An index of citations given at conclusion of articles. Available on-line.)

Other Important Sources

Review Volumes These important and useful secondary sources are reviews, typically done annually, by authorities who survey the year's research, summarize it, and make comments and recommendations. There are comprehensive bibliographies.

Review volumes have advantages for the beginning of a literature search since the list of references provides a convenient starting point for the search.

Formerly it was difficult to locate some kinds of reviews, since they were not necessarily issued as separate publications but might have been included within a volume of a journal.

Today, however, there is an index published by the Institute for Scientific Information (ISI), the *Index to Scientific Reviews*, which gives more than 23,000 review articles published each year in science.

In addition, there are annual review series published by Wiley, Academic, Pergamon, Springer-Verlag, Plenum, Annual Reviews, Inc., and other publishing houses.

Wiley publishes an *Advances in . . .* series each year, including *Advances in Analytical Chemistry and Instrumentation*, *Advances in Biomedical Engineering and Medical Physics*, and *Advances in Environmental Sciences*.

Academic Press publishes many titles that are annuals. *Advances in Applied Mechanics*, for instance, has been issued by Academic Press since 1948. Each year there are five to ten articles reporting on the year's progress, and each article includes extensive references.

CRC Press publishes critical reviews, as does the Chemical

Society. The American Chemical Society has published *Chemical Reviews* monthly since 1925.

Table-of-Contents Journals The leader is *Current Contents*, referred to in *Trends in Biochemical Sciences* as "virtually irreplaceable" in rapidly developing fields such as biochemistry. *Current Contents* is a weekly service publishing the tables of contents for outstanding journals within particular fields. (See Figure 7-5, p. 140.)

There are several issues of interest to scientists and engineers, among them *Current Contents: Engineering and Technology*, *Current Contents: Life Sciences*, and *Current Contents: Physical and Chemical Sciences*. All *Current Contents* are published by the ISI in Philadelphia.

Tear sheets for most articles are available through the related OATS service (see Figure 7-6, p. 141), or through sending the author a postcard (see Figure 7-7).

The American Chemical Society also publishes biweekly a table of contents, called *Chemical Titles*, for 700 chemical journals.

Proceedings Proceedings are a third important source. These volumes, often unedited and published rapidly in the wake of conferences or meetings, are useful because of their timeliness, and often displace monographs solely through the promptness with which they can be put on the shelf.

Patent Information

Derwents is an abstracting and retrieval service for chemical and related patents that can be used manually or on-line. Derwents publishes both the *Central Patents Index* and the *World Patent Index*.

There are also traditional sources for patent information, including the *Manual of Classification* (U.S. Patent Office, Superintendent of Documents, Washington, D.C.), a loose-leaf volume listing the numbers and titles of the main classes and subclasses used in the subject classification of patents; and *Official Gazette: Patents* (U.S. Patent Office, Superintendent of Documents, Washington, D.C.), which lists recent patents with illustrations, abstracts, and name of patentees.

Chemical Abstracts also lists and abstracts patents in chemistry.

HT788

International Archives of Allergy and Applied Immunology
Articles and Abstracts in English

VOL. 60 NO. 4 1979

Original Papers

Attallah, A.M.; Malinin, G.I.; Houck, J.C.; Johnson, J.B., and Petricciani, J.C. (Bethesda, Md./Washington, D.C.): Kinetics and Cell Killing in Dividing and Nondividing Leukemic Cells in vitro and in vivo by Natural Splenic Cytotoxic Factor 361

Attallah, A.M.; Johnson, J.B.; Malinin, G.I.; Houck, J.C., and Petricciani, J.C. (Bethesda, Md./Washington, D.C.): Cytochemical and Ultrastructural Alteration of Leukemic Cells by a Naturally Cytotoxic Factor from Spleen 371

Attallah, A.M. and Folks, T. (Bethesda, Md.): Interferon Enhanced Human Natural Killer and Antibody-Dependent Cell-Mediated Cytotoxic Activity 377

Kimura, M. and Takaya, K. (Toyama): Ultrastructure of Basophilic Leukocytes and Mast Cells in Normal and Cutaneous Basophil Hypersensitivity-Reacted Guinea Pig Dermis 383

Gray, B.N. and Walker, C. (Fitzroy): Augmentation of Lymphocyte Surface Immunogenicity following Treatment with Dimethyl-Sulphoxide 390

Rudofsky, U.H.; McMaster, P.R.B., and Pollara, B. (Albany, N.Y./Bethesda, Md.): Studies on the Pathogenesis of Experimental Autoimmune Renal Tubulointerstitial Disease in Guinea Pigs. VI. Induction of Renal Lesions by Active or Passive Immunization of Strain 2 Guinea Pigs 398

Sandberg, G. and Ernström, U. (Stockholm): Mitotic Activity of Thymocytes in a Synthetic Tissue Culture Medium. Effect of L-Alanine 407

Rozenfarb, E. and Eidinger, D. (Kingston): Heterotoxicity of Human Serum. IV. Role of the Alternative Complement Pathway and Natural Antibody in the Lethal Toxicity of Human Serum for Mice 414

Rozenfarb, E. and Eidinger, D. (Kingston): Heterotoxicity of Human Serum. V. Development of Hematological Abnormalities in Mice Suggestive of Disseminated Intravascular Coagulation and Thrombotic Thrombocytopenic Purpura 427

Garrido, M.J. and Moreno, C. (Beckenham): The Use of Hapten-Polysaccharide Conjugates for the Induction of B-Cell Tolerance Involving IgE Responses. III. Specific Tolerance Induced by Sulphonamide-Substituted Levan in the Guinea Pig 441

Johansson, S.G.O.; Deuschl, H., and Zetterström, O. (Uppsala): Use of Glutaraldehyde-Modified Timothy Grass Pollen Extract in Nasal Hyposensitisation Treatment of Hay Fever 447

Short Communications

Ennis, M. and Pearce, F.L. (London): Effect of Cyclic AMP on Histamine Release Induced by Compound 48/80 461

Kimura, I.; Yamamoto, S., and Yamura, T. (Hiroshima): In vitro Release of Eosinophil Chemotactic Factor of Anaphylaxis (ECF-A) from Guinea Pig Skin 465

HU420

Medical Laboratory Sciences
Abstracts in English

VOL. 36 NO. 4   OCTOBER 1979

Uniform requirements for manuscripts submitted to biomedical journals. **International Steering Committee of Medical Editors** 319

Cell Hybrids: an important new source of antibody production. **A. D. Blann** 329

Factors influencing the inhibition by Digoxin of ^{86}Rubidium uptake into human red cells. **J. R. Cowie** 339

An improved electronic counting method for bovine leucocytes. **W. G. Halliday, J. G. Ross and J. M. Gibson** 353

The crystalline nature of histology waxes: the effects of microtomy on the microstructure of paraffin wax sections. **R. T. Allison** 359

A reappraisal of ammoniacal silver nitrate staining for microglia and neuroglia. **T. Scott** 373

Short technical notes

Automated capillary blood spot glucose estimation. **P. West, I. Marsland and P. Bradshaw** 379

Specificity of commercial kits for estimation of thyroid stimulating hormone (TSH). **R. Henley and D. Kisgyorgy** 381

CONTINUED

140

CURRENT CONTENTS®
Ⓟ 1979 by ISI®

FIGURE 7-5   Page from *Current Contents. (Courtesy ISI.)*

oats ORDER CARD
Original Article Tear Sheet

Price Structure - 1980
Per article of 20 pages or less, ordered with ISI® Accession Number:
   $4.50* - U.S.A., Canada and Mexico.
   $5.50* - All other locations (price includes airmail delivery).
 • For every additional 10 pages or fraction, add $2 per article.
 • For Hotline Service (telephone or Telex orders), add $1 per article.
 • For orders placed without ISI Accession Numbers, add $1 per article.
 • For a small number of journals, a royalty surcharge for photocopies will be applied.
 *Rates may vary and are subject to change.
 Payment must accompany OATS orders placed by mail.

OATS File # _____

Name _____
Organization _____
Address _____
City _____ State/Province _____ Zip _____
Country _____ Telephone _____
For ISI use only:
©1979 ISI OFC-5/7042 A-62
C|T|P|R| |C|A|F|N|O₁|O₂|A|P| |M|O|O|T|P| |C|C|

Fill in oval with ISI Accession Number
Journal _____
Volume No. _____ Issue No. _____
Pages _____ Date _____
Author _____
☐ I need ISI Stamps. Send me:
___$5.50's ___$4.50's ___$2.00's ___$1.00's
___$ .50's ($50 minimum order)
Total payment in stamps or check $_____
Please send me ___OATS Order Cards.

Pay for your OATS order the convenient way - with ISI Stamps. Place them here.

Please send the following article:

FOR A PERMANENT RECORD OF YOUR ORDER fold back this panel and insert carbon paper.

Amount _____
Check No. _____
Date _____

Need extra-fast service?
Use **oats** Hotline
Service Numbers:
Telephone-215-386-4399
Telex-84-5305

FIGURE 7-6   OATS provides original tear sheets or photocopies of articles reported, abstracted, or indexed in ISI publications such as *Current Contents*.

Dear Doctor Eisenberg :

I would appreciate receiving a reprint of your article
7 rules: how to write a poor proposal.
Trends Biochem. Sci. 5 XII (1980)

Thank you for this courtesy.

Sincerely,

W. A. Smith, D. Phil.

sent 11/20/80

Smith

Department of Anatomy
West Virginia University
Medical Center Drive
Morgantown, West Virginia 26506
U.S.A.

FIGURE 7-7   You may simply send a postcard to the author requesting reprints.

Summary

"To be creative," P. B. Medawar writes, "scientists need libraries, and laboratories, and the company of other scientists" [2].

Laboratories and colleagues are usually familiar territory to the beginning researcher; the library, on the other hand, may be daunting.

If you feel it is easier to rediscover a fact than to look it up, consider instead a plan for learning to handle library resources. Begin with the regular reading of several journals within your field; subscriptions are usually available through student or regular memberships in the professional society.

Background information abounds in specialized encyclopedias and handbooks; these volumes are invaluable beginning points for the researcher using the reference collection. As one moves into a subject, there are many excellent on-shelf abstracting and indexing sources to help direct and focus the search: devices such as the *Citation Index*, for instance, will prove enormously helpful in locating and screening sources.

In the beginning, you may feel overwhelmed by the amount of information available; practice with search strategies, though, will in time help you to wend your way through the collection. In so doing, you will have mastered an integral part of the writing process itself, for most complex writing jobs begin not, as it might be supposed, at the typewriter, but in literature searches and related reading available through the library.

Literature Cited

1. E. Bright Wilson, Jr., *An Introduction to Scientific Research*, McGraw-Hill, New York, 1952, p. 10.
2. P. B. Medawar, *Advice to a Young Scientist*, Harper & Row, New York, 1979, p. 40.

Exercises

1. Assume you need to do background reading on a subject; select a topic such as "scientific instruments" and compare information available through (*a*) a general encyclopedia and (*b*) a specialized encyclopedia such as the *Harper Encyclopedia of Science*, the *McGraw-Hill Encyclopedia of Science and Technology*, or *Van Nostrand's Scientific Encyclopedia*. Analyze and compare differences in the approach and scope of the information according to the sources you consulted. Which of the science encyclopedias was most useful? Were there differences in the scope and focus among the science encyclopedias?

2. Select a subject from the *Encyclopedia of Chemical Technology* (Kirk and Othmer) such as "High Temperature Alloys" or "Holography." How many items are in the bibliography? What use might this bibliography serve for the researcher? What tables and figures are given? Are they useful for an introduction to the subject? Why? Is the encyclopedia a useful starting point for research? Why?

3. Choose a topic and consult a relevent handbook. What sort of coverage is given in the handbook? How does handbook information help the beginning researcher?

4. Assume your subject is "Polymers" and that you are interested in background reading. Look in the latest annual of *Applied Science and Technology Index* and in the latest annual of *Engineering Index*. Is the type or quantity of information different in the two indexes? How? In which cases might you find the *Engineering Index* more useful? Take three sources from each of the indexes and translate them—that is, write out the abbreviations in the citations so that you become accustomed to the formats used.

5. Choose a recent issue of *Current Contents*, either in *Engineering, Technology and Applied Sciences*; in *Physical, Chemical and Earth Sciences;* or in *Life Sciences*. What is the "ISI Press Digest"? What is a "citation classic"? How can you obtain copies of articles that you think may be useful?

6. Consult an abstracting service in your field, such as *Chemical Abstracts, Engineering Index, Biological Abstracts*, or *Metals Abstracts*. Select a subject within this field, and then use the abstracting service to collect six to eight references that might be useful for a state-of-the-art paper on the subject. As you

pick your way through the volumes, note the answers to these questions: Are there differences in the ways information is listed monthly vs. annually? What function does the abstract number serve? How are subject headings useful?

7. Choose a subject of interest to yourself. Pick a book or article pertinent to the subject. If you don't have a book or article at hand, use an abstracting or indexing service, the library catalog, or a technical report. Once you have the author and title of a pertinent article, enter the *Citation Index* section of the *SCI Science Citation Index,* using the author's name.

   1. List five or six works which cite your starting reference.
   2. Explain all notations in one of these citations.
   3. Trace the five or six cited works to the *Source Index* section of the *SCI Science Citation Index* and copy the full bibliographic information.

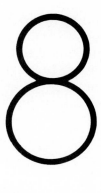

Style

Clearness is secured by using the words . . . that are current and ordinary.

Aristotle

Can you translate these three sentences into plain English?

It is limited in length.
We have experienced growth.
These are aircraft with lower noise emission characteristics.[1]

These are examples of inflated style—the sort of writing Churchill said compressed "the largest amount of words into the smallest amount of thoughts."

Why is such language so congested? What happened to "It is short," sacrificed at the altar of "It is limited in length"?

---

[1]   It is short.
    We grew.
    These are quieter aircraft.

A good style in technical writing should be as far from the florid or roundabout as possible.

The components of technical style can be summed up in an abbreviation, ABC—accuracy, brevity, and clarity. All three of these virtues apply to general prose but have particular application in scientific and technical writing.

Accuracy

Accuracy is essential in technical writing. Check figure references and citations, column heads and column totals—any items that cause a small warning buzzer to go off in your head.

In a prose that is stripped to the bones, it is essential that the bones be labeled correctly.

Brevity

Sydney Smith comments: "In composing as a general rule, run your pen through every other word you have written; you have no idea what vigor it will give your style."

But brevity isn't the rule in our society. In the past, we deposited money in checking accounts and received receipts. Now we receive a "Corporation Name Banking Record." Four words for one. People used to put out cigarettes. Now they "extinguish all smoking materials." My favorite example is a note I received commenting that a manuscript had been "wordy and verbose"!

Just as we consume a lot of junk food in this country, we also consume a lot of junk language. Fortunately, scientists have one defense against the general wordiness of the society. Parsimony has always been a virtue in scientific prose. Historically scientists have sought the most economical explanations in the formulation of theories and laws, the maximum simplicity for their explanations. The parsimony of the scientific method extends itself to the prose, which can be counted on—for page charges if for no other reason—to be briefer than writing used outside scientific and technical areas.

Clarity

Donald Hall writes, "When the smoke of bad prose fills the air, something is always on fire somewhere."

And in a similar vein, Jonathan Swift, noted for his lucid style and avoidance of frills and affections, says that when a writer is not clear, it is "usually on purpose."

Writers can hide behind bad prose. Each profession generates its own jargon, in part because members talk to each other and naturally develop a kind of verbal shorthand, and in part because jargon is useful as a means of excluding others. Lawyers are famous for their involuted, congested verbal styles. The history of the language of chemistry is a typical example of the piling up of trade secrets into a professional code. Chemistry had two origins, in the study of alchemy (hence the word *chemist*) and in the study of commercial processes such as tanning. The processes were closely guarded family secrets, protected by codes —scrambled languages for members only.

But while people often deliberately use esoteric language to hide rather than to communicate, there are also other reasons for congested style.

Consider, for instance, the case of the famous scientific passive.

Let's start with a sample sentence:

The man was let go.
            retrenched.
            asked to leave.

With a little thinking, one can translate it into

The man was fired.

But this sentence is missing a very important piece of information. It doesn't tell *who* fired the man. Compare the impact of the original with a rewritten version:

The man was fired.

vs.

I fired the man.

The second sentence is much clearer. It is written with what grammarians call an active verb. The verb is *fired*, and it's active because it comes with a subject—*I*. The order of the sentence is SVO—subject, verb, object.

The other sentence has what's called a passive verb—a combination of the verb *to be* with a past participle: *was + fired*. When you use a passive, you eliminate the subject. You take away the doer.

This construction presented a great advantage in scientific

writing since it helped develop the so-called objective tone, providing a stylistic way to make the scientist invisible. With the person removed, the prose has a more impersonal or objective flavor. Thus, instead of saying, "I saw," scientists took to writing, "It was seen." In short order, the passive became a hallmark of scientific prose.

The institutionalization of the passive voice in scientific prose is not a nefarious scheme to avoid responsibility, although in general prose the passive often functions this way. Its use does, however, congest scientific writing. It interferes with subject-verb order, making comprehension more difficult, and it adds words: To explicate an action one must use a *by* phrase—as in "The man was fired *by me.*"

There are other reasons why scientific prose is difficult to understand. How much explication is one allowed? The style in scientific writing is toward a deliberately limited use of examples and explanations, and yet the reader is typically less knowledgeable than the writer and more in need of examples. Bright adjectives, figurative language, anecdotes, humor—the tools of the trade in general writing—are avoided in scientific writing.

How then does one develop clarity in technical prose? Here are some suggestions.

Seven Ways to Trim Useless Language

Ideas are difficult enough to understand without useless language to further complicate the reader's job.

George Orwell was a passionate advocate of clear English. His first rule was

If it is possible to cut a word out, always cut it out.

It was followed by

Never use a long word where a short one will do.

Orwell is the author of a famed satire on prefabricated phrases, stale and mixed images, humbug and vagueness. Here is his parody—he's taken a verse from *Ecclesiastes* (9:11) and rewritten it in his essay, "Politics and the English Language."

ORIGINAL
I returned, and saw under the sun, that the race is not to the swift, nor the battle to the strong, neither yet bread to the wise, nor yet riches to men of understanding, nor yet favor to men of skill; but time and chance happeneth to them all.

ORWELL'S REWRITE
Objective consideration of contemporary phenomena compels the conclusion that success or failure in competitive activities exhibits no tendency to be commensurate with innate capacity, but that a considerable element of the unpredictable must inevitably be taken into account.

You can trim away useless language in your own writing. Be ruthless. Cut to the bone. Here are some suggestions that will help to sharpen your eye for the "wordy and verbose":

1. Eliminate Redundant Expressions Redundancy is unnecessary repetition—for example, a "dead corpse" (the result, no doubt, of a "fatal slaying").

The amount of redundancy in normal prose is astonishing. Cast a cold eye on your own work, and edit heartlessly. You've no idea how it will improve your style.

Here are some garden variety examples that are among my favorites:

end results, final results, consequent results (use *results*)
estimated at about, estimated at nearly, estimated more or less at (use *estimated*)
as a general rule, usually as a rule (how about "estimated at nearly 10, as a general rule"?)
in a range of between
circular in shape, round in form (how about "a round-shaped ring"?)
white in color, white-colored, whitish colored (use *white*)
basic fundamentals
such as chloride, etc.
refer back (can you refer forward?)
modern world of today
two months' time, two months' duration

2. Purge Inflated Expressions Why use five words when one will do? Instead of *owing to the fact that*, try the simple *because*. Here is a list of some common examples:

Inflated	*Deflated*
owing to the fact that	because
at this point in time	now
at that point in time	then
in the near future	soon
in many cases	often
in most cases	usually
in the event of	if
in the vicinity of	near
despite the fact that	although
during the time that	while
for the reason that	because
in all cases	always
in many cases	often
in most cases	usually
he is a man who	he
this is a finding which	this finding
only a limited number	few

3. Shun Bureaucratese "Bureaucratese," or doublespeak, is the wildly inflated language that characterizes government pronouncements.

An author received a request from the government to help them revise their publications. Here is what they said: "The purpose of this form is to solicit beneficial comments which will help achieve procurement of suitable forms."

Bureaucratese is endemic to government publications. Don't allow it in your writing. Avoid such nonwords as

> apprised
> disseminate
> implement
> utilization

There is a parody of such empty phrases called the Systematic Buzz Phrase Projector.

0. Integrated	0. Management	0. Options
1. Total	1. Organizational	1. Flexibility
2. Systematized	2. Monitored	2. Capability
3. Parallel	3. Reciprocal	3. Mobility
4. Functional	4. Digital	4. Programming
5. Responsive	5. Logistical	5. Concept

6. Optional	6. Transitional	6. Time-Phase
7. Synchronized	7. Incremental	7. Projection
8. Compatible	8. Third-Generation	8. Hardware
9. Balanced	9. Policy	9. Contingency

These three columns of pompous words can generate many pompous phrases. You can take any three numbers and then match the numbers with the three columns. The result: instant nonlanguage. For example, 157 would be "total logistical projection." Try it out. Be sure to get your options synchronized before you begin.

4. Do Not Use Meaningless Phrases   Here are some examples:

in this connection, it may be observed that
as already stated, as already said, as already pointed out
hopefully, it is expected that
necessitates the indication of

5. Use Active Verbs   There are occasions when you'll have to use the passive. Many publications require

x is reacted with *y*.

rather than

x reacted with *y*.

One of the products of the struggle for objectivity in science was this enshrining of the passive voice; it's a sort of syntactic outgrowth that is now entrenched in the rhetoric.

However, the use of passive verbs slows down the pace, requires more words, and tends to make the going more difficult for your reader. Therefore, use the passive only when you're writing for a formal occasion. On all other occasions, use active verbs.

Here is an example of how active verbs reduce verbiage:

The pipes corroded.

vs.

Corrosive action has been noted in the pipes.

or

It has been observed that there is corrosive action in the pipes.

The expression *it has been observed* is rife in scientific prose. It is one of the leeches of scientific language, in company with other empty phrases such as *it has been found* and *it has been concluded.* Avoid such expressions, and instead simply state the observation, finding, or conclusion.

6. Uncover Your Verbs. Prefer active verbs to nouns or adjectives made from these verbs. For example, use *investigate* instead of *investigation, corrodes* instead of *has a corrosive effect upon, analyze* instead of *conduct an analysis of.* Buried verbs are called "nominalizations." Here are some examples of nominalizations and the verbs they stand for; notice the vigor of the original verbs and how this force is lost in the nominalizations.

The research team conducted an investigation of the problem.
An investigation of the problem was conducted by the research team.
    The research team *investigated* the problem.

Ice served to have a congesting effect on the canal.
The congestion occasioned by ice was observed to be in the canal.
    Ice *congested* the canal.

We did an analysis of the data.
An analysis of the data was performed.
A data performance analysis was done.
    We *analyzed* the data.

When you combine buried verbs, wordiness, and passives, you have an awesome product. Consider, for instance, the following:

Water rusts iron pipes.

which can be inflated to

Iron pipes are known to be rusted by water.

which can be inflated to

It has been observed that iron pipes are known to be rusted by water.

which can be ballooned into

It has frequently been observed to be a condition that iron pipes are rusted by water.

7. Be Positive Negative statements require more words; they are also more difficult to understand. For instance, compare

did not recall

with

> forgot;

> not useful

with

> useless

Or consider these expressions:

1. It is not unlikely that there will be many occurrences of this strain.
2. It is not unusual to find many involuted sentences of this sort in professional journals.

Invert these sentences so they are positive. You'll save words, and be clearer in the bargain. In these cases, the edited versions would read

1. This strain will probably occur frequently.
2. Involuted sentences are common in professional journals.

Always avoid the "not un-" trap, as in "It is not uncommon," "It is not unlikely," and "It is not unusual."

Summary

Be accurate, be brief, and be clear. Avoid redundancy and inflated language. Use active, undecorated verbs.

Be ruthless. "Do not be afraid to seize whatever you have written and cut it to ribbons," E. B. White writes in *The Elements of Style*. "It can always be restored to its original condition in the morning."

Perhaps the best—and most cynical—advice in this quarter was given by Samuel Johnson. "Read over your composition," he advises, "and when you come to a passage you find particularly fine, strike it out."

Exercises

1. Rewrite these wordy statements:

    (a) The name John Patrick McPhee is not unknown in the annals of today's modern science.

(b) Vitrine is effective in reducing ketones.

(c) Superovulation is a factor of some importance during the luteal phase of the cycle.

(d) The end results of this report are not uninteresting.

(e) In consequence of the fact that we've had equipment breakdowns in the department, we estimate the delay at about six to eight weeks.

(f) It has been recommended by the board that the conclusions be adopted.

(g) Quite a limited number of articles were received.

(h) The footsie is a plastic toy with a plastic hoop that is red in color and circular in shape.

2. There is a fine quote from Samuel Johnson buried in the following paragraph. Remove the passives, do some judicious pruning, and the original fine language should appear.

> It has been found that your paper is both good and original. Unfortunately, it has been concluded that the part that is good is not original; further, it has been observed that the part that is original is not good.

3. There is a quote from Albert Szent-Gyorgi buried in this piece of doublespeak. Can you find it?

> It should be manifest by now that for the most part, as far as we are aware, discovery may be said to consist in seeing what everybody has seen, and in consequence of this fact thinking what nobody has thought.

4. Here is a quotation from a journal for English teachers. Rewrite it.

> Despite what is being done, however, the fact is easily observed that few students are able to use their dictionaries with anything like efficiency.

5. This quotation comes directly from the flyer for a new journal. Rewrite it.

> Our publication will issue periodically on a 4-month time basis. It should be of interest to intense readers in whatever field who want to be apprised of the latest thinking in fields outside their own.

6. Correct this memo.

To: Lab Assistant

From: P. K. Squeleth, Supervisor

This is to inform you that we have a serious mouse problem in this building and we would like to have your laboratory exterminated on Thursday, August 9, so please empty all cabinets. Please contact the office for permission to enter. Thank you very much.

7. Select three or four paragraphs of an author whose style you admire, and three or four paragraphs from an author whose style you dislike. Write a short (two to three pages) paper discussing the differences in style, and why you prefer one type of writing to the other.

THREE

Reports
and
Proposals

Writing an Abstract

More is in vain when less will serve.
Sir Isaac Newton

Samuel Johnson once said, "Depend upon it, sir, when a man knows he is to be hanged in a fortnight, it concentrates his mind wonderfully."

Writing abstracts concentrates the mind, too. Apprentice technical writers are often trained through abstract writing. They learn in this way how to distill the information into a brief, clear presentation.

Often a "short" of this kind is the only part of the paper that will be read. Much medical copy, for instance, is sent to doctors in abstract form. Doctors say they don't have time to read entire papers. Instead, they skim over the abstract and decide on that basis whether to read the entire paper.

The ability to write a clear, correct abstract is useful in two ways. First, it concentrates writing, teaching one how to search papers systematically for their essential parts and then present the information in as few words as possible.

It also yields a useful product. Much technical and scientific information is presented in abstract form whether the original source is an industrial report or a scientific article.

Definitions and Formats

An abstract is not a summary. Summaries are a part of the text and usually come at the end of an article or report. An abstract, on the other hand, is a brief statement of the contents of a scientific or technical work which comes *before* the work.

It may exist independently of the paper or report. Often abstracts are collected under subject headings in services, such as *Chemical Abstracts*.

The abstract is the decisive part of a paper or report because the prospective reader will look at the abstract and then decide whether or not to consult the original paper.

The format is traditionally one paragraph, typed single-spaced, with a maximum of 200 words. Two- and three-paragraph formats have recently come into use, although they are not so common.

The abstract is often written after the paper is complete. The writer selects the most important points and then expresses them in clear, concise language.

The abstract should include brief statements of the following:

1. Objective
2. Results
3. Conclusions
4. Implications

It may also give an indication of the theoretical or experimental framework.

A good abstract serves two basic purposes:

1. It presents sufficient information so that those interested in the subject can decide whether to read the original paper.
2. It gives those readers only peripherally involved in the subject sufficient information so that they will not need to read the original work.

Two Types of Abstracts

There are two types of abstracts: indicative and informative.

Indicative abstracts are actually tables of contents in narrative form. They simply list the topics described in the original work without supplying exact information. This type of abstract is widely used for reviewing book-length works. The following shows an example from *Mathematical Reviews*.

A source book in classical analysis. 57 #9395
Edited by Garret Birkhoff.
With the assistance of Uta Merzbach.
Harvard University Press, Cambridge, Mass.,
1973. xii + 470 *pp.* $25.00.
This excellent book outlines the development of classical analysis in the 19th century by means of judiciously chosen selections from the writing of leading 19th-century analysts. The selections are grouped into 13 chapters: Foundations of real analysis, Foundations of complex analysis, Convergent expansions, Asymptotic expansions, Fourier series and integrals, Elliptic and Abelian integrals, Elliptic and automorphic functions, Ordinary differential equations (two chapters), Partial differential equations, Calculus of variations, Wave equations and characteristics, Integral equations. All selections not originally in English have been given first-rate translations. The various sections are well provided with penetrating introductions, and the selections themselves are amply annotated.   R. P. Boas, Jr. (Evanston, Ill.)

Here is a second example of an indicative abstract.

ABSTRACT
This report presents an analysis of the principles of magnetic refrigeration with application to air conditioning. A comparison with conventional evaporation-condensation gas cycle devices is presented. Conclusions concerning the applicability of magnetic refrigeration to air conditioning are made.

The author says a comparison *is presented*, rather than giving the actual comparison, that conclusions *are made* rather than giving actual conclusions. Thus a listing of the types of information is given rather than the information itself.

Informative abstracts, in contrast, actually provide a distillation of the information in the document—a condensed account of the objective, procedure, results, conclusions, and implications. Thus they contain the principal ideas and data, unlike the indicative abstract, which is generalized and does not have qualitative or quantitative data.

Below are two examples of informative abstracts (courtesy of American Chemical Society).

CA abstract number — 88: **99848j** **The relationship between the renal effects of cadmium and cadmium concentration in urine among the inhabitants of cadmium-polluted areas.** Nogawa, Koji; Kobayashi, Etsuko; Inaoka, Hiromi; Ishizaki, Arinobu (Dep. Hyg., Kanazawa Med. Univ., Ishikawa, Japan). *Environ. Res.* 1977, 14(3), 391–400 (Eng). In 221 female inhabitants of Cd-polluted areas, sorted according to their urinary Cd concns. (expressed in μg Cd/g creatine), the incidence of proteinuria, glucosuria, proteinuria with glucosuria, tubular proteinuria, and aminoaciduria increased distinctly with increasing Cd in urine. Probit linear regression lines between urinary Cd concn. (μg Cd/g creatine) and renal effects were obtained. The same relation was not obsd. when urinary Cd concns. were expressed as μg Cd/L.

Labels: Article title; Authors' names; Abbrev. journal title; Language of article; Work; site; Year of publication; Volume (issue) numbers; Inclusive page numbers

The original article was in *Environmental Research,* volume 14, number 3, 1977, on pages 391 to 400. It was written in English. The abstract gives the findings—that the incidence of proteinuria, glucosuria, tubular proteinuria, and aminoaciduria increased distinctly with increased concentrations of cadmium in the urine.

The second example shows a longer informative abstract. The original article appeared in *Infection and Immunity.* The authors are Klipstein and Engert; their affiliation is the School of Medicine at the University of Rochester.

90: **20213m** **Protective effect of active immunization with purified Escherichia coli heat-labile enterotoxin in rats.** Klipstein, Frederick A.; Engert, Richard F. (Sch. Med., Univ. Rochester, Rochester, N. Y.). *Infect. Immun.* 1979, 23(3), 592–9 (Eng). The protective effect of active immunization by different routes with a purified prepn. of the polymyxin-release form of *E. coli* heat-labile toxin was evaluated in rats. Immunized animals were challenged by placing toxin into ligated ileal loops at dosages which produced either 50% or the max. secretory response in unimmunized rats. Immunization exclusively by the parenteral route yielded significant protection. Rats were also protected when parenteral priming was followed by boosting given either directly into the duodenum or perorally 2 h after intragastric cimetidine, but not when the peroral boosts were given with bicarbonate. Immunization administered entirely by the peroral route with cimetidine yielded protection but only when the immunizing dosage was 5-fold greater than that found effective in the parenteral-peroral approach. Rats immunized exclusively by the parenteral route and those boosted perorally with cimetidine were also tested, and found to be protected, against challenge with viable organisms of strains that produce either heat-labile toxin alone or both heat-labile and heat-stable toxin, but they were not protected against a strain which produces just heat-stable toxin. Geometric mean serum antibody titers were increased by ≥16-fold over control values in those groups of rats in which protection was achieved, with the exception of those immunized exclusively by the peroral route. Thus, active immunization with purified *E. coli* heat-labile toxin results in significant protection against both this toxin as well as viable organisms which produce it, but not against viable strains which produce heat-stable toxin only, and concomitant ablation of gastric secretion by the use of cimetidine renders the peroral route of immunization effective. Prophylactic immunization against diarrheal disease caused by heat-labile toxin-producing strains of *E. coli* may be feasible in humans.

This abstract can be broken into the following components:

1. Objective
2. Procedures and results for a series of related experiments
3. Conclusions
4. Implications

90: **202123m   Protective effect of active immunization with purified Escherichia coli heat-labile enterotoxin in rats.** Klipstein. Frederick A.; Engert, Richard F. (Sch. Med., Univ. Rochester, Rochester, N. Y.). *Infect. Immun.* 1979, 23(3), 592–9 (Eng). The protective effect of active immunization by different routes with a purified prepn. of the polymyxin-release form of *E. coli* heat-labile toxin was evaluated in rats.   **Objective**

Immunized animals were challenged by placing toxin into ligated ileal loops at dosages which produced either 50% or the max. secretory response in unimmunized rats. Immunization exclusively by the parenteral route yielded significant   **Procedures and results** protection. Rats were also protected when parenteral priming was followed by boosting given either directly into the duodenum or perorally 2 h after intragastric cimetidine, but not when the peroral boosts were given with bicarbonate. Immunization administered entirely by the peroral route with cimetidine yielded protection but only when the immunizing dosage was 5–fold greater than that found effective in the parenteral-peroral approach. Rats immunized exclusively by the parenteral route and those boosted perorally with cimetidine were also tested, and found to be protected, against challenge with viable organisms of strains that produce either heat-labile toxin alone or both heat-labile and heat-stable toxin, but they were not protected against a strain which produces just heat-stable toxin. Geometric mean serum antibody titers were increased by ≥ 16-fold over control values in those groups of rats in which protection was achieved, with the exception of those immunized exclusively by the peroral route.

Thus, active immunization with purified *E. coli* heat-labile toxin results in significant protection against both this toxin as well as viable organisms which produce it but not against viable strains which produce heat-stable toxin only, and concomitant ablation of gastric secretion by the use of cimetidine renders the peroral route of immunization effective.

Conclusions

Prophylactic immunization against diarrheal disease caused by heat-labile toxin-producing strains of *E. coli* may be feasible in humans.

Implications

The pattern of objective, procedures and results, conclusions, and implications is followed routinely in informative abstracts. There are cases, however, when the author begins the abstract with the findings, dispensing with any information about the objective, the procedures, or the theoretical or experimental framework. This format presumes a very sophisticated reader and is usually followed only by highly specialized publications.

An Exercise in Writing an Abstract

Below you will find a copy of a famous document. It is Joseph Lister's presentation of the antiseptic principle in the practice of surgery. He read this paper before the British Medical Association in Dublin in August 1867. Lister's findings had a tremendous influence on the practice of surgery.

In the paper he follows the classic format by stating objective, procedures, results, and conclusions.

Read through this document and then write an abstract. An efficient way to do this is to

1. Underline key points—objective, salient procedural details, conclusions—as you read. Then transcribe them, attempting to condense the language.
2. Stitch these points together with appropriate connectives such as *first, second, thus*.
3. Concentrate on the findings. Don't dwell on procedural details.
4. Edit the abstract so that it is concise but preserves the tone of the author's original language.

ON THE ANTISEPTIC PRINCIPLE IN THE PRACTICE OF SURGERY

In the course of an extended investigation into the nature of inflammation, and the healthy and morbid conditions of the blood in relation to it, I arrived, several years ago, at the conclusion that the essential cause of suppuration in wounds is decomposition, brought about by the influence of the atmosphere upon blood or serum retained within them, and, in the case of contused wounds, upon portions of tissue destroyed by the violence of the injury.

To prevent the occurrence of suppuration, with all its attendant risks, was an object manifestly desirable; but till lately apparently unattainable, since it seemed hopeless to attempt to exclude the oxygen, which was universally regarded as the agent by which putrefaction was effected. But when it had been shown by the researches of Pasteur that the septic property of the atmosphere depended, not on the oxygen or any gaseous constituent, but on minute organisms suspended in it, which owed their energy to their vitality, it occurred to me that decomposition in the injured part might be avoided without excluding the air, by applying as a dressing some material capable of destroying the life of the floating particles.

Upon this principle I have based a practice of which I will now attempt to give a short account.

The material which I have employed is carbolic or phenic acid, a volatile organic compound which appears to exercise a peculiarly destructive influence upon low forms of life, and hence is the most powerful antiseptic with which we are at present acquainted.

The first class of cases to which I applied it was that of compound fractures, in which the effects of decomposition in the injured part were especially striking and pernicious. The results have been such as to establish conclusively the great principle, that all the local inflammatory mischief and general febrile disturbance which follow severe injuries are due to the irritating and poisoning influence of decomposing blood or sloughs. For these evils are entirely avoided by the antiseptic treatment, so that limbs which otherwise would be unhesitatingly condemned to amputation may be retained with confidence of the best results.

In conducting the treatment, the first object must be the destruction of any septic germs which may have been introduced into the wound, either at the moment of the accident or during the time which has since elapsed. This is done by introducing the acid of full strength into all accessible recesses of the wound by means of a piece of rag held in dressing-forceps and dipped in the liquid. This I did not venture to do in the earlier cases; but experience has shown that the compound which carbolic acid forms with the blood, and also any portions of tissue killed by its caustic action, including even parts of the bone, are disposed of by absorption and organization, provided they are afterwards kept from decomposing. We are thus enabled to employ the antiseptic treatment efficiently at a period after the occurrence of the injury at which it would otherwise probably fail. Thus I have now under my care in the Glasgow Infirmary a boy who was admitted with compound fracture of the leg as late as eight and a half hours after the accident, in whom nevertheless all local and constitutional disturbance was avoided by means of carbolic acid, and the bones were firmly united five weeks after his admission.

The next object to be kept in view is to guard effectually against the spreading of decomposition into the wound along the stream of blood and serum which oozes out during the first few days after the accident, when the acid originally applied has been washed out, or dissipated by absorption and evaporation. This part of the treatment has been greatly improved during the last few weeks. The method which I have hitherto published consisted in the application of a piece of lint dipped in the acid, overlapping the sound skin to some extent, and covered with a tin cap, which was daily raised in order to touch the surface of the lint with the antiseptic. This method certainly succeeded well with wounds of moderate size; and, indeed, I may say that in all the many cases of this kind which have been so treated by myself or my house surgeons, not a single failure has occurred. When, however, the wound is very large, the flow of blood and serum is so profuse, especially during the first twenty-four hours, that the antiseptic application cannot prevent the spread of decomposition into the interior unless it overlaps the sound skin for a very considerable distance, and this was inadmissible by the method described above, on account of the extensive sloughing of the surface of the cutis which it would involve. This difficulty has, however, been overcome by employing a paste composed of common whitening (carbonate of lime) mixed with a solution of one part of carbolic acid in four parts of boiled linseed oil, so as to form a firm putty. This application contains the acid in too dilute a form to excoriate the skin, which it may be made to cover to any extent that may be thought desirable, while its substance serves as a reservoir of the antiseptic material. So long as any discharge continues, the paste should be changed daily; and, in order to prevent the chance of mischief occurring during the process, a piece of rag dipped in the solution of carbolic acid in oil is put on next the skin, and maintained there permanently, care being taken to avoid raising it along with the putty. This rag is always kept in an antiseptic condition from contact with the paste above it, and destroys any germs that may fall upon it during the short time that should alone be allowed to pass in the changing of the dressing. The putty should be in a layer about a quarter of an inch thick, and may be advantageously applied rolled out between two pieces of thin calico, which maintain it in the form of a continuous sheet, that may be wrapped in a moment round the whole circumference of a limb, if this be thought desirable, while the putty is prevented by the calico from sticking to the rag which is next the skin. When all discharge has ceased, the use of the paste is discontinued, but the original rag is left adhering to the skin till healing by scabbing is supposed to be complete. I have at present in the hospital a man with severe compound fracture of both bones of the left leg, caused by direct violence, who, after the cessation of the sanious discharge under the use of the paste, without a drop of pus appearing, has been treated for the last two weeks exactly as if the fracture were a simple one. During this time the rag, adhering by means of a crust of inspissated blood collected beneath it, has continued perfectly dry, and it will be left untouched till the usual period for removing the splints in a simple fracture, when we may fairly expect to find a sound cicatrix beneath it. . . .

The next class of cases to which I have applied the antiseptic treatment is that of abscesses. Here, also, the results have been extremely satisfactory, and in beautiful harmony with the pathological principles indicated above. The pyogenic membrane . . . forms pus, not from any inherent disposition to do so, but only because it is subjected to some preternatural stimulation. In an ordinary abscess, whether acute or chronic, before it is opened, the stimulus which maintains the suppuration is derived from the presence of the pus pent up within the cavity. When a free opening is made in the ordinary way, this stimulus is got rid of; but when the atmosphere gaining access to the contents, the potent stimulus of decomposition comes into operation, and pus is generated in greater abundance than before. But when the evacuation is effected on the antiseptic principle, the pyogenic membrane, freed from the influence of the former stimulus without the substitution of a new one, ceases to suppurate . . . , furnishing merely a trifling amount of clear serum, and, whether the opening be dependent or not, rapidly contracts and coalesces. At the same time any constitutional symptoms previously occasioned by the accumulation of the matter are got rid of without the slightest risk of the irritative fever or hectic hitherto so justly dreaded in dealing with large abscesses.

In order that the treatment may be satisfactory, the abscess must be seen before it has opened. Then, except in very rare and peculiar cases, there are no septic organisms in the contents, so that it is needless to introduce carbolic acid into the interior. Indeed, such a proceeding would be objectionable, as it would stimulate the pyogenic membrane to unnecessary suppuration. All that is necessary is to guard against the introduction of living atmospheric germs from without, at the same time that free opportunity is afforded for the escape of discharge from within. . . .

It would carry me far beyond the limited time which, by the rules of the Association, is alone at my disposal, were I to enter into the various applications of the antiseptic principle in the several special departments of surgery.

There is, however, one point more that I cannot but advert to—namely, the influence of this mode of treatment upon the general healthiness of a hospital. Previously to its introduction, the two large wards in which most of my cases of accident and of operation are treated were amongst the unhealthiest in the whole surgical division of the Glasgow Royal Infirmary, in consequence, apparently, of those wards being unfavourably placed with reference to the supply of fresh air; and I have felt ashamed, when recording the results of my practice, to have so often to allude to hospital gangrene or pyaemia. It was interesting, though melancholy, to observe that, whenever all, or nearly all, the beds contained cases with open sores, these grievous complications were pretty sure to show themselves; so that I came to welcome simple fractures, though in themselves of little interest either for myself or the students, because their presence diminished the proportion of open sores among the patients. But since the antiseptic treatment has been brought into full operation, and wounds and abscesses no longer poison the atmosphere with putrid exhalations, my wards, though in other respects under precisely the same circumstances as before, have completely changed their character; so that during the last nine months not a single instance of pyaemia, hospital gangrene, or erysipelas has occurred in them.

As there appears to be no doubt regarding the cause of this change, the importance of the fact can hardly be exaggerated.

There are many ways to write an abstract of this article. One student solved the problem in the following way. First, the student read through the article, underlining the salient details. The student then strung the information together and edited it so that it was brief but comprehensive.

The student began with the conclusion (first sentence), then added a one-sentence summary of the procedure (second sentence), and then gave the results (final sentence). Here is the final version:

> **On the antiseptic principle in the practice of surgery.** Lister, Joseph. *British Medical Journal*, vol. 2, p. 246.
>
> The essential cause of suppuration in wounds is decomposition brought about by the influence of the atmosphere and may be avoided by applying as a dressing material capable of destroying the life of floating particles. To stop the spread of infection, carbolic or phenic acid is applied to the injuries by means of a rag, a piece of lint covered with a tin cap, or by a paste, depending on whether these are open wounds, compound fractures, or abscesses. In the nine months since the introduction of antiseptics in two large wards of Glasgow Royal Infirmary, which was previously among the unhealthiest, not a single instance of pyaemia, hospital gangrene, or erysipelas has occurred.

Commercial Abstracts

The commercial abstract usually comes at the beginning of TBRs (technical business reports); sometimes it is prepared by managers who write a set of "highlights" for the department's monthly work.

This abstract is slightly different from the research abstract. It is still informative—it gives the salient points cleanly and clearly—but the pattern shifts to deal with commercial problems.

It usually answers these questions:

1. What is the problem?
2. What is the solution?
3. How do the results compare with the competition?
4. What are the commercial implications?

Example Here is an example where you can use these questions to write a commercial abstract:

Situation Suppose that your group has developed a new test to diagnose heart attacks. Simple, quick and relatively inexpensive, it relies on measuring the concentration in blood serum of

LDH-1, a specific lactate dehydrogenase isoenzyme released when heart muscle cells are damaged or killed.

You've dubbed the test Isoheart.

There's a market for the product. Present clinical tests measuring lactate dehydrogenase aren't specific for heart attack (myocardial infarction) because they don't distinguish readily among the five isoenzymes released by damaged muscle tissue other than the heart. But Isoheart is specifically for LDH-1, released *only* by the heart muscle cells.

When a coronary artery is blocked during a heart attack, the flow of oxygen-rich blood to the heart muscles is cut off. If the muscles are damaged by oxygen starvation, they release LDH-1. In fact, the isoenzyme appears in the blood about eight hours after initial symptoms. The test has advantages. It uses only about $1 worth of chemicals. It can be performed in less than 15 minutes. It doesn't use electrophoretic separations, which are time-consuming. Instead it uses highly specific antibodies that react with and remove the four interfering isoenzymes. The LDH-1 remaining after treatment is quantitatively determined using standard techniques. The method is virtually 100 percent accurate for heart attacks, because the rise in LDH-1 serum level reflects only the breakdown of heart muscle cells.

Using this typical set of "notes," you might write a four-sentence commercial abstract according to the following solution.

Solution

1. What is the problem?
   Present clinical tests measuring lactate dehydrogenase are not specific for heart attack because they don't distinguish readily among the five isoenzymes released by damaged muscle tissue other than the heart. (Sentence 1)
2. What is the solution?
   A new test, Isoheart, actually measures the concentration in blood serum of LDH-1, a specific lactate dehydrogenase isoenzyme released when the heart muscle cells are damaged or killed. (Sentence 2)
3. How do the results compare?
   Unlike other tests, Isoheart is specifically for LDH-1, released only by the heart muscle cells. (Sentence 3)
4. Commercial implication?
   Simple, quick, and relatively inexpensive, the tests uses only $1 worth of chemicals, and can be performed in less than 15

minutes. The method is virtually 100 percent accurate for heart attacks. (Sentence 4)

Summary

Follow these guidelines as you write informative abstracts:

1. Concentrate on the objective, the findings, and the implications. If your audience is sophisticated, you may simply begin with a statement of the findings.
2. Do not belabor the procedures. Compress these details as much as possible.
3. Pick out key points and express them in language that is clear and concise.
4. If you are writing a commercial abstract, concentrate on these questions: What is the problem? What is the solution? How do the results compare? What are the commercial implications?

Exercises

1. The following article by David P. Cowan first appeared in *Science* (vol. 205) in September 1979. First, write an informative abstract to preface this article. Then compare your abstract with the ones at the end of this chapter; reprinted are (1) the abstract that appeared before the original article in *Science*, (2) a sample abstract written by a student.

> SIBLING MATINGS IN A HUNTING WASP: ADAPTIVE INBREEDING?
> Among sexually reproducing animals, outcrossing is the rule. Indeed, high frequencies of close inbreeding are known for only a few forms such as gregarious parasitoid Hymenoptera, among which choice seems largely restricted to siblings. In these generally tiny insects, siblings develop in close proximity on the same host. Males are often flightless (indicating inability to join a general mating pool), reach adulthood before the females, remain in the natal area, and inseminate their sisters, which then seek out new hosts on which to oviposit. Because of the near universality of outbreeding by sexual organisms, and its known benefits, biologists have tended to consider sibling mating systems as forced (in an

evolutionary sense) on the species in question by low population densities and thus low chances of females finding suitable mates away from the natal area. I here report frequent brother-sister matings in an abundant, nonparasitic, solitary wasp, *Euodynerus foraminatus* (Saussure) (Vespidae), which does not seem forced to inbreed since both sexes are strong fliers and capable of dispersing widely. This case raises questions because inbreeding has important genetic consequences with regard to sex determination, sex ratios, the maintenance of sexual reproduction, and rates of evolution and speciation; it is not obvious that costs are offset by benefits.

Normally, females of *E. foraminatus* nest in vacant insect tunnels in wood. Within the tubular hole, a female sequentially constructs and provisions a series of linearly arranged cells separated by mud partitions. Inside each cell she first lays an egg and then provides enough paralyzed caterpillars for the complete growth of the single wasp larva. When foraging, a female may fly several hundred meters to locate and sting caterpillars. Nesting wasps readily accept sticks with drilled holes (trap nests) as nest sites. Through the use of such nests, population density can be manipulated, and trap nests can be opened for study. Female wasps usually rear both sexes in the same nest hole; females in the innermost and males in the outer cells. The sexes are not intermixed. Controlled arrangement of the sexes is possible because of the haplodiploid genetic system found in the Hymenoptera. Diploid females are produced when eggs are fertilized at the time of oviposition by sperm stored in the female's spermatheca. Haploid males are produced when sperm are withheld so that unfertilized eggs are deposited. Even though females are provisioned first, males in the outer cells develop more rapidly and emerge from the nest several days ahead of their sisters. Emergence occurs in the morning, and it is usually synchronized so that all individuals of the same sex exit on the same morning within a fairly short period.

When a single nest produces two or more males, they interact aggressively: one brother drives away the others. The fights are brief, and in a matter of seconds the issue is permanently decided. The dominant male becomes resident at the nest and assumes an activity pattern that he maintains for about a week. He usually spends nights away from the nest; but each morning, as the temperature rises, he returns and awaits the emergence of his sisters. He may make periodic short flights from the nest and patrol nearby flowers or vegetation, but he returns to the nest after a few minutes. As the morning passes, these flights away from the nest increase in frequency and duration; and by noon the male no longer returns to the nest but continually patrols plants. The subordinate brothers spend the entire day patrolling vegetation:

though they may remain in the area of the natal nest, they do not again challenge their territorial brother.

The females' emergence from the nest is heralded by vibrations they make as they chew through the mud partitions between the cells. At this time the resident male remains standing over the nest hole. As a female exits, the male mounts and copulates with her for 1 to 2 minutes. After mating, if the female has carried him away, the male returns directly to the nest hole and waits for the next female. If another female is already out of the nest, the male initiates copulation directly. Females do not wait for the male and sometimes leave the nest area without copulating. I saw 42 females emerge from 19 nests while each nest was being attended by a resident male. Thirty-three females mated with the resident males (nearly four-fifths), three emerged and flew off while the male was away temporarily, and six emerged and departed while the resident was occupied with another female at the nest. Thus, a male resident at his natal nest inseminates a high proportion of his emerging sisters. Females, after leaving the nest and whether mated or not, usually fly to a nearby leaf or flower where they groom or feed on nectar. At these locations, patrolling males probably find and inseminate the willing females.

Significant inbreeding will result from sibling matings if females do not mate more than once. Were females to mate again after dispersal, it is likely that their mates for these copulations would not be closely related. The available evidence, however, indicates that females of *E. foraminatus* mate once and are thereafter unreceptive. (i) That males compete to be the first to mate with females suggests that subsequent matings by females either do not occur or are less important to the production of offspring. (ii) Freshly mated females successfully reject males by curling their abdomens forward under their thoraxes so that males cannot link genitalia. (iii) Nesting females are not sexually receptive. I never observed males frequenting areas where females were provisioning nests, but on several occasions I saw females initiate nests in holes where males were waiting, at their natal nest, for the emergence of virgin sisters. These nesting females and waiting males were always quarrelsome and never mated.

I estimated the proportion of sibling matings by scoring the emergence of females from trap nests placed in the field at stations 50 feet apart. Forty-five nesting females provisioned 71 nests, and 198 adult wasps emerged from 50 of these nests. From this total, 104 females emerged from 36 nests. Table 9-1 categorizes these females as to whether or not they mated with a brother before dispersal. Forty-one females emerged from 16 nests from which males failed to emerge, and 11 females emerged from five nests from which males emerged but failed to wait at the nest for their

TABLE 9-1 CLASSIFICATION OF 104 FEMALES FROM 36 NESTS WITH RESPECT TO SIBLING AND NONSIBLING MATINGS

Nest Situation	Mated with Brother	Left without Mating
No male at nest		
No males produced		41
Abandoned by males		11
Brother at nest		
Females observed	14	5
Other females	24	9
Total	38	66

sisters. These 52 females probably mated with unrelated males at flowers. The remaining 52 females emerged from 15 nests while the nest was attended by a brother. I could keep only one nest under observation at a time; consequently, some females emerged and left their nests while I was away temporarily. I observed the actual emergence of 19 of these females; 14 of the 19 mated with a brother (three-fourths), and five flew away without mating. By extrapolating, I assigned the remaining unobserved 33 females as sibling mating (24 females) or nonsibling mating (9 females) according to the proportion of females observed mating. Thus, approximately two-fifths of the copulations were between siblings as estimated for the wasps from these 50 nests (Table 9-1).

The distribution of nesting females, and thus the distribution of emerging males and virgin females, affects the extent of sibling mating. When females nest in isolation, their sons emerge and readily become established at their natal nest; once established as resident, a male is resistant to being displaced. Occasionally, patrolling males attacked resident males, but the residents prevailed and returned to their position after a skirmish. However, males that have just emerged from the nest seem to be driven off easily by intruders, who then assume typical resident behavior at the nest they usurped. Vulnerability of callow males to displacement is apparent only during their first morning out of the nest, perhaps because they are not yet oriented to the area. When nests provisioned by different females of the parental generation are nearby, the chance that callow males will be discovered and driven away by intruders increases because territorial males are constantly in the area, and males are less able to monopolize their emerging virgin sisters. Sometimes, males from nearby nests emerge and become established before discovering each other. Once established, these males are reluctant to yield, and over a period of several days they may fight many times during the morning hours without one's finally driving off the other. When males were distracted by constant quarreling, females were more likely to emerge and disperse before mating; when rival males are in the area constantly, copulations may be interrupted, further reducing the amount of sibling mating.

Reports on the behavior of other abundant, strong flying species suggest sibling mating is probably more important than generally realized, and inbreeding by species that are not constrained by a scarcity of mates after dispersal indicates that the evolutionary role of sibling mating needs to be more carefully considered. A female that mates with a brother increases her relatedness to her offspring, and thus may increase her genetic representation in subsequent genetic representation in subsequent generations relative to outcrossing females. A male gains because he encounters more females by remaining at the natal nest but still participates in a general mating pool. Also, the sex ratio control afforded by haplodiploid genetic systems allows hymenopteran females to gain further by shifting their reproductive effort toward daughters once inbreeding has begun.

The selective forces acting on these wasps may be similar to those that led to an alternation of sexual and asexual generations in organisms such as aphids or gall wasps. Inbreeding combined with sex ratio control and bias toward females is comparable to parthenogenetic reproduction; reproductive effort is diverted from "excess" sons to the production of more daughters which are genetically more similar to the parents. This results in a higher rate of increase for the genetic line than would occur under outbreeding, but it occurs at the expense of genetic variability. The regular occurrence of mating between nonrelatives at flowers ensures that new genetic combinations are continually generated. It seems that for *E. foraminatus* the costs of reduced genetic variability, resulting from partial inbreeding, are outweighed by the benefits of large numbers of daughters with high genetic relatedness to the parents.

2. Here is a set of notes based on an actual product discussed in the press. Write a commercial abstract based on these notes.

Situation

Grow Group, Inc., is one of the country's leading independent manufacturers of chemical coatings. Enviro-Spray is their product. It is an aerosol with a compartmentalized plastic sack, pressurized by carbon dioxide, produced when citric acid reacts with pellets of sodium bicarbonate.

The product developed after the ban of chlorofluorocarbon

aerosols was announced two years ago. Although the ban did not go into effect until last April, many fluorocarbon substitutes appeared on the market, including pump sprays, Freon aerosols, units that use a pressurized rubber balloon to dispense products, and hydrocarbon propellants.

Of these, hydrocarbon sprays were the most popular, since they offered many of the advantages of fluorocarbons without threatening the earth's ozone layer. But hydrocarbons have decided disadvantages. For one thing, since they are petroleum-based, they are incompatible with food products. Further, when combined with volatile products such as hairsprays, alcohol-based colognes, and spray paints, they pose the potential hazard of turning into miniature flame throwers when used too close to a heat source. Finally, they can explode from overheating or incineration after use, leading to skyrocketing insurance rates for factories and warehouses that manufacture and store them.

Enviro-Spray is based on a principle familiar to anyone who has used baking soda and vinegar as a fuel to power toy boats across the bathtub.

Here is how the product works: During manufacture, the sack is initially pressurized with a small amount of carbon dioxide. Then, as the product is dispensed, the sack expands, progressively breaking the heat seals of the compartments holding the tiny bicarbonate pellets. These then drop down into the citric acid at the bottom of the sack, where they react to form more CO_2 which in turn further expands the sack.

The advantages include safety. Because CO_2 is not flammable, it does not produce miniature flame throwers and therefore can be used with insecticides and similar products. Further, the product, whether it is shaving cream or cheese spread, never comes into contact with the propellant, since the acid-sodium bicarbonate reaction is confined to the plastic sack.

It is not limited by the size of the container or the thickness of the product. You can dispense a full keg of beer with it, or a caulking compound. In addition, because Enviro-Spray aerosols can be sterilized at temperatures up to 250°F, they would seem to be suitable candidates for pharmaceutical products and even for use in the operating room. Testing also finds that the Enviro-Spray can discharges 90 percent of its product in any position, even upside down.

3. Reread the Lister article reprinted in the chapter. Underline salient details and then write your own abstract of the article.

4. Return to Chapter 1, Exercise 5. Reread the article and then write an abstract. Compare your abstract with the one that appeared before the original article in *Science*, reprinted at the end of this chapter.

5. Write an informative abstract of "Long-term recall of father's song by female zebra finches," Chapter 5.

Solution: Exercise 1

(*a*) This is the original abstract that appeared before the article:

Abstract. Upon emergence as adults, brothers of *Euodynerus foraminatus* compete among themselves for the microterritory around their natal nest. The winning male inseminates his sisters as they emerge several days later. Unlike most species that inbreed in a similar fashion, both sexes of this common wasp are strong fliers. The possibility is raised that siblings may be preferred as mates even when outbreeding is possible.

(*b*) This is a sample abstract written by a student:

Sibling Matings in a Hunting Wasp: Adaptive Inbreeding? Cowen, David P. (Museum of Zoology, University of Michigan, Ann Arbor, Mich.) 1979 (Eng). Observed are frequent brother-sister matings in an abundant, nonparasitic, solitary wasp, *Euodynerus foraminatus*, which does not seem forced to inbreed since both sexes are strong fliers and capable of dispersing widely from the natal nest. Significant inbreeding results from sibling matings if females do not mate more than once, as is the case with *E. foraminatus*. In scoring the emergence of wasps from 50 trap nests, it was observed that approximately two-fifths of the copulations were between siblings. The reproductive effort results in the production of more daughters than sons, and these daughters are genetically more similar to the parents. This results in a higher rate of increase for the genetic line seemingly at the expense of genetic variability, which is ensured, however, by the matings of nonrelatives.

Solution: Exercise 4

Abstract. Precipitation in and around St. Louis was investigated to study urban influences on summer precipitation conditions. Prerain winds were used to define the "downwind area" where influences would be greatest, and wind-sorted rains were combined into monthly and summer totals. Seventy-five percent of the 16 rain patterns revealed a rainfall maximization downwind of the city, and the rainfall in the downwind area was 22.7 percent more than the rainfall upwind of St. Louis where no urban influences existed. Various statistical tests of the summer rainfall distribution reveal the downwind rainfall to be significantly greater than elsewhere and supportive of other findings that St. Louis increases rainfall.

10

Report Writing

Careful learning, accurate method, and extreme sobriety of statement.
Said of Newton's work by John Maynard Keynes.

The patterns of writing discussed thus far—definition, description, example, contrast, analogy, process—are basic rhetorical patterns that are used in technical writing.

They are parts of a whole.

The larger product that they fit into is reports—technical reports, research reports, trip reports, letter reports, memo reports. The word *report* means "to bear or bring back." To report is to return with the news of something observed. As short stories are staples in literary writing, reports are basic in technical and scientific communication.

The format for reports originated in antiquity, probably for forensic situations—situations occurring at courts of law. In these investigations, one asked, Did the event occur? If so, what was its nature? What was the significance? One searched for evidence that events occurred and then evaluated the evidence.

The information was based on this format:

1. Introduction
2. Exposition—the circumstances defining the issue
3. Proposition—the one-sentence statement that the discourse established
4. Division—the short outline of main points to be covered
5. Proof
6. Refutation of anticipated objections
7. Summary

This classic structural scheme developed in antiquity fits almost exactly the present format for a scientific or technical report.

The report has certain hallmarks: It is verifiable—you can, if you wish, confirm its accuracy. Its goal is not to excite the emotions of the reader, but to explain something in a way capable of verification. Both logarithmic tables and car maintenance books are, in this sense, reports. Clearly they do not have to meet criteria of liveliness and pace associated with literary writing.

The style of the report is unadorned, unemotional, economical. Unlike more romantic modes of writing that are inspirational, imaginative, intuitive, report style is in the classic mode of fact rather than feeling. Careful proportion, thorough analysis, and economical presentation are guiding principles.

Types of Reports

Companies, government funding agencies, and publications have various names for types of scientific and technical reports. Although there is no universally accepted nomenclature, reports can be divided into the five following categories. The divisions are arbitrary, and in some cases characteristics overlap.

1. *Progress reports.* These are submitted during the course of a project (see Figure 10-1). Usually you'll prepare them at fixed times—monthly, quarterly, semiannually, or annually. They are customarily short and to the point, although the interval between reports may to some extent determine length.

   Monthly reports begin with a summary of the month's work. They discuss problems and proposed solutions, comment

REPORT OF RESEARCH CORPORATION GRANT

(Please check one)   (Submit original and one legible copy)   . . . .

☐ Interim Report

☐ Terminal Report

INSTITUTION AND ADDRESS

PRINCIPAL INVESTIGATOR   PHONE

ACADEMIC RANK AND DEPARTMENT

SHORT TITLE OF RESEARCH SUPPORTED BY GRANT

STARTING DATE . . . .

SUMMARY OR PRINCIPAL FINDINGS AND THEIR SIGNIFICANCE (State succinctly in language understandable to one not necessarily expert in this field. Include extent to which original goals have been realized and any changes to original plan made or contemplated.)

FIGURE 10-1   Format for a progress report to the Research Corporation

on the study in terms of the schedule, and conclude with an overview of work in coming months.

Quarterly reports begin with a summary of the work that's been done in the three months. Usually a formal analysis section with results and interpretation follows. This may be supplemented by visual aids such as diagrams, tables, or sketches. The writer then recommends further actions, relating the results to the ultimate objective.

Interim reports are written when you've completed a part of the job rather than at a preordained time. The format is summary, data, and interpretation. The results are presented in the context of ultimate objectives.

2. *Trip or field reports.* These are written after you've visited a site. Typically a product or process for which you are responsible is given a trial. Give your observations in an orderly manner: objective of trip, list of those attending, conditions of visit, attitudes of people involved, findings.

3. *White papers.* These are presentations on developments in your area. You may do a literature search on a topic and then write up the findings. The paper may later be the groundwork for a new R&D project. Or you may prepare a white paper on instrumentation in your area, and later use it to justify the purchase of a new piece of equipment. A white paper is a report on the state of the art in a subject.

4. *Manager's report.* You may pick out several significant developments by your team and report on them, or you may report on new business.

5. *Final technical reports.* When the job is done, you'll prepare a report. The format will vary according to your audience. Final reports may be divided into three types: business reports, journal reports and contract reports. While all three types share similarities in style and purpose—that is, they are unadorned, verifiable accounts of something witnessed—there are also certain differences.

> *Business reports.* These have a more diversified audience than do journal articles. For instance, readers may include workers in other labs within the same company, sales/marketing/ production staff, and executives. Business reports follow the traditional order of introduction, procedure, results, and conclusion, but modify the design for commercial purposes.
>
> *Journal reports.* Reports on experimental findings prepared for journals follow the pattern of abstract, statement of the problem, related literature, materials and methods, results, and conclusions.
>
> *Contract reports.* These are prepared at the end of projects They follow highly specific guidelines issued by the funding agency. The work may be done by a research team with different members writing different sections of the final report.

Because of the importance of business, journal, and contract reports, separate sections follow discussing each.

Technical Business Report

The technical business report (TBR) is ubiquitous in industry; it's the project write-up, done after the assignment is completed.

At one time, TBRs were rare, but as staffs grew and diversified, reports became (1) a way of introducing and explaining products to sales and marketing people, (2) an *apologia* for R&D groups constantly under pressure to explain results of investments in their long-range programs, and (3) an all-purpose communications tool for highly diversified management and executives, who are often at different levels of scientific and technical training.

TBRs can be issued either formally, with introduction, procedure, results, conclusions, and recommendations; or informally, in the format of memos (internal) or letters (to people outside the organization).

Parts of the TBR   The TBR is usually aimed at wide corporate distribution. While the standard parts of a research paper are its basis, these parts are modified to broaden their appeal.

The abstract that prefaces journal articles becomes a summary in the TBR. This summary should give the findings briefly and clearly. It's important that the findings be stated in relation to business objectives.

The introduction differs from that of a journal article in which the problem is stated in relation to a review of literature in the field. Instead, the problem in a TBR is stated in relation to business or commercial considerations. Again, the market is primary. If there is a literature survey, it can be put in an appendix.

In this section, you should answer the questions, What is the nature of the problem? Why have I chosen method x to address this problem?

The procedure is not as detailed as in journal articles. In scholarly articles, a complete account of the procedure is fundamental; the replicability of your experiment rests upon the information you give. But the general reader of a TBR is not interested in replicating an experiment. Instead he or she wants only the gist of what you've done. Those with a specialized interest can consult the appendix—where you can attach procedural details. In the body of the report, simply make a short statement of the procedure, and get on with the results.

The results and discussion should be put briefly and clearly. Do not give exhaustive data. Remember, in a business report you do not need to give all information in the body of the text. Instead, use the appendix for lengthy supporting information and amplified statements of results.

Conclusions should address commercial aspects of the problem. You may do this in a separate recommendations section where you take the findings and apply them to business situations.

Format for Formal Business Reports

If the report is four or more pages, it cannot be done handily in the informal style of a memo. Instead, most companies use some version of this standard format:

1. The front matter includes the title page, abstract, table of contents, list of figures, list of tables, and list of abbreviations. Front matter is numbered with lowercase Roman numerals.

2. The body of the report includes the information contained under the first-, second-, third-, and fourth-level headings, footnotes, acknowledgments, and references.
3. The back matter includes the bibliography and appendixes.

Front Matter

Title Page   Formats vary. The minimum information includes name of presenter, date, and title. Be careful in arriving at a title. Such expressions as *a study of* and *results of an experiment to*, for instance, are unnecessary. Instead, be as specific as possible, avoid unfamiliar acronyms, and try to hold the total number of words to 14 or less.

Abstract   Include an informative abstract of between 25 to 200 words. (See Figure 10-2 for a title page incorporating an abstract.)

Table of Contents   Necessary only for long and complicated reports, the table of contents should list all first- and second-level headings; the abstract; the lists of figures, tables, and abbreviations and the pages on which they occur; and the appendixes. (See Figure 10-3 for a typical table of contents.)

List of Figures   If the report has more than five or six figures, drawings, charts, graphs, or photographs, list these at the front on a separate page.

List of Tables   If the report has more than five or six tables, list these at the front on a separate page.

List of Symbols, Abbreviations, Acronyms   If understanding of the report depends upon technical symbols or abbreviations that may be unfamiliar to the reader, include a list before the front matter.

Body of Report   Many agencies and companies specify the kinds of headings they want. Here are two types that are in common use:

FIRST-LEVEL HEADING

Second-Level Heading.   The text follows the heading.
Third-Level Heading.   The text follows the heading.
Fourth-Level Heading.   Text follows the heading.

June 30, 1972   TR 31.204

WHY SOME IBM PROFESSIONALS WRITE ARTICLES AND PAPERS, AND SOME DON'T -- RESULTS OF A SURVEY

by

Mason P. Southworth

ABSTRACT

To learn about why some technical professionals write articles
and papers, and some don't, a questionnaire was distributed at
20 IBM laboratories and plants in the U.S. and Europe. Ninety
authors and 20 non-authors responded. Professionals who become
authors say they do so primarily for recognition and prestige,
and to communicate their results to others. The benefit of
authorship cited most often is enhanced reputation in the technical community. Fewer professionals think that authorship
has helped their careers, and there is disagreement about how
much authorship counts in the company. Writing appears to help
a professional in his work because it develops a better understanding of the subject and opens lines of communication that
keep him informed of new developments. Eight out of 10 professionals who have tried authorship say it is worth the effort.
In comparing the three principal external media available to
professionals, authors like the prestige of journals, the wide
circulation and honorariums of technical magazines, and the
chance a conference paper offers to meet other professionals
at the conference. On the negative side, authors are critical
of the journals' slowness and strict requirements, the magazines' lower status and popularization, and the transient
nature, small audience and time and expense of a conference
presentation. Non-authors give two main reasons for not
writing: lack of time or motivation, and lack of a subject.

IBM

International Business Machines Corporation
Systems Development Division, Harrison, New York

FIGURE 10-2   Title page and abstract *(Courtesy IBM)*

TABLE OF CONTENTS

Page

PREFACE iii

ABSTRACT iv

LIST OF FIGURES vi

LIST OF TABLES vii

LIST OF EXHIBITS viii

S1 CONVERSION UNITS ix

1. INTRODUCTION 1

    1.1 Background   1
    1.2 Purpose   2
    1.3 Scope and Approach   3

2. ALTERNATIVE METHODS OF ESTIMATING REHABILITATION COSTS 5

    2.1 Average Costs and Costs Indices   5
    2.2 Parametric Cost Estimating Procedures   9
    2.3 Probabilistic Cost Estimating Procedures   17
    2.4 Cost Functions   26

3. CRITIQUE OF ALTERNATIVE METHODS OF ESTIMATING
   REHABILITATION COSTS 35

    3.1 Impact of Changing Job Size   37
    3.2 Treatment of Productivity   42
    3.3 Markup and Its Determinants   45
    3.4 Assessment of Reliability   46
    3.5 Treatment of Risk   48

FIGURE 10-3   Sample table of contents

I. FIRST-LEVEL HEADING

A. Second-Level Heading

     The first line of the paragraph is indented five spaces under the heading.

     1. Third-Level Heading. Text follows the heading.

     2. Fourth-Level Heading. Text follows the heading.

If you want to divide material within a paragraph, use a list.
(1) List items, using Arabic numerals in parentheses, indenting as you would for a paragraph.

(2) Make sure there are at least two items if you choose to number in this way.

You may also use bullets, or large dots.

● Indent for these as for a paragraph.
● Use them for items of equal importance.

Footnotes If you wish to explain further but don't want to interrupt the flow of the text, use a footnote. Indicate the footnote by typing an asterisk or double asterisk. Type the symbols slightly above the line. Then single-space the footnote at the bottom of the page. Many publications discourage footnotes because they interrupt the flow of the text; therefore, when possible integrate the information in the narrative itself.

Acknowledgements These follow immediately after the text. Include the names of those people or organizations who were helpful as well as any permissions received for reprinting materials.

References At the end of the work, you must give a list of your sources. To do this efficiently, cite references sequentially in the text using superscript Arabic numerals and then give the references in the same sequence in the reference list. If you are citing two references, use a comma between numerals. If you are citing more than two references, use a dash. Do not place such superscripts above symbols in cases in which it might be interpreted as an exponent. Here is the opening of a paper in which the references are given in superscript; the actual citations appear at the end of the paper.

LONG-TERM RECOGNITION OF FATHER'S SONG BY FEMALE ZEBRA FINCHES

Recently, attention has been directed at the question of how sexual imprinting, or the development of mating preferences, affects assortative mating within polymorphic species[1-3] and regulates the extent of inbreeding and outbreeding in a population[4-6]. It may be selectively advantageous for a young organism to learn individual characteristics of parents and/or siblings to avoid subsequent mating with kin as well as to avoid hybridisation by not mating with individuals that differ greatly from rearing partners[4-6]. I report here that adult female zebra finches (*Taeniopygia guttata*) can recognise the song of their own father after a period of early exposure followed by more than 2 months of separation while attaining sexual maturity.

Note that references 1 to 3 are indicated with a dash (1–3), rather than as 1, 2, 3.

If you wish, you may indicate references in the text by citing the author's name and the publication date in parentheses. Then arrange the reference list alphabetically, presenting works of each author chronologically.

> Corbin (1970) compares the . . . , while Leitner, Allen, and Jones (1980) suggest that. . . . Recent studies (Corbin, 1978; Leitner et al., 1980). . . .

The reference list should be prepared according to the guidelines your business or professional society specifies, since requirements differ even among such standard works as the *Handbook for Authors* of the American Chemical Society, the *Style Manual for Guidance in the Preparation of Papers* of the American Institute for Physics, and the *Publication Manual* of the American Psychological Association. Here are examples of the reference format provided by McGraw-Hill, which are appropriate if the publication for which you are writing does not specify a format:

Ferdinand P. Beer and E. Russell Johnston, Jr., *Mechanics for Engineers,* vol. 2: *Dynamics,* 3d ed., McGraw-Hill, New York, 1976, p. 486, fig. 12.19.	Books
Bradford Perkins, "Planned Parenthood: How to Beget and Raise a Branch or Subsidiary," *Architectural Record,* August 1976, pp. 53–57.	Periodicals and newspapers
E. S. Miliaras, *Power Plants with Air-Cooled Condensing Systems,* Monographs in Modern Electrical Technology, no. 7, MIT Press, Cambridge, 1974, pp. 75–79.	Serial publications
Proposing an Amendment to the Constitution of the United States Providing for Four-Year Terms for Members of the House of Representatives, 89th Cong., 2d Sess., S.J. Res. 126, Jan. 20, 1966, p. B-1.	Legislative and legal citations
J. R. Nall and J. W. Lathrop, "The Use of Photo-lithographic Techniques in Transistor Fabrication," Diamond Ordnance Fuze Lab. Rep. TR-608, ASTI Doc. AD-159233, June 1, 1958.	Technical reports

Back Matter

Bibliography   Unlike a reference list, which contains only the names of works cited in the paper, a bibliography is a listing for background or further reading. Like the reference list, it should be prepared according to the guidelines your business or professional society specifies.

Appendixes Identify these as Appendix A, Appendix B; cite all appendixes in the body of the report.

Format for Informal TBR: Memo and Letter

Memo Format You may write a technical brief or report in the form of a memorandum. This is common (1) when you want to report in-house to more than one person, and (2) when the information you are reporting can be encapsulated in one to three pages.

In memo format, use a to/from/subject line as the heading; the subject line functions as the title (see Figure 10-4).

If the memo can be kept to a page, begin with a clear opening that states the point. That is, present the gist of the matter first in a highly readable fashion. Then develop any points that you decide are necessary. Append supporting material only if essential. Remember, a memo is supposed to be brief and to the point. Resist the temptation to turn it into a 15-page technical report.

It's particularly important to present the opening statement clearly and directly in a memo. There are two useful techniques you can use to present the point at the top in a memo if it is two or three pages long.

Abstract/Introduction/Road Map/Subheadings

1. Write a simple (20- to 25-word) abstract at the top.
2. Follow with an introduction stating the problem in brief.

FIGURE 10-4 Memo format

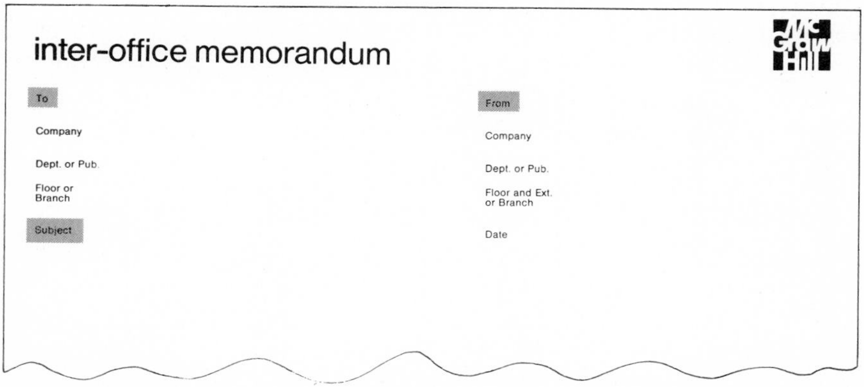

inter-office memorandum

To

Company

Dept. or Pub.

Floor or Branch

Subject

From

Company

Dept. or Pub.

Floor and Ext. or Branch

Date

3. Close the introduction with a "road map" giving the divisions or limitations: "This memo accordingly considers *x* and *y*," "This memo is restricted to the following considerations."
4. Use two or three subheadings to divide the material into coherent and readable units. These subheadings should be the same as those stated in the road map.

Objective/Scope/Introduction

1. Write a statement of the objective.
2. Write a statement of the scope of the memo. This is the same as a road map: it gives the major divisions of the paper, or states the areas to which it is restricted.
3. Follow with a brief introduction.
4. Use two or three subheadings to divide the materials into units. These subheadings should be the same as those stated in the scope statement.

Here is an example showing how to use either of these techniques to form a longer memo.

> **Situation**   You are sent by your company to visit one of its bottling plants. The plant bottles Slenderella, a low-calorie salad dressing, and during the five-hour sampling period last week, 20 percent of the bottles coming off the line were below declared volume. This was, of course, a serious problem, and the manager of the plant, George Fox, immediately began searching for the error. Eventually he located the source of the problem, experimented with various solutions, and chose one. His solution was to overfill at a later stage of the bottling process until the machinery causing the problem could be modified.

Your company asks you to report on the problem and the solution. You return from the visit and write this report in the form of a memo. It is three single-spaced pages. However, it is missing a clear introduction telling readers what they are going to read. You can provide this information either with an *abstract/ introduction/road map/subheadings* or an *objective/scope/introduction* line.

ABSTRACT/INTRODUCTION/ROAD MAP/SUBHEADINGS

To: Date:
From: Distribution:
Subject: Slenderella-Union Visit
           1 March 1980

Abstract: On 18 January Slenderella-Union discovered 20 percent of their bottles were coming off the line below declared volume. The problem was traced to foam and trapped air that appeared at the aqueous stage of the process. The solution adopted after a series of experiments was to overfill at the oil stage to compensate for air at the earlier phase. The solution is effective as a temporary measure until the machinery is modified.

I visited with George Fox, Quality Control, on 26 February. He explained that _____.

This memo is accordingly divided into three parts: _____; _____; and _____.

OBJECTIVE/SCOPE/INTRODUCTION

To: Date:

From: Distribution:

Subject: Slenderella-Union Visit
                 1 March 1980

Objective: This memo describes a trip to Union Bottling to evaluate the temporary adjustment in their bottling process of Slenderella to compensate for underfill of vinegar at the aqueous stage.

Scope: The report is restricted to three areas: (1) an account of the source of the error, (2) an evaluation of Fox's temporary solution, and (3) recommendations.

I visited with George Fox, Quality Control, on 26 February. He explained that _____.

(The author would then use three subheadings as suggested by the scope statement.)

Letter Format   If you are reporting outside of your organization and the information can be put briefly, you may do a technical report in the form of a letter. Essentially you will be saying "I was at x, got results y, analyzed them, and here's what it looks like. I'm therefore recommending z." If you are including this information in a letter, state your findings clearly in the opening. Above all, do not make the letter an eight-page, anecdotal account of your discoveries. State the objective (what), the reason (why), and what you did (how). Summarize the results and give recommendations.

If this is going to take more than three pages, do a separate letter of transmittal and attach the report using standard TBR format.

For a more complete discussion of the letter format, see Chapter 14.

Journal Report

Reports on experimental work are traditionally written in the manner of technical and scientific journals.

While TBRs are written for varied readership, journal reports are not. In a journal-style report, the readers are assumed to be one's peers. The prose tends to be compressed and the content highly specialized.

The *abstract* is first. It is a statement of the findings, customarily no more than 200 words in length. Although the abstract appears first, you should write it last, after you have finished the paper. Take your findings directly from the report, stitching sentences together with appropriate connectives.

The *introduction* gives the rationale. It clearly states the nature of the problem with a relevant theoretical and historical framework. Ask yourself: Have I stated the problem? Did I relate it to other works in the field? Have I demonstrated an adequate background both for the work and for my approach to the problem? Be selective in your literature citations; beginning writers have a tendency to cite excessively.

The introduction should explain why you conducted the experiment, and relate it to other investigations in the area.

The *procedure* section—also known as the *materials and methods* section—should answer the questions, What did I do? How did I do it?

Describe the experimental techniques used. Standard laboratory equipment and reagents should be mentioned without detail. Describe apparatus only if it is not standard.

Write this section so clearly that an informed person can replicate your experiment based upon it. You are writing for your peers. People in other fields will not read this section in the same way. They will know your findings and methodology from the abstract and will only skim this section. But people who work in your area will go over this prose carefully, judging the quality of your work by the type of detail you have included. Knowledge counts here. Write this section carefully, knowing that it will be scrutinized.

Results or *results and discussion* should be given succinctly. State the findings and then give supporting data. Do not comb through all of your tables column by column; cite only figures that are essential to a brief, clear presentation. Don't discuss implications in this section unless you are doing a combined results and discussion.

Conclusions It is here that you interpret your results. You will want to compare and contrast your findings with those of others in your field and discuss discrepancies. Include any limitations of your study. Answer this question directly and clearly: How has this study contributed to the original problem?

References Take the time to check and double-check these. Since references will typically be copied and recopied three or four times in the transition from original notes to typed manuscript, it is easy to garble information. Proofread your final manuscript against the original citations before shipping the paper off.

The accompanying table summarizes the differences between a technical business report and a journal report.

BUSINESS REPORT vs. JOURNAL REPORT

Section	Technical Business Report	Journal Report
Abstract	Written for broad readership; includes commercial objective.	Written for peers; highly specialized language and content.
Introduction/ Problem Statement	Rationale based on both technical and commercial considerations; related literature given in brief or placed entirely in appendix.	Justification; survey of related literature.
Procedure/ Materials and Methods	Given in brief. Full account put into appendix.	Fully detailed.
Results	Given in brief. Full account in appendix if necessary.	A crucial section. Don't repeat data from tables and graphs.
Discussion/ Conclusions	Combine technical and business aspects. Use a separate section for recommendations.	Recommendations rare.
Attachments	Appendixes give details of related literature, procedure, results.	Reference list obligatory.

Contract Report

If you are awarded money through a city, state, or federal agency, you'll be obliged to submit interim and final reports.

The format for these reports is highly standardized. The funding agency issues guidelines explaining line by line how to proceed with the paperwork.

As an example, here are guidelines for contract reports from the U.S. Department of Transportation. Their format, based on the American National Standards guidelines, is as follows:

1. *Front matter.* Summary page, table of contents, list of illustrations, list of tables, list of abbreviations and symbols.
2. *Body.* Introduction, main text, conclusions, recommendations.
3. *Back matter.* Appendixes, glossary, notes, references, bibliography, index.

A cover page is shown in Figure 10-5.

The order and content of each element in the report are clearly specified. The government uses a summary or documentation page to replace a traditional title page and abstract. Directions for filling out this page are exhaustive. Figure 10-6 shows a typical documentation page. The abstract is item 16. Key words, item 17, are the phrases by which the document will be indexed in information retrieval systems. These terms are listed in the *Thesaurus of Engineering and Scientific Terms.*

The body of the text is divided into the traditional sections of introduction—here called *work objectives* and *background information*—followed by procedure, apparatus, tests, results, conclusions, and recommendations.

Appendixes begin immediately without a separate page to announce them. If more than one appendix is included, designate them Appendix A, Appendix B, and cite them in the table of contents and at the top of each page on which they begin.

Handling Sources in a Report

In the problem statement of a formal paper, you will probably refer to published sources. The knack for interweaving such references gracefully within the narrative is easily acquired by some writers; others have difficulty.

Two guidelines may be helpful:

Report No. CG-D-14-74

Title

REMOTE SENSING OF

Subtitle (if any)

OIL SLICKS

Author(s)

John R. Doe

*Performing
organization
name and address*

**ABC Laboratories, Inc.
405 Main Street
Zedburg, TN 37000**

Insignia (if any)

Date

SEPTEMBER 1974

Type of report

FINAL REPORT

*Distribution
statement*

Document is available to the U.S. public through
the National Technical Information Service,
Springfield, Virginia 22161.

Prepared for

Operating element

U.S. DEPARTMENT

OF TRANSPORTATION

*Headquarters element
and address*

**UNITED STATES COAST GUARD
Office of Research and Development
Washington, D.C. 20590**

FIGURE 10-5   Sample cover for final report

1 Report No. FAA-RD-74-74,I	2 Government Accession No.	3 Recipient's Catalog No.
4 Title and Subtitle ANALYSIS OF PREDICTED AIRCRAFT WAKE VORTEX TRANSPORT AND COMPARISON WITH EXPERIMENT Volume I - Wake Vortex Predictive System Study		5 Report Date April 1974
		6 Performing Organization Code
7 Author(s) M.R. Brashears, N.A. Logan, S.J. Robertson, K. R. Shrider and C.D. Walters		8 Performing organization Report No. LM-74-2B
9 Performing Organization Name and Address Lockheed Missiles & Space Company, Inc.* Huntsville Research & Engineering Center 4800 Bradford Drive Huntsville, AL 35807		10 Work Unit No. (TRAIS) FA405/R4115
		11 Contract or Grant No. DOT-TSC-593
		13 Type of Report and Period Covered
12 Sponsoring Agency Name and Address U.S. Department of Transportation Federal Aviation Administration Systems Research and Development Service Washington, DC 20590		Final Report April to December 1973
		14 Sponsoring Agency Code FAA/ARD-500
15 Supplementary Notes　　U.S. Department of Transportation *Under contract　　Transportation Systems Center to:　　　　　　　Kendall Square 　　　　　　　　Cambridge MA 02142		

16 Abstract

　　　A unifying wake vortex transport model is developed and applied to a wake vortex predictive system concept. The fundamentals of vortex motion underlying the predictive model are discussed including vortex decay, bursting and instability phenomena. A parametric and sensitivity analysis is presented to establish baseline uncertainties in the algorithm to allow meaningful comparison of predicted and measured vortex tracks. A detailed comparison of predicted vortex tracks with photographic and groundwind vortex data is presented. Excellent agreement between prediction and measurement is shown to exist when sufficient wind data are available. Application of the Pasquill class criteria is shown to be an effective technique to describe the wind profile in the absence of detailed wind data. The effects of wind shear and the Ekman spiral on vortex transport are discussed. It is shown that the combination of wind shear and ground plane may be possible mechanisms underlying vortex tilting and a theoretical explanation is advanced that is somewhat supported by comparison with the experimental data. Finally, recommendations for further vortex data collection in the vicinity of an airport are presented.

　　　Volume II, 246 pages, contains appendices.

17 Key Words Vortices　　　　　　Ground Plane Aircraft Wakes　　　Vortex Tilting Wake Turbulence　　Vortex Transport Wind Shear Wake Vortex Predictive System		18 Distribution Statement Document is available to the U.S. public through the National Technical Information Service, Springfield, Virginia 22161		
19 Security Classification Unclassified		20 Security Classification Unclassified	21 No. of Pages 256	22 Price

FIGURE 10-6　Completed documentation page

1. *Do not quote to excess.* Beginning writers commonly read about their subject, transcribe useful quotations and information, and end up citing far more than necessary.
2. *Do not quote or paraphrase a source without acknowledging this source.* Include a page number for all direct quotations, a complete citation for any paraphrase. If certain texts were important in formulating your ideas but are not quoted directly, you can acknowledge these sources in the text and include the complete citation in the reference list.

There are a number of ways to handle the technicalities of citation. First, here is an example of what you *cannot* do. The information given in the example has been taken from the *McGraw-Hill Encyclopedia of Science and Technology;* however, the writer has failed to acknowledge the source. Except for the introductory sentence, the passage is unchanged.

Illegitimate Use of Quotation

A microphone is an electroacoustic device containing a transducer which is actuated by sound waves and delivers essentially equivalent electric waves. Modern conventional microphones may be classified as pressure, gradient, combination pressure-gradient, and wave types. A pressure microphone is one in which the electrical response is caused by variations in pressure in the actuating sound wave. In a gradient microphone the electrical response corresponds to some function of the pressure difference between two points in a sound wave. A wave microphone is one in which the response depends upon sound wave interaction.

Here is the source from which the quotation was drawn:

MICROPHONE

An electroacoustic device containing a transducer which is actuated by sound waves and delivers essentially equivalent electric waves. Modern conventional microphones may be classified as pressure, gradient, combination pressure-gradient, and wave types. A pressure microphone is one in which the electrical response is caused by variations in pressure in the actuating sound wave. In a gradient microphone the electrical response corresponds to some function of the pressure difference between two points in a sound wave. A wave microphone is one in which the response depends upon sound wave interaction.

Here are acceptable alternatives:

Direct Quotation

According to the *McGraw-Hill Encyclopedia of Science and Technology,* a microphone is

> . . . an electroacoustic device containing a transducer which is actuated by sound waves and delivers essentially equivalent electric waves. Modern conventional microphones may be classified as pressure, gradient, combination pressure-gradient, and wave types. A pressure microphone is one in

> which the electrical response is caused by variations in pressure in the actuating sound wave. In a gradient microphone the electrical response corresponds to some function of the pressure difference between two points in a sound wave. A wave microphone is one in which the response depends upon sound wave interaction. (p. 425)

This style of quotation used for citations of three or more lines is called *block format*. Notice the margins are shortened, single spacing is used, and the page number is given at the close. No quotation marks are used.

However, long quotations of this sort should be used sparingly. When possible, reduce them by quotation and paraphrase, or simply by summary.

Quotation and Paraphrase

According to the *McGraw-Hill Encyclopedia of Science and Technology*, a microphone is an "electoacoustic device containing a transducer which is actuated by sound waves and delivers essentially equivalent electric waves." Typically microphones are divided into pressure, gradient, pressure-gradient, and wave types, depending upon the causes of the electrical response.[1]

Summary

The function of a microphone is to transduce pressure waves into an electrical signal. Microphones are typically classified into pressure, gradient, pressure-gradient, and wave types, depending on what causes the electrical response.[1]

You may handle the citation either by a footnote, or by marking the text with either the date of publication (1977) or a number [1] and then including the full citation in the reference list.

Summary

Whether you are writing a technical business report or a journal report, these general guidelines should be useful.

1. *Title*. Beginning writers tend either to omit titles entirely

---

[1]"Microphone," *McGraw-Hill Encyclopedia of Science and Technology*, McGraw-Hill, New York, 1977, p. 425.

or to make them far too general. Instead, be explicit. Focus on your subject. Titles such as "photometers" or "light-scattering photometers" are too general when your actual subject is "Evaluation of Light-Scattering Photometers at the Rivington Laboratories."

Titles are important. They identify your subject for the reader. Think of how difficult it would be to read the newspaper without headlines, and be guided accordingly.

If you are writing an article for a journal, be warned that article titles tend to expand, and for good reason—wise authors use as many key words as possible in the title as an aid to the vital retrieval and indexing services that will provide an afterlife for their articles. Many journals therefore ask authors to confine their titles to 14 words or less.

2. *Opening*. Use clear, direct language, and state your point simply and clearly at the beginning. Many writers think they have to delay a statement of their findings because otherwise they'll "spoil the suspense." Technical reports are not murder mysteries. Your reader wants to know at the outset the gist of the matter, how you arrived at your method, and salient supporting points. To focus your report, use either an abstract or an objective/scope line.

3. *Subheads*. Follow up your introduction with an explanation of what, who, where, and why. If this information takes more than three paragraphs, use subheads to guide your reader. Use such standard heads as "Nature of Problem," "Analysis of Data," "Market," "Recommendations."

Subheads are useful both for reader and writer. They break up the wall of type and permit the reader to skim the text and use it selectively. As a writer, you'll find they help you keep to the point; they function as labels telling what does and does not belong in a particular section.

4. *Tone*. Who is your audience? Consider this question every time you write. The bulk of reports are written for executives. If they are your audience, you need to write the report differently than you would for your peers. Executives are besieged by paper and have little time to give to any one document. They will skim the report quickly, looking for the point. Furthermore, you can't assume they will have a detailed technical knowledge of the area you're treating. Anyone who spends all day working in a particular technical area is going to have a more specialized knowledge of it than someone who supervises a number of areas.

Therefore, if the report is for sales, marketing, or other administrative branches, be simple, clear, and direct. Avoid overloading the body of the report with detailed technical information. Put it in the appendix instead. What most of your readers will be doing is shopping for kernels of information. Don't jam in background materials that are unnecessary. Remember how much information goes over their desks each day, and be guided accordingly.

5. *Layout.* Neatness counts! A memo may be the only way someone higher on the ladder knows you. Make it attractive— clear, easy to read, carefully laid out. Avoid uninterrupted text. The use of subheads, white space, and generous margins is a courtesy to the reader.

6. *Flow.* State the point in the introduction. Explain why you took a particular approach. This will lead you logically to the procedure. After you state how you did the study, give the results with as much economy as possible. When you've told how you solved the problem, briefly discuss the implications. Don't overload any one section with technical detail unless you are preparing the report for a journal. Instead, place lengthy supporting information in an appendix.

Exercises

1. Select a research report from a technical or scientific journal. Analyze the parts of the paper. Is there an abstract? A statement of the problem? A review of literature? What are the major divisions of the paper? Has the author developed each section effectively? If you are studying in a group, pool research papers. Analyze the different parts so that you are thoroughly familiar with the standard sections of a report.
2. Here is a sample format for a progress report.

Grant No. _____

Subject _____

Period Covered _____

Summary	One to two sentences identifying project objectives and giving gist of work done in period.
Results	Short and clear.
Conclusions	Brief discussion of findings in terms of overall objectives.

Situation

You are preparing a monthly progress report for the Department of Energy on the events of December 1979. Your DOE grant number is F1376.

Your research team has been studying ways to clean emissions from coal-fired boilers. In particular, your group has been working on one way to remove oxides of sulfur (SO_x), an air pollutant that results when coal is burned.

You are testing the Heyman-Wright process. In a series of six tests conducted during the past month, your group has found that 80 percent of the sulfur originally contained in the stack gas can be converted to a concentrated stream of sulfur dioxide. Not only does the Heyman-Wright process appear to deliver most of the sulfur originally contained in the stack gas as a concentrated stream of sulfur dioxide; this stream can then be converted into sulfuric acid, elemental sulfur, or liquid sulfur dioxide. All of these have a market value. The selling of them would help with the operating costs of the recovery system.

Assignment

Write this information up in the form of a progress report.

3. Here is a sample format for a trip report:

Subject:

People Attending:

Testing Procedure:

Results:

Conclusions:

Recommendations:

Situation

The Metropolitan Transit Authority is testing one of your products, a graffiti remover called X-It. They want to know if one of its components, methylene chloride, is within the limits set by the Federal Occupational Safety and Health Act (OSHA). If they find the exposure to the product is safe for the workers who scrub graffiti off subway cars, they are going to order a lot of X-It.

You attend the field test. Here are your notes:

September 19, 1979. Field test of X-It. Present—James Killington, foreman. Fleet engineer—R. Leeds. Chemist for MTA —Richard Steinberg. Supervisor, Susan Rhodes. Safety coordinator, L. Myrvaggnes. Director of safety, M. T. Oliveri. All from the Met Trans Authority. The test was at the Met's Bushwick Junction Garage, Broadway at 103 St., Brooklyn. Test was for the toxicity of methylene chloride in X-It. OSHA limits are 500 ppm. Would we comply?

First test an imitation of their standard operating procedure for cleaning graffiti off subway cars. Graffiti removed from a specific area, then rinsed with soap and solution. Both interior and exterior areas done. First the X-It applied. Then rinsed with soap solution. For the interior the reading was 80 ppm. Then the reading for the exterior—10 to 20 ppm.

Then the nonstandard operation. That is, they set up at the most extreme conditions they imagine a worker might be exposed to using X-It. The cleaner was simply told to scrub the entire right rear quarter of the subway car. Then he was told to clean the entire right rear quarter of the exterior. He did the two jobs in sequence. First the X-It, and then a rinse. For this one the reading for the interior after 10 minutes was 70 ppm. For the exterior after 15 minutes it was 10 to 20 ppm. So we're well within the guidelines.

Assignment

Write this information up in the form of a trip report.

4. Here is a sample format for a one-page report in memo style.

To: Names, Titles   Date:

From: Distribution:

Subject:

Introduction: State point clearly and directly. Follow with one to three paragraphs giving background and implications.

Situation

Your R&D group has worked for the past six months on a simple, inorganic additive for concrete that extends the life of reinforced concrete structures. You've made progress, and have decided to present your findings in the form of a one-page memo to your supervisor.

Assignment

Write a one-page memo designed for distribution within your company, using the following information.

The product, Corrosion Inhibitor, works by covering the anodic loci of the steel reinforcement bars with a thin coating of gamma ferric oxide, or iron oxidized to its highest oxidation state. There is a market for the product. Bridge decks (driving surfaces) are notoriously fragile. When road crews apply salt to melt ice, the resulting corrosion problem is severe. The salt seeps into the concrete during the winter and then spurs corrosion when the weather warms in spring. It does this by setting up an electrolytic reaction on the steel reinforcing rods in the concrete. The corrosion causes the steel rods to expand, cracking the concrete surface and thus leading to deterioration of the structure.

Bridge decks, parking garages, buildings, and many other structures in which steel reinforcing is used are obvious applications. A recent General Accounting Office report of June 1979 states that one-third of the bridges in the United States have badly deteriorated. This includes 162,622 bridges in 32 states, 29,000 of them on interstate highways.

The product is unusual because it is the first time a chemical bonding protection process has been offered in the United States for reinforcing rods in concrete. Furthermore, the new product is relatively inexpensive. It will add only about $5 to the cost of concrete when mixed 2 to 5 percent by weight, a 2 to 3 percent increase per cubic yard. A cubic yard of concrete costs about $200.

The new additive is calcium nitrite.

5. *Situation*

You are the manager for a divison which has developed a new device. You want to prepare a brief report on it for sales and marketing people.

Assignment

Using the following information, write a one-page memo.

The product is a sensor, an electrode that measures the pH of water at temperatures from 100° to 285°C, and pressures as high as 1200 pounds per square inch. Previously the maximum operating temperature for practical pH sensors was below 150°C. This sensor has run continuously in pressurized water at 285°C for as long as two weeks.

Possible applications include monitoring pH of coolant water in nuclear reactors, detecting changes in the "mud" that lubricates oil-well drilling rigs, monitoring manufacturing processes in chemical plants, and measuring pH in steam-based power-generation plants to help prevent corrosion.

The sensor measures pH at extremely high temperatures and pressures, conditions under which ordinary glass electrodes cannot be used because glass membranes dissolve in superheated, pressurized water.

Zirconia ceramic is used in the sensor. Although this material has been used in the fabrication of high-temperature fuel cells and high-temperature oxygen sensors, this is its first application to pH electrodes to extend the range of conditions under which they operate.

The new electrode owes its inertness to a sealed outer tube membrane of zirconia ceramic that has been stabilized in the cubic crystalline form by the addition of magnesium oxide or calcium oxide. While the outer tube is novel, the inside is conventional, consisting of a silver wire coated with silver chloride immersed in a buffered solution of potassium chloride. The sensor is used in conjunction with a reference electrode that is similarly constructed except that a porous plug seals the end of the tube that is placed in water.

6. Here is a memo-report on truck ride evaluation. While the author has provided all necessary information, the memo still needs some final touches. Specifically, it needs either an abstract/introduction/road map/headings approach or an objective/scope/introduction/headings approach. Either will serve to give the paper the focus it needs. Write the opening

statement for the paper. Supply headings as needed and any necessary changes in the text.

To: Date:

From: Distribution:

Re: Assessment of ride quality in trucks

Truck drivers today seem to feel a kinship to the horseback riders of the western plains. Anyone who has spent time in the cab of a truck, being jarred back and forth as well as up and down, can recognize the similarity between the harsh vibration one can experience in a truck and the movement one is subjected to on horseback.

As the wheels of a truck revolve on the road, any irregularities in the wheels, tires, or road can set up repetitive impulses in the truck. As the speed of the truck increases, the frequencies of impulses increase and vibrations are transmitted to the cab and driver. (Other vibrations can come from the trailer attached to the cab.) As the velocity of the truck runs from 0 to 65 or 70 miles per hour, the frequency of vibration transmission can run from 0 to 16 or 17 hertz. If the frequency input through the wheels hits any natural frequency of the vehicle, strong cab vibrations result.

There are three main natural frequencies which can be set up in the vehicle. At lower frequencies (0 to 3 hertz and 0 to 20 miles per hour) the truck vibrates as a rigid body in a vertical direction. This vibration is termed *bounce*. As the velocity of the truck increases to 20 to 40 miles per hour, the input frequencies rise to 3 to 5 hertz. The truck then tends to pivot around a single point (still as a rigid body). This vibration is called *pitch*. The third natural frequency possible in trucks usually occurs at 5 to 16 hertz (50 to 70 miles per hour). In this phenomenon, the truck and frame bend as a beam—flexing around two nodal points. This type of vibration is *beaming* (see Figure 10-7).

At our engineering center, truck evaluation is done in two ways, subjectively and objectively. Subjective evaluations are performed on the road. Technicians and engineers rate the truck on a scale from 1 to 10 for movement in two directions—vertical and fore and aft—after sitting in the driver's seat and in the passenger seat.

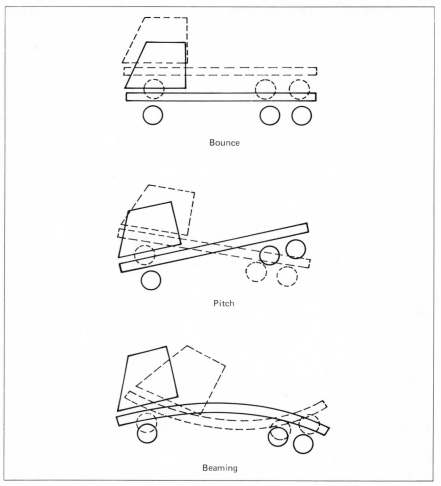

Bounce

Pitch

Beaming

FIGURE 10-7   Natural vibrational frequencies for trucks

The objective evaluation is a recently developed computer program containing seven parts and attempting to quantify the truck ride with 12 values.

Data for this program are collected by placing accelerometers in various locations on the cab. These data may be fed directly into the system or taped on a multitrack recorder for later computer analysis.

The first part describes vibration at various frequencies. The average power spectrum is calculated and integrated, and the square root taken (root mean square value). The result is a single digital "ride meter value" in the vertical direction and in the fore and aft direction.

The second program part is the same process with a weighting applied to the power spectrum frequencies which cause less pleasing human response. Thus the ride meter value may more closely resemble human evaluation. This part also gives a value for vertical and a value for fore and aft. In the first two tests, the higher the ride meter value, the lower the truck rating.

The rate at which energy is transferred to the human body during vibration is measured by the third part of the program; the more power the body must absorb, the more harsh the ride. Again a value is given for the vertical direction and the fore and aft; the higher the value, the worse the ride.

Combining the vertical and fore and aft results of the previous test into one result establishes another value of truck ride analysis.

In order to determine what amplitudes of vibrations are encountered, a range of amplitudes is divided into several bands. Using a level discriminator on the time history of response, the computer calculates the amount of time in each amplitude band. Then a percentage of time between two specified amplitude cutoff points can be calculated for vertical and fore and aft vibrations; the higher the percentage, the better the ride quality.

This procedure is also repeated using human response weighting factors applied to the time history, and again the percentage of time between two cutoff amplitudes is calculated.

The final part of the program checks the root mean square acceleration calculated in the first part of the program and determines the amount of exposure time permitted in each frequency band for human working proficiency. The lowest possible amount of time is then used to quantify the ride; the higher the number of hours, the better the ride.

At present, data are insufficient to use this computer program to predict human response to truck ride. However, with more data and development, it is hoped that this will be a future possibility.

7. *Situation*

You are hired by a small consulting firm of engineers. The week after you come to work, your boss sees an attractive ad for a home computer and decides it's high time to replace the office typewriter (an IBM Selectric) with a word processing unit. You're asked to do the spadework—the necessary telephone calls and letters, the gathering of spec sheets—and to prepare a two- to three-page memo-report on several possible systems. The boss does not want to spend more than $10,000 for the start-up equipment, that is, for the computer, terminal, software, and printer. The goal is a word processing unit that will handle not only typing but also accounting, payroll, proposals, and mass mailings.

Assignment

Write a memo-report comparing two possible systems. You may want to present the two alternatives by companies—for instance, an Apple system vs. a NorthStar or Radio Shack system. Or you may want to present two combinations made by the same company—a NorthStar system using one type of terminal and printer vs. a Northstar system using another type of terminal and printer. Whichever way you choose, remember to organize the report so that each alternative is presented clearly.

To do this properly, begin with a statement of the ojective and scope of the memo. You may do this using an objective/scope approach, or using an abstract/introduction approach. Afterward, introduce and describe the first alternative in a nutshell. Include costs. Then do the same for a second system. Then give your recommendations. Use appropriate headings such as "Objective," "Description of System *x*," "Description of System *y*," "Comparison," "Recommendations."

You are free in doing the assignment to write any company you wish to get its current literature. Most answer promptly; Mini Micro Mart, Inc., for instance, 1618 James Street, Syracuse, N.Y. 13203, has an extensive catalog which they will mail to prospective customers. Larger towns also have authorized dealers carrying both literature and demonstration models of the larger word processing manufacturers.

Remember, you are not interested in optional accessories: these will come later. For the present, you need gather information only on (1) a computer with a 64k memory, (2) a terminal, (3) a printer, and (4) a basic software package.

8. *Situation*

You work for a large consulting firm in a community that is considering building a liquefied natural gas (LNG) terminal. There are many risks associated with the venture, however.

LNG is a flammable substance, and potentially dangerous situations include the possibility of flameless vapor explosions if LNG comes in contact with water. The community has applied for a planning grant and has received encouragement from Washington, but needs a report addressing the question, What is the public risk associated with handling liquefied natural gas? The community asks your company to supply the statement, and you are assigned the job.

Assignment

Write the report. It should be no longer than ten typed pages. Begin with an abstract summing up your conclusions. State the problem in the introduction, then develop each point using subheads.

You'll find useful data in such articles as "Assessing the Risk of a LNG Terminal," *Technology Review*, October 1978, and "The Importance of Liquefied Natural Gas," *Scientific American*, April 1977. You may quote from these and other articles, but credit all sources.

Include a title page, table of contents, abstract, introduction, body, and reference list.

9. *Situation*

Your company is interested in hot dry rock (HDR) geothermal energy, and you are asked to prepare a state-of-the-art report on the subject.

Assignment

Prepare this report, using such sources as "Mining Earth's Heat: Hot Dry Rock Geothermal Energy," *Technology Review*, February 1979; or "Theory of Heat Extraction from Fractured Hot Dry Rock," *Journal of Geophysical Research,* vol. 80, 1975.

State your conclusions at the beginning in the form of an abstract. Then state the problem in the introduction and give a road map, or division, of the paper. This format of introduction and division is followed in many well-written papers. For instance, here is part of the opening of a report in *American Scientist* on barrier islands:

Understanding the natural dynamics of barrier islands is the key to recognizing and estimating both the short-term and long-term hazards of living on them. The purpose of this paper is to summarize the current information on barrier island dynamics and to show relationships between these dynamics and environmental hazards. We will begin with a review of the geomorphological history of barrier islands—how these land-forms were created, how they have undergone change, and why they will continue to change in spite of our efforts to halt the natural processes.

This introduction follows the classic format of proposition and division. Use this format for your introduction: State the purpose of the report and then announce the major divisions.

Include a title page, table of contents, abstract, introduction, body, and reference list.

10. *Situation*

You work for an engineering consulting firm that is proposing a new set of elevators for a large business. You are part of the team that is preparing the proposal.

Assignment

Your job is to do the field report on the state of the present elevator service. Use the elevators at your own school or institute as the basis for the report.

You'll need a physical description of the elevators, captioned drawings showing the location of the elevators, and easily understood tables showing peak times of use and maximum number of people that can be carried at these times. To get this data, interview staff at the location, do timed observations of the elevator(s), and read necessary background information.

Encapsulate your findings as an abstract at the beginning of the report. Then divide the information by subheads and develop each topic logically. Conclude with recommendations based on the data.

Length: Give five to ten pages, typed. Include a title page, table of contents, abstract, introduction, body, and reference list.

11. Your company is planning a commitment for a multiple synthetic fuel plant and is considering both coal and shale as sources. You've been asked to prepare a brief report on the comparative costs and benefits of the two types of synthetic liquid fuels—coal vs. shale. Prepare this state-of-the-art report. Credit all sources.

12. Write a five- to six-page (typed) formal report on the aerodynamics of the curve ball.

13. Your company is interested in recent innovations in loudspeaker design, primarily in the use of materials and enclosures. Prepare a four- to seven-page (typed) report on the topic. Credit all sources.

14. Prepare a state-of-the-art report of six to eight pages on one of the following topics:

    (a) Acid rain
    (b) Electronic sorting of mail
    (c) Plastics fabrication
    (d) Magnetic levitation trains (mag lev trains)
    (e) Electrostatic precipitators

    Include an abstract and an introduction that ends with a road map, or division of the parts. Use headings for each major section. Credit all sources.

15. Prepare a report on a subject at your school or place of business which requires direct observation, interview, and assembling of data. Weave the information into a six- to ten-page technical document with abstract, introduction, headings, and conclusion. Some possible topics include role of a bursar's office; role of a registrar's office; organization and functions of a technical library.

16. Write a two- to three-page memo on energy consumption in your school or place of business. Give the gist of the report in the opening paragraphs. Use headings as necessary to divide the information.

11

Effective Illustration

Illustrations are tricky—they can be so effective that they transcend the text, or so poorly conceived that they cloud the message.

Whether they succeed or fail, however, they do have one thing in common: all are expensive to produce. And therefore most illustrations are subject to the question, Is this illustration window-dressing, or will it help the reader?

If all pictures were worth a thousand words, there would be no problem; but this is rarely the case. Instead, illustrations range from useless to superb; you, the writer, will need to cast a cold eye upon them. Accordingly, this chapter presents basic guidelines a writer can use to evaluate the effectiveness of graphs and charts, photographs, tables, and other illustrations prepared for written reports.

Graphs and Charts

Graphs are effective if you want to show a trend—particularly if you want the reader to extrapolate. They also permit vivid comparisons.

Good graphs are simple, with lines and wording kept to a minimum. Since their purpose is to help the reader grasp the significance of the data, criticize them on that basis. If they don't do the job, either edit them or eliminate them.

Figure 11-1, for instance, is a poor illustration. The lines are not distinguishable, and neither are the points. The figure fails to do its job—to make differences between the groups clear. Rather than convey information graphically, it is a jumble, or, as one student called it, "fruit salad."

Figure 11-2, in contrast, is effective; that is, the reader can see the drift of the data.

FIGURE 11-1   Confusing illustration. Neither lines nor points are distinguishable. Good graphs, in contrast, are simple and direct, and are particularly effective in showing trends.

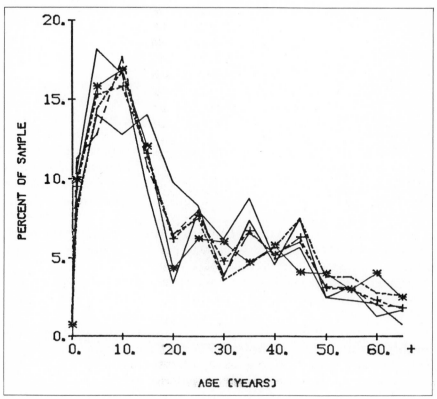

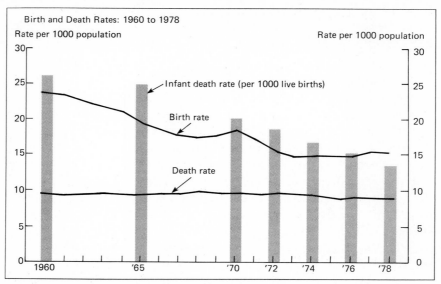

FIGURE 11-2   Effective illustration. The reader can see trends and make comparisons. Graphs and bar charts can often be combined in illustration. (*U.S. Bureau of the Census*)

Graphs, bar charts, and area and volume charts can all play a part in effective illustration.

Graphs show relationships between variables, using either straight lines, curves, or both. The graph is plotted on coordinate paper as a series of points standing for values of the variables.

Bar charts are useful for data that can be separated into such clear-cut divisions as, for instance, months of the year or number of ships in the Navy. Then these divisions may be shown on the chart by heavy lines or bars in lengths that correspond to the quantities.

All bars should be the same width. If the width of any bar is exaggerated, the reader may compare areas rather than length and in the process will be misled.

Area or volume charts include pie charts, those sector diagrams that are particularly popular when a presenter wants to convey the relationship of the parts to the whole (Figure 11-3).

Like bar charts, area and volume charts can present a problem: the reader can be easily misled. For instance, a diagram may use triangles where it is the height of the triangles that

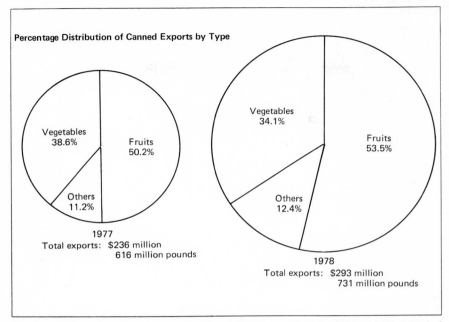

Percentage Distribution of Canned Exports by Type

Vegetables
38.6%

Fruits
50.2%

Others
11.2%

1977
Total exports: $236 million
616 million pounds

Vegetables
34.1%

Fruits
53.5%

Others
12.4%

1978
Total exports: $293 million
731 million pounds

FIGURE 11-3   Pie charts are a simple way to show distribution or relative size of parts of a whole. These charts compare relative sizes of two totals. (*U.S. Industrial Outlook, 1980*)

matters. However, if the illustrator varies the volume of the triangles, the reader may be led to assume it is the areas of the triangles that are being compared.

Here are some guidelines to use when planning and evaluating the effectiveness of graphs and charts:

1. In graphs, use different lines to distinguish variables (see Figure 11-4). This procedure will help you avoid the fruit-salad effect. If the lines are far apart, you may be able to use labels, as is done in Figures 11-2 and 11-4.

2. If you decide to show points on a graph, make sure the points clarify rather than clutter the presentation. One good technique is to use different symbols to distinguish variables, choosing them from simple template data symbols ($\bigcirc$, $\bullet$, $\triangle$, $\blacktriangle$).

3. Make sure letter size and symbol size are compatible. Graphs are often reduced for publication to fit either a single-column or a single-page format. When the letters are reduced, will the

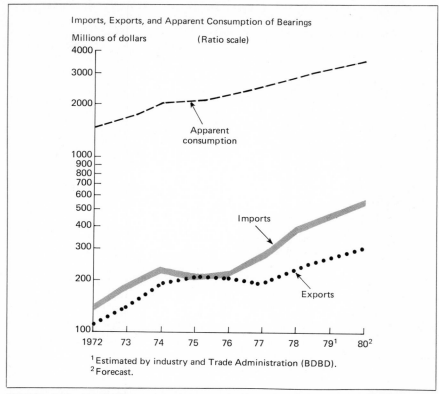

Imports, Exports, and Apparent Consumption of Bearings

FIGURE 11-4   Use different lines to distinguish variables in a graph. (*U.S. Industrial Output, 1980*)

symbols still be readable? If the lettering is small, reduction may make the accompanying symbols almost illegible (see Figure 11-5).

4. If you are doing a sketch that will be redrawn by the publisher, guide the draftsperson with suggestions in the margins, preferably in a color different from that of the drawing itself (Figure 11-6).

5. Captions count! Figures and captions are the first items most readers inspect. Therefore, make captions informative and direct so that the subject is identified immediately and specifically for the reader. Ideally, the captions should be so well prepared that the figure can be understood independently of the text. Since figures and captions may be processed separate-

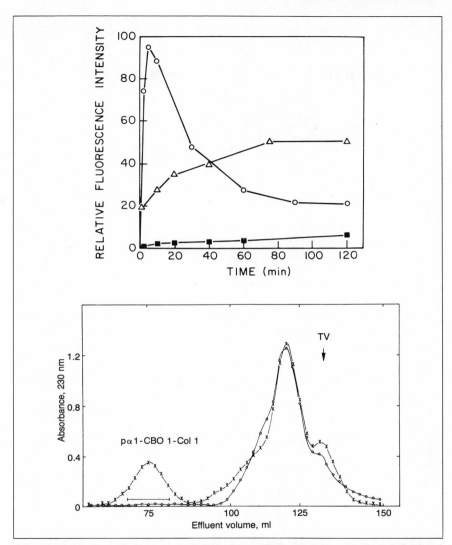

FIGURE 11-5   Illustration in which symbols and letters are proportionately sized vs. illustration in which symbols are disproportionately smaller than letters. (*American Chemical Society*)

ly, with captions going to the typesetter and illustrations to the art studio, do the figure captions two ways: (1) pencil the number and caption on the back of the figure; and (2) type each figure number, title, and caption consecutively and attach at the end of the text.

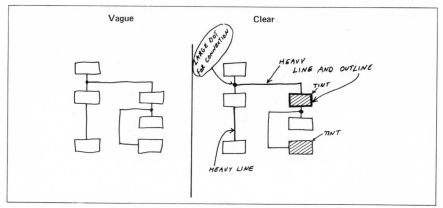

FIGURE 11-6   In the first sketch, the author has not indicated which lines should be emphasized or which boxes shaded. The second sketch has the author's directions.

6. Combine figures when possible if the combination will convey the same information since space is at a premium in most publications. The combination may mean that the drawing loses impact. Figure 11-7, for instance, loses some effect in order to conserve space. The combination is, however, preferred to its alternative—two separate figures conveying the same information.

FIGURE 11-7   The figure is crowded but clear. (*American Chemical Society*)

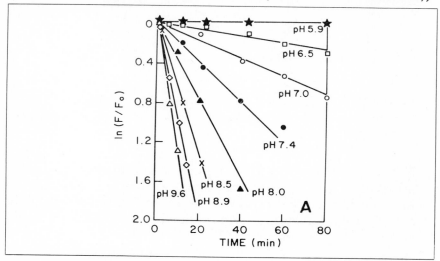

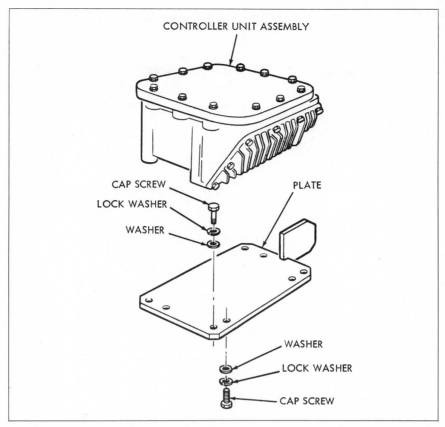

FIGURE 11-8 Callout refers to the list of labeled parts in a drawing. In this exploded view, the callout is handled on the picture itself rather than below it in a separate index or legend. (*Department of Defense.*)

Callouts and Instructions

Callout is the technical term for the list of labeled parts in a drawing. In Figure 11-8, for instance, the callout is written directly on the illustration itself. Government manuals call this *nomenclature callout.*

If the item is too complicated to allow for direct labeling, the callout may be handled with item numbers and a separate index or legend. Complicated callouts follow the government suggestion of beginning item numbers at 11 o'clock and then proceeding clockwise. Usually item numbers and leaders (lines connecting the item number to the part) are outside the boundaries of the parts being itemized.

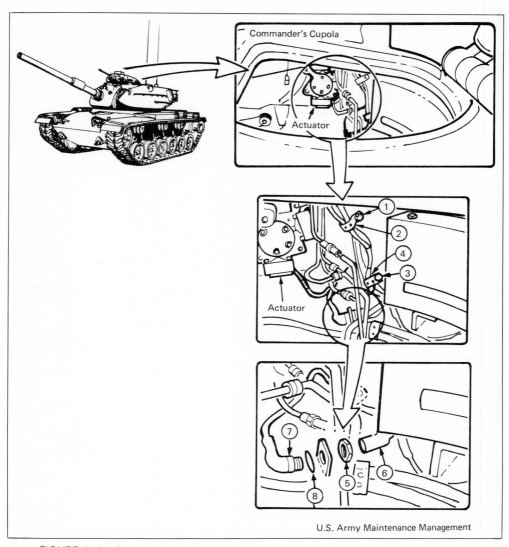

FIGURE 11-9   Successive locators use circles and arrows to lead the reader from the general to the specific. (*U.S. Army Maintenance Management*)

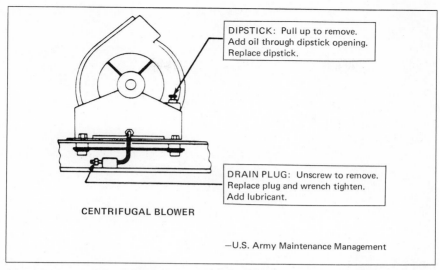

DIPSTICK: Pull up to remove.
Add oil through dipstick opening.
Replace dipstick.

DRAIN PLUG: Unscrew to remove.
Replace plug and wrench tighten.
Add lubricant.

CENTRIFUGAL BLOWER

—U.S. Army Maintenance Management

FIGURE 11-10   Instructions are connected to the illustrations by boxed text and leaders. (*U.S. Army Maintenance Management*)

Before calling out the names of parts, you may need to lead the reader from an overall view to a specific part. In government manuals this is accomplished by a device known as a *successive locator* (Figure 11-9), in which a series of arrows is used to help inexperienced technicians pinpoint locations. The successive locator ends with an exploded view—a line drawing of a part that has been separated into its component parts. For some simple devices, an exploded view may replace written text or instructions entirely.

Instructions are effective when placed on the same page as the illustration. In Figure 11-10, instructions are connected to the illustration by boxed text and leaders.

FIGURE 11-11 This reproduction is from the original photo of the crater Yuty, Mars.

Photographs

The original print should be of studio quality: high-contrast, glossy, black and white, 8 × 10 inches.

To see how rapidly the quality of the reproduction deteriorates according to the quality of the original print, see Figures 11-11 and 11-12. Figure 11-11 shows a reproduction made from an original high-contrast, glossy, black and white, 8 × 10 inch photograph of Mars taken by Viking 1. Figure 11-12 is a poor reproduction. In this case, a reproduction of the photograph from a journal was used instead of the original photograph. Tear sheets, offset reproductions, xerographic copies, color slides, color prints—all are difficult to handle. They should be avoided as sources of illustration if a studio-quality black and white print is available.

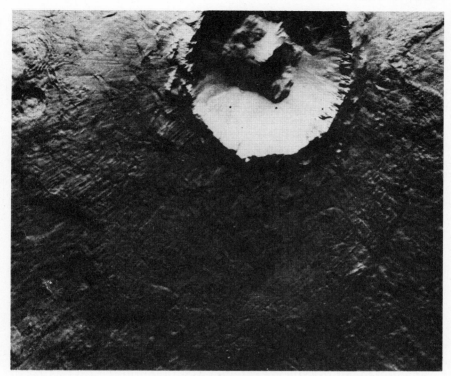

FIGURE 11-12   This is a poor reproduction done from a printed copy of the photograph rather than from the original.

Not only should the print be of high quality; it should also be accompanied by arrows, labels, or other instructions for the viewer if there is any possibility of confusion. Such instructions, which can make a tremendous difference in the impact the final reproduction will have, can be written on a transparent overlay and placed on top of the photograph.

If you are assembling photographs, identify each with a figure number and a caption. This may be done in either of two ways: (1) place a typed sheet with figure number and caption on the back of the print, taking care not to make an impression on the photograph, or (2) attach a list of figure captions in consecutive order at the end of the article or chapter. In either case, lightly mark figure numbers on the back of each photograph. Do not use a ball-point pen or any other writing instrument that can mar the surface. Do not staple or paper-clip overlays or captions in place.

Tables

Tables are useful because

They allow a reader to see relationships and make comparisons.
They can be clear, effective summaries.
They inform without interrupting the narrative.

While graphs are excellent for trends, tables are ideal vehicles for showing detail. The usefulness of a table in presenting detailed information can be shown by a comparison of two ways of presenting data on death rates for accidents and violence.

Narrative Method   What were death rates from accidents and violence between 1960 and 1977? The answers may surprise you. There were 91.3 deaths per 100,000 population among white males in 1960, 101.9 in 1970, 96.9 in 1975, and 96.8 in 1977. In sharp contrast, among nonwhite males, the death rate per 100,000 population was 136.6 in 1960, 174.3 in 1970, 157.3 in 1975, and 144.2 in 1977. The suicide and homicide rates were in contrast when one compared white and nonwhite males. Among white males, the suicide rate per 100,000 population was 17.6 in 1960, 18.0 in 1970, 20.1 in 1975, and 21.4 in 1977. Among nonwhite males the suicide rate per 100,000 population was 7.2 in 1960, 8.5 in 1970, 10.6 in 1975, and 11.4 in 1977.

Tabular Method   See Table 11-1. Ideally, tables should be understandable independently of the text and should supplement text rather than repeat it.

TABLE 11-1   DEATH RATES FROM ACCIDENTS AND VIOLENCE: 1960 TO 1977 [per 100,000 population]

Sex, Cause of Death, and Age	White				Black and Other			
	1960	1970	1975	1977	1960	1970	1975	1977
Male, total	91.3	101.9	96.9	96.8	136.6	174.3	157.3	144.2
Motor vehicle	31.5	39.1	32.2	34.1	34.4	44.3	33.8	33.8
Other accidents	38.6	38.2	35.5	32.7	60.6	60.7	50.2	45.4
Suicide	17.6	18.0	20.1	21.4	7.2	8.5	10.6	11.4
Homicide	3.6	6.8	9.1	8.7	34.5	60.8	62.6	53.6
15–24 years	105.2	130.7	129.7	135.4	147.8	224.3	179.5	157.6
25–44 years	88.5	107.1	103.4	102.5	200.1	275.4	256.4	230.1
45–64 years	118.6	121.4	104.0	98.0	185.1	236.8	203.3	184.8
65 years and over	223.5	216.9	185.3	176.5	202.0	218.0	200.5	188.4

Source: U.S. National Center for Health Statistics, *Vital Statistics of the United States,* annual.

Parts of the Table

Titles Titles are important in tables since they help make the tables clear enough so that the information can be understood independently of the text. They are placed above tables and numbered consecutively.

Stub Column The first column on the left is the stub column (see Table 11-2). Usually it lists the items described in the horizontal rows to the right. If it has a heading, it is called the *stub head.* However, if a heading is unnecessary, the space may be left blank (see Table 11-4).

To subdivide categories without using new columns, indent within the stub column to show subordination (see Table 11-5).

Column Heads Although the stub head is optional, column heads are not. Each column should have a heading; abbreviate units of measurement and set them off by commas. The first word is usually capitalized and the head aligned at the bottom. Experiment with wording in headings since the number of characters affects column width.

Rules Use rules below title, column heads, and at bottom of table. Avoid unnecessary horizontals and verticals, although especially complex tables may need them for clarity (Table 11-3). Use a straddle rule to clarify column heads. This is a rule which extends only the width of the columns that it straddles, unlike the three standard horizontal rules that run at the top, the bottom, and under column heads.

Footnotes Use lowercase letters for footnotes, unless the rules of a particular publication specify otherwise. Do not use numbers since superscripts are easily confused with those in the tables.

Numbers Don't use columns of data that can be calculated easily from given columns. For example, the second column in the accompanying table is unnecessary since it can be computed easily from the data in the first column.

Percent with	Percent without
43	57
86	14
19	81

TABLE 11-2 COMBINED EARNINGS OF FOUR FIRMS ROSE 175 PERCENT IN 1979

Stub head————Firms

Firms	Net Sales 1979	Change from 1978, %	Net Income 1979	Change from 1978, %
Canadian Industries	$880.0	18	$36.3[b]	38
Celanese Canada	353.6	22	21.2[c]	221
Du Pont Canada	879.6	33	59.0	478
Union Carbide Canada	685.9	30	57.8	188
TOTAL	$2799.1	23	$174.3	175

Stub column

Footnotes————[a]Net income as percentage of sales.
[b]Excluding extraordinary gain of $12.0 million.
[c]Excluding extraordinary loss of $3.0 million.

Math table with both vertical and horizontal rules

TABLE 11-3 RESULTS OF COMPUTATIONS OF EQUIVALENT RIGIDITIES FOR EXAMPLE 1

Parameters and equivalent rigidities	Frame 1	Frame 11
$\dfrac{l^3(1 + 2k)}{96EI_l(2 + k)}$	$\dfrac{3.06^3(1 + 2 \times 1.51)}{96 \times 3 \times 10^6 \times 0.0452(2 + 1.51)}$ $= 2.70 \times 10^{-6}$	$\dfrac{3.06^3(1 + 2 \times 2.23)}{96 \times 3 \times 10^6 \times 0.069(2 + 2.23)}$ $= 1.88 \times 10^{-6}$
$\dfrac{3l}{8GA_l}$	$\dfrac{3 \times 3.06}{8 \times 10^6 \times 0.58} = 1.98 \times 10^{-6}$	$\dfrac{3 \times 3.06}{8 \times 10^6 \times 0.83} = 1.38 \times 10^{-6}$
Deflection of frame beam at center of span under action of unit force, m	$(2.70 + 1.98) \times 10^{-6} = 4.68 \times 10^{-6}$	$(1.88 + 1.38) \times 10^{-6}$ $= 3.26 \times 10^{-6}$

Title placed above table and numbered consecutively.

TABLE 11-4 TYPICAL PRODUCTIVITY OF VARIOUS CULTIVATED AND NATURAL ECOSYSTEMS*

Stub head blank

Straddle rule separates levels of column heads.

Cross heads: Heads which do not apply to specific columns.

| | Net Primary Production, g/m^2 | |
	Per Year	Per Day
Cultivated		
Wheat	344	0.94 (2.3)
Oats	926	2.54 (6.2)
Corn	412	1.13 (2.3)
Hay	420	1.15 (2.3)
Potatoes	385	1.10 (2.6)
Sugar beets	765	2.10 (4.3)
Sugar cane (Hawaii)	3430	9.40 (9.4)
Noncultivated		
Giant ragweed	1440	3.95 (9.6)
Tall spartina salt marsh	3300	9.0 (9.0)
Forest, pine	3180	6.0 (6.0)
Forest, deciduous	1560	3.0 (6.0)
Tall grass prairies	446	1.22 (3.0)
Seaweed beds	358	1.98 (1.0)

Place footnotes at bottom of table, not bottom of page.

*Values represent world average where crops are widespread, otherwise areas of highest yield. Values in parentheses are rates for growing season only.

Explanatory footnote dropped from table title.

TABLE 11-5 RECOMMENDED DOSAGES

Procedure

Infiltration
  Percutaneous
  Intravenous regional
Central neural block
  Epidural
    Thoracic
    Lumbar
      Analgesic
      Anesthesia

Do not use zeros unless there is a zero reading. Otherwise use three center dots plus a footnote explaining that no information was available. Prefer decimals to fractions, unless the decimal implies a greater accuracy than that achieved.

Keep decimal points in a vertical line.

Do not use ditto marks.

In some countries, commas are used instead of decimal points. Therefore, to eliminate confusion, when you have five or more digits to the right or left of the decimal point, break the number into groups of three counting from the decimal point.

10 968	0.649 50
5 465	0.988 45

Placement Since you cannot be sure in advance where the table will be placed, refer to it by saying "see Table 1" or "Table 1" or "the accompanying table" rather than "the table above" or "the table below."

Do not prepare tables as part of the running text. Instead, have each prepared separately and placed at the end of the paper.

Try to design tables so they can be viewed upright rather than sideways.

If you are sending the table off for publication, you can assume that it will be reduced to half its size. Will the type still be clear? For most journals, tables are reduced to go in either single- or double-column widths. A standard single column is 8.5 centimeters, or 50 to 75 characters. The normal double column is 17.5 centimeters. If you plan to have the tables published in a journal, you should find out in advance the exact size of columns.

Summary

1. Your illustrations or tables will probably be reduced. Therefore, all artwork and tabular matter should be prepared so that if it is reduced by one-third, the type will still be readable.
2. Put titles on tables; put captions on figures. Make these titles or captions as long as necessary to guarantee that the figure or table will be comprehensible independently of the text.
3. Although you cannot determine where tables and illustrations will be placed if you are submitting an article or book for publication, you can put figure or table citations at the first mention so that the reader will be alerted.
4. Submit tables separately, one to a page. Submit figures separ-

ately, one to a page. For the latter, prepare a caption list and lightly pencil captions and figure numbers on the back of each figure.

Exercises

1. Discuss the strengths and/or weaknesses of the accompanying illustrations (Figure 11-13a to c).
2. Prepare a set of instructions using boxes and lines for one of the following jobs:

   (a) Filling a fountain pen
   (b) Changing the lead in a mechanical pencil
   (c) Filling a stapler
   (d) Your choice

3. Do an exploded view of a familiar object such as

   (a) the wheel of a car
   (b) a doorknob
   (c) a phonograph tone arm
   (d) a bicycle derailleur
   (e) the firing mechanism of a rifle

   Label this object so that the person reading the description can either assemble it or perform some task with the object. Then write instructions for the particular task beneath the exploded view. For example, you may show how to mount a doorknob or how to adjust a bicycle derailleur. Identify parts using either nomenclature callout or item numbers.
4. Do either a cutaway or a close-up of

   (a) the mechanism of a drill press or other power tool
   (b) a living organism

   Label the parts of the drawing.
5. Prepare a set of illustrations in two parts: (a) an introduction to the object, and (b) how to use the object. Choose a compass, a contour map, or some other process, mechanism, or organism with which you are familiar.
6. If you are studying in a group, gather statistics on the group—such as age, height, weight—and arrange the informa-

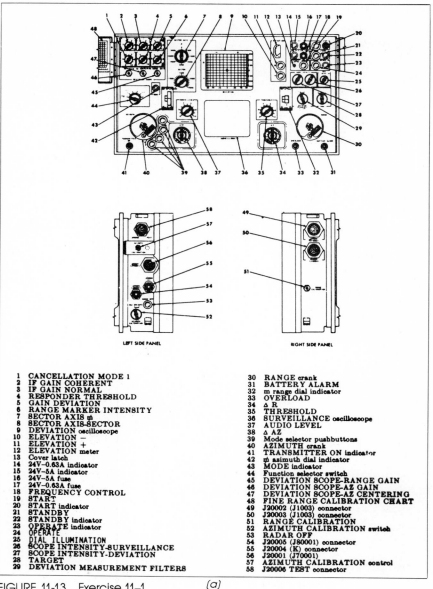

1 CANCELLATION MODE 1
2 IF GAIN COHERENT
3 IF GAIN NORMAL
4 RESPONDER THRESHOLD
5 GAIN DEVIATION
6 RANGE MARKER INTENSITY
7 SECTOR AXIS ₥
8 SECTOR AXIS-SECTOR
9 DEVIATION oscilloscope
10 ELEVATION −
11 ELEVATION +
12 ELEVATION meter
13 Cover latch
14 24V−0.63A indicator
15 24V−5A indicator
16 24V−5A fuse
17 24V−0.63A fuse
18 FREQUENCY CONTROL
19 START
20 START indicator
21 STANDBY
22 STANDBY indicator
23 OPERATE indicator
24 OPERATE
25 DIAL ILLUMINATION
26 SCOPE INTENSITY-SURVEILLANCE
27 SCOPE INTENSITY-DEVIATION
28 TARGET
29 DEVIATION MEASUREMENT FILTERS

30 RANGE crank
31 BATTERY ALARM
32 ₥ range dial indicator
33 OVERLOAD
34 Δ R
35 THRESHOLD
36 SURVEILLANCE oscilloscope
37 AUDIO LEVEL
38 Δ AZ
39 Mode selector pushbuttons
40 AZIMUTH crank
41 TRANSMITTER ON indicator
42 ₥ azimuth dial indicator
43 MODE indicator
44 Function selector switch
45 DEVIATION SCOPE-RANGE GAIN
46 DEVIATION SCOPE-AZ GAIN
47 DEVIATION SCOPE-AZ CENTERING
48 FINE RANGE CALIBRATION CHART
49 J20002 (J1003) connector
50 J20003 (J1003) connector
51 RANGE CALIBRATION
52 AZIMUTH CALIBRATION switch
53 RADAR OFF
54 J20005 (J80001) connector
55 J20004 (K) connector
56 J20001 (J70001)
57 AZIMUTH CALIBRATION control
58 J20006 TEST connector

FIGURE 11-13 Exercise 11-1   (a)

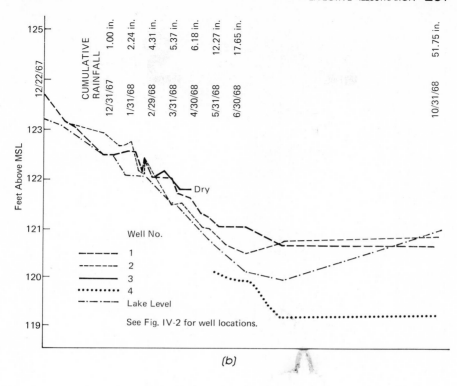

(b)

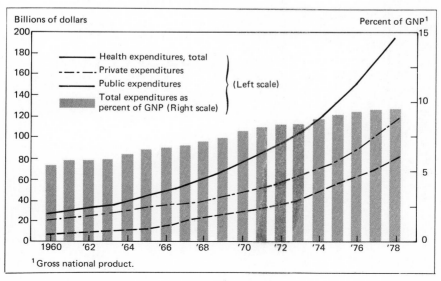

(c)

In millions of dollars. Direct investment abroad means ownership or control, directly or indirectly, by one U.S. person or business enterprise of 10 percent or more of the voting securities of an incorporated foreign business enterprise or an equivalent interest in an unincorporated foreign business enterprise. Direct investment position is value at year end of U.S. parents' claims on the equity of, and receivables due from, foreign affiliates less foreign affiliates receivables due from U.S. Income consists of U.S. parents' shares in earnings (net of foreign income taxes) of their foreign affiliates plus net interest on intercompany accounts, less withholding taxes on dividends and interest.]

Type of Industry	Direct Investment Position							Income						
	1966	1970	1974	1975	1976	1977	1978	1966	1970	1974	1975	1976	1977	1978
All industries	1325	1912	2854	3200	2976	3230	3712	108	146	394	455	70	322	597
Mining and smelting	95	127	83	80	89	98	97	17	2	33	16	9	9	14
Petroleum	29	10	18	22	17	26	11	(z)	2	8	7	2	4	9
Manufacturing	927	1380	2173	2442	2218	2391	2753	75	121	291	348	22	201	448
Food products	107	132	191	223	224	207	229	8	13	32	47	23	21	36
Chemicals and allied products	261	375	652	720	654	699	785	20	39	91	101	1	60	101
Primary and fabricated metals	72	129	194	224	213	219	244	7	10	27	33	6	13	
Machinery	177	264	427	480	451	451	512	13	30	59	72	5	20	92
Transportation equipment	121	151	240	267	221	298	370	8	12	19	22	−7	29	82
Other manufacturing	190	330	469	528	455	517	612	19	18	62	72	−7	58	101
Trade	136	207	400	476	448	502	503	8	13	45	67	19	87	77

Source: 1598, 1599; U.S. Bureau of Economic Analysis, *Survey of Current Business,* various monthly issues.

Z Less than $500.00.

tion in a table. Compare your table with that of others in your group.

7. Analyze a set of tables or illustrations from either a professional journal or technical magazine. What are the strong points? the weak ones?

8. The accompanying table contains information on U.S. direct investment in Mexico. To emphasize particular trends or aspects, accompany this comprehensive data with charts or graphs illustrating selected details.

   (a) Make a pie chart showing relative incomes of U.S. direct industrial investment in Mexico for 1975.

   (b) Draw a bar chart showing income of mining and smelting industries for 1966 to 1978.

   (c) Draw a graph showing direct investment position of mining/smelting and petroleum for 1966 to 1978.

12
Preparing a Proposal

I can think of no one objection that will possibly be raised against this proposal—
Jonathan Swift, *A Modest Proposal*

In grade school I wrote "compositions"; in high school, "themes"; in college, "term papers." Then I landed an industrial job and discovered I was supposed to know how to turn out proposals.

I drew a complete blank. Proposals? What were they? The only one I could recall reading was by Jonathan Swift. Called *A Modest Proposal*, it ironically offered to solve the Irish problem of hunger by baking all the Irish children and serving them in pies. "A most delicious, nourishing and wholesome food," Swift explains, "whether steamed, roasted, baked or boiled."

I have since brushed up on the form and content of proposals. But of all the new kinds of writing I encountered when I went to work, proposals were the most unfamiliar.

What's a Proposal?

A proposal is actually a hybrid—it combines the formality of a technical report with the persuasiveness of a sales pitch.

As the name suggests, a proposal is an offering, from *pro*, meaning "forth," and *poser*, "to place or put."

A proposal is that which you put forward. Usually it's written to solicit new business; to compete for research money; to bid for a government contract; or to justify a new expenditure, typically for equipment.

A proposal is a bid for a job, for services, for a cash award, for research money—for attention in a crowded field. Although it is rarely included in a writing class, it is a basic form in the marketplace. Think of it this way: at the end of the job, you write the report, but *to get the job, you write a proposal.*

Who Is the Audience?

For a *research proposal*, the audience is a panel of peer reviewers, specialists in your field who are invited by the sponsor—an agency such as the National Science Foundation—to read and evaluate your paper. The reviewing may be done either by mail or by panel sessions where all the reviewers travel to one location and read the proposals together. Usually, at least three people read each proposal.

Sometimes the entire process is done twice. First there is a preliminary review, done by mail or panel. Then those people with the highest scores are asked to submit a formal proposal, and the entire review process is repeated. The procedure is highly competitive, and only those proposals with the best scores will make it through.

Whether you win or not, you can have copies of the reviews sent to you.

For some kinds of *contract bidding*, you will respond to nationally advertised RFPs—requests for proposals—that appear in *Commerce Business Daily*. Proposals are usually read by the program staff of the agency with the aid of specialists. There may not be a formal panel.

For *new business*, the audience is the prospective customer.

For *in-house* proposals, the audience is management.

Parts of the Proposal

You'll need to adapt the proposal to the audience, but there is a standard list of parts which you can use as a guide:

1. Problem statement, or rationale ⎫ Introduction
2. Objectives ⎭
3. Procedure: Technical discussion
4. Evaluation
5. Follow-up
6. Qualifications
7. Budget
8. Attachments

Section 1: The Problem Statement

The key part of the proposal is the idea you seek to develop. This idea should address itself to

Something important that has not been done, or
Something important that has been done poorly, or
Something important that has been done incompletely

The core of the proposal is usually called the *needs assessment, rationale,* or *problem statement.*
Answer these questions in your problem statement:

1. What is the problem?
2. Why is it significant?
3. Who else has studied this problem? What have they found? What is the supporting empirical evidence? What are the theoretical underpinnings?

Remember, you are addressing yourself to a *problem*—to something not done, or done incompletely, or done poorly.
To do this effectively, you must state immediately what the problem is and then explain its significance. When appropriate, you need to add any finding from related literature that supports this basic statement.
You may need to argue special needs for a local population, or there may be national needs that you are addressing. In arguing significance, you may use statistics, a survey, or a thorough search of the literature in your field:

If it is a proposal to develop a new rust inhibitor for the steel loci used in reinforced concrete, you may demonstrate need by quoting national statistics on the corrosion of paved surfaces during the winter on highways and parking decks.

If it is an educational project, you may cite declining reading scores throughout the nation, and declining scores among your local population.

If it is a model recruitment project on women in engineering, you may cite the lack of women in engineering, both nationally and locally.

The problem statement is crucial. If you have "a problem with your problem," you're going to have trouble with the entire proposal because objectives, methodology, and evaluation flow logically from the problem statement. Therefore, take time with this section; think it through carefully before proceeding.

Section 2: Objectives

You need not only a statement of the problem and its significance but also a statement of your goals within the context of the problem.

You need, in other words, objectives.

List your objectives clearly and specifically. Divide them into short-term and long-term goals if necessary.

Section 3: Procedure

How will you carry out your objectives?

A reviewer for a national agency reports that many proposals begin with excellent, carefully reasoned statements of the problem but have only the skimpiest of details on how the objectives are to be carried out.

Don't make this mistake. Instead, make this section highly specific. This part of the proposal should state who will do what, and when.

1. List each objective, and under it state exactly how you plan on realizing it.
2. Use simple devices such as month-by-month timetables, schedules, or time lines so the reader can see what your activities will be over the year. (See Figure 12-1.)

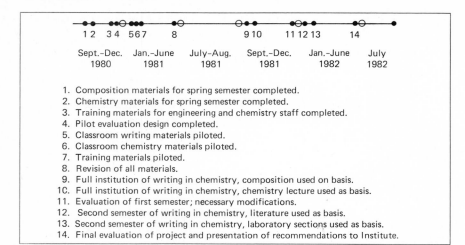

FIGURE 12-1   Time line. This simple device matches the two years of the project with the fourteen program objectives.

3. Use a simple chart that matches up the time schedule with the list of people responsible for each job. In this way, a reviewer can see who is actually going to do what. If the project is complicated, make up a simple management plan showing the steps you'll take and who will be responsible at each critical decision point. (See Figure 12-2.)

4. Include all necessary technical detail. You may have an extensive technical discussion in this section, complete with instrument documentation, testing schedules, and the like. Such technical discussions are read carefully by the specialist who evaluates the project, and they need to be accurate and convincing to establish your technical competence. However, you need not include all of the information in the narrative. If possible, boil the methodology down to two to three pages, including all important features, and then attach supporting technical information in an appendix.

Section 4: Evaluation

How do you plan on evaluating your project. How will you answer the question, Did it work?

In most cases, it's possible to measure change. But there are instances where evaluation is difficult. Suppose, for example, you are proposing a new chemistry curriculum for first-year students.

	Job 1	Job 2	Job 3	Job 4	Job 5	Job 6	Job 7	Job 8	Job 9	Job 10	Job 11	Job 12	Job 13	Job 14
	1	2	3	4	5	6	7	8	9	10	11	12	13	14
Person 1	A	A	A	A	A	A	A	A	A	A	A	A	A	A
Person 2	I			C	C			I		I		C	C	
Person 3		I	I		I		I	C	I	C		I	I	
Person 4			C			I	C		C		C			I
Person 5		C				C					I			C

Legend
A = Accountable for overall project
I = Initiates activity
C = Coordinates activity

FIGURE 12-2   Responsibility chart. This chart matches the 5 people heading the project with their level of responsibility for jobs 1 to 14.

How will you test the new curriculum against the old one to see which is more effective?

Because educational gains are so difficult to measure, it is common to hire specialists to do the evaluation. The practice is encouraged in the guidelines for most educational grants, and specific stipulations are allowed in the budget.

Section 5: Follow-Up

What will you do when the project is over?

If you are undertaking a research contract, how will you guarantee to tell others of your results? Will you send the document to a retrieval center so that others can learn from your work? Will you attend professional conferences and present papers on your findings?

In governmentese, this is called "disseminating the results." That means, how do you plan on getting the news out locally, nationally, even internationally?

There is a second question you may need to answer in this section. If you are undertaking an educational project, you will need to explain how your institution or organization will follow up on the proposed program. Suppose you have applied for a project to recruit women into engineering professions. Will the school continue this project after the funding is over, or will the entire effort collapse?

Section 6: Qualifications

Who will do the work? What qualifies them for the job? What kinds of organizational support do they have? What kinds of physical facilities are involved? Are they appropriate?

In this section you are making a case for your own competency. What makes you and your institute or company the right spot? You'll answer this question in three areas: (1) the qualifications of the project leaders, (2) institutional support, and (3) appropriateness of facilities and support staff.

Personnel   Describe key personnel who will take leadership, stressing their qualifications. These qualifications should be related to the specific tasks that they have been assigned in the procedures. Include in the narrative a paragraph on professional background for each key person, and in addition attach vitae as supporting documents in the appendix.

Organizational Support   It is rare to carry out a project alone, with no collaborative effort. You may need the help of another department in your corporation, another division in your school district. You may need letters from the Board of Education or the Chemists' Club saying that your project is valuable, that their services are open to you if you undertake the job.

You'll need to do the legwork necessary to get support for your project; then state in the proposal that you have this support. To prove it, attach letters in the appendix demonstrating that appropriate people or organizations have been contacted and that they have given the project their blessing.

Resources   Do you have the appropriate facilities, laboratories, classrooms? The space, equipment, and support personnel to handle the job?

Be specific in this section. You need to demonstrate that you have the resources to solve the problem.

Do you have enough people to do the job? Is their training adequate to solve the tasks you have set for them? Will it take more time than you have allotted in the schedule for completion? This section will help you answer such questions. If necessary, you may need to revise your timetable and adjust your budget based on your assessment of discrepancies between (1) the job that needs to be done, (2) the time you've allotted, and (3) the qualifications of the staff.

Section 7: Budget

The budget is the kingpin in the proposal. It should follow logically from the narrative—that is, the allocations should match the objectives and the way you have proposed to go about realizing the objectives. To make sure this happens, go back to the part of the proposal where you laid out the objectives and list of actions. How much will each objective cost? Figure the cost both in terms of personnel and in terms of computer time, laboratory costs, paper, supplies, and the like.

You need to ask two kinds of questions:

1. Is the project cost-effective? That is, does the project make the largest impact for the smallest amount of money?
2. Will the project still work with integrity if you reduce the amount of the request? You may find, on looking over the bottom line, that the sum you need is larger than the sum available. Can you do a proper job under these circumstances?

In general, follow these guidelines in completing the budget:

1. *Be realistic.* Try to decide how much money you will actually need to carry out your objectives. Trim when you must, but remember that you won't be able to do the research unless you pay the researchers. If your project will cost more money than is available, you have to decide: Do I want to do this for less money? Will I be able to carry it out successfully? How much can I realistically expect of half-time workers? of graduate students? Deal with these questions while you are preparing the project.
2. *Accompany figures with words.* Write a budget justification in which you explain *each item*. Account for the cost of each person's time.

The budget is often negotiated again after the proposal is awarded. You can expect to spend weeks fiddling over it, refining each term.

The Abstract

At this point, circle back and write a clear abstract stating the problem, the objectives, the methodology, and the plan for evaluation.

Never send out a proposal without an abstract. It is essential for reviewers to have a nutshell description of the proposal before they begin reading.

In addition, the abstract will be a valuable tool for you, the writer. As you go through your proposal seeking key sentences to excerpt, you will often discover you have left out important parts of the statement. In the midst of writing, you may have neglected to state the objectives directly, or you may have left out a key sentence on the method. This is common when you are knee-deep in a narrative. You will also tend to leave out lead sentences. The abstract will point out these shortcomings and help you to tighten your arguments.

At some companies, the abstract is called a summary. One large corporation puts their summaries on blue paper. The document is written in a direct, conversational style, never goes over one page, and is pegged directly for management.

Summary

The advantages of writing proposals are many, even if you don't get the contract, new equipment, or research money.

It is a superb way to clarify your thinking, to do imaginative planning about a problem that arises within your sight as a professional.

You may turn the proposal into a paper or exploratory article. You may recycle it as an application for a fellowship. Or you may revise it and send the edited product to another company or agency.

Whether your proposal succeeds or not, you will learn how to think crisply and clearly about a problem. And the proposal itself will become tangible evidence of your ability to think critically.

The accompanying table summarizes parts of the proposal and the questions you need to answer.

PARTS OF THE PROPOSAL AND QUESTIONS TO ANSWER

Section Title	Questions to Answer
Problem statement, or rationale	What is the problem? Why is it significant? Who else has studied this problem? What did they find?
Objectives	What are your specific, measurable goals? Is each goal or expected outcome listed separately?
Procedure	How will each objective be realized? Is this information given separately and specifically for each objective? Is there a step-by-step schedule for completion?
Evaluation	How will you measure what you did? How will you answer the question, Did it work?
Follow-up	What will you do when the project is over? Will you publish your results? Will supporting organizations maintain the project beyond formal termination?
Qualifications	Who will work? What qualifies them? What kinds of organizational support do you have? Are the facilities appropriate?
Budget	How much will each objective cost? Is your overall figure adequate, and adequately cushioned?
Attachments	Technical Discussion? Vitae? Letters of Support?

Exercises

1. Write a preliminary proposal (five pages) for The National Science Foundation competition described below.

Type of Competition

Most communities don't have a place for scientists and citizens to meet to discuss important issues. The National Science Foundation (NSF) wants to support such places, which they call Science for Citizens Public Service Science Centers.

This competition is to encourage such Science Centers.

Anyone who writes a proposal needs to think about a way to

1. Meet the needs of citizens who lack access to scientific expertise by
2. Bringing together scientists and nonscientists to identify, discuss, and resolve issues of public concern.

Therefore, the proposer is essentially a matchmaker for groups and resources which have previously had little contact.

You, the proposer, need to figure out a way—through seminars or workshops, for instance—to bring together the x (scientists and engineers) with the y (citizens).

How to Proceed

1. Pick your community. Consider, for instance, where you live or work. Chances are the people in one of these two places don't have the sort of access to scientific information the NSF wants to encourage. That is in fact why the NSF mounted the competition. And you probably know the churches, block associations, or other ways your community is organized. You could contact some of these organizations to find out the science issues that concern them.
2. Pick your sponsor. You will need to write the proposal on behalf of a nonprofit group. The perfect vehicle is a professional society or honorary society in which you are active. For instance, you may be in a branch of the IEEE, ASME, or ACS—any of these groups is perfect for sponsoring a series of workshops. Community groups are also acceptable sponsors.
3. Decide on your issues. Significant ones will depend on the people you involve.

Bring these three items together and write a proposal. It is an assignment that combines one's knowledge of a community with one's scientific expertise, and can be accomplished either by undergraduates or by professionals.

Some Examples

One student lived in Petersburg, Virginia, and was concerned about the dumping of toxic waste in the community. This formed a nucleus for the proposal he wrote through the student branch of a professional society.

Another student living on Long Island proposed four problems of concern to residents—solid waste disposal, location of nuclear power plants, beach pollution and erosion, and drinking water quality. The problems were the basis for a community-sponsored proposal.

Explicit Guidelines

Here are the guidelines actually distributed by the NSF for the competition. Please follow their directions in preparing your preliminary proposal.

PROGRAM ANNOUNCEMENT: SCIENCE FOR CITIZENS (SFC) PUBLIC SERVICE SCIENCE CENTERS

NSF Support for Public Service Science Centers   NSF support is intended to provide seed money to enable communities to establish centers, rather than to create institutions that will require continuing federal support. Therefore, PSSC awards will be made on a continuing and matching basis for a three-year period. We hope to make approximately five new awards for centers in Fiscal Year 1981, but the number of awards to be made in this and subsequent years will depend upon the availability of program funds.

In general, the maximum award for any 12 month period will be $100,000; the total maximum award will be $300,000. Yearly budgets are not required to be equal. Special justification can be presented for a yearly award in excess of $100,000, to a maximum of $150,000. One such justification might be a demonstration that the project area is one where expenses are considerably higher than average; another, a demonstration of a special one-time opportunity. In making this justification, proposers should remember that one important review criterion is whether the centers' public service science activities are likely to continue after this initial funded period.

PSSC applicants should prepare an overall three-year budget and three yearly budget breakdowns. NSF will support 100 percent of the budget for the first year; 80 percent for the second year; and 60 percent for the third year. Second and third year funds will be awarded contingent on the satisfactory completion of activities in the preceding year and on the provision of in-kind or monetary support for the remaining percentage of the second and third year budgets.

The matching requirement can be met by monetary or in-kind commitments to the PSSC project. These commitments can come from individuals or from private or public, local or regional organizations. For instance, an educational institution can agree to allow faculty members to do public service science work for a certain portion of their time. So may a business or labor organization, a regional planning commission, or a neighborhood organization. A public library or community center may donate space or personnel for public service science activities. Local foundations, charities, and service organizations may set aside funds to support public service science initiatives. Local or state governments may allocate money or assign personnel to the center. Local, regional, or state agencies may allocate federal "pass through" monies to the center. Support from agencies of the federal government for specific and limited activities will not satisfy the SFC matching requirement.

Who May Apply   You may apply if you are a tax-exempt citizens' group; an educational institution (such as a college, university, public library or museum); a professional or trade association or trade union; a unit of state or local government; or an organization which: (1) is operated primarily for scientific, educational, service, charitable or similar purposes in the public interest; (2) is not organized primarily for profit; and (3) uses all income exceeding costs to maintain, improve, and/or expand its operation.

In accordance with the Joint Explanatory Statement of the Committee of Conference of the U.S. Congress on the NSF Authorization Act of 1978, no award will be made to groups requesting support solely or principally for the purpose of intervention in any judicial or administrative proceeding by contesting any action or decision before any court of law or federal, state, or local executive agency or instrumentality. . . .

PREPARATION OF PROPOSALS

Preliminary Proposals   A preliminary proposal is treated as an informal document. It implies no commitment on the part of either the applying organization for the Foundation. Its narrative should be no more than five pages long . . . and should indicate briefly:

1. the need for the project and its objectives;
2. the work plan—what specific activities are contemplated, who will direct them, and when they will occur;
3. management procedures—what organizational representatives will be involved in project oversight, management, and review;
4. the results or products to be anticipated;
5. plans for determining whether the project is achieving its objectives and whether the results are worthwhile;
6. the purpose and nature of the sponsoring and cooperating organizations or institutions.

You should also include a tentative budget and a brief

statement of the qualifications of important project staff, consultants, advisors and co-sponsors or cooperating organizations.

2. Here are National Institutes of Health guidelines for a research proposal, followed by a sample research proposal written for the NIH. Write a research proposal following these guidelines.

NIH GUIDELINES

BIOGRAPHICAL SKETCH

This information is used by reviewers in evaluating the adequacy of project staff.

Prepare the biographical sketches as concisely as possible for all professional personnel. If an individual is not a citizen of the United States, explain visa status and any effect this may have on the project. Under research and/or professional experience, list in reverse chronological order the individual's professional background and employment. List all research support for each individual including requests now being considered, as well as any proposals being planned, regardless of relevance to this application. Include also current or pending contracts, fellowship awards, research career program awards, training grants, regardless of the source of support. List grant number, title of project, amount for current year, total funds for the entire project period, estimated percentage of effort the individual devotes to the project, and the source of the support.

List support provided by the applicant institution, including any support received from NIH General Research Support or Biomedical Sciences Support grants. If an application pending elsewhere is identical or substantially similar to the proposal described in this application, explain the duplication.

Provide for each person a chronological list of all or the most representative of his [or her] publications. List the authors in the same order as they appear on the paper, the full title, and the complete reference as these usually appear in journals. *The complete biographical sketch, including bibliography, should not exceed three pages for each individual.*

RESEARCH PLAN

The principal investigator should use continuation pages to describe the proposed project.

Complete information should be included to permit review of each application without reference to previous applications.

Reviewing groups are assisted materially in their evaluation of applications when the research plan is arranged under a uniform pattern of captions. The principal investigator should prepare the program narrative according to the suggested outline insofar as possible.

The reviewing groups will consider the information provided as an example of the principal investigator's approach to a research objective and as an indication of ability in this area of research.

A. Introduction:
1. Objective: State the overall objective or long-term goal of the proposed research.
2. Background: Review the most significant previous work, and describe the current status of research in this field. Document with references. In a new application, describe any preliminary work the principal investigator has done which led to this proposal.
3. Rationale; Present concisely the rationale behind the proposed approach to the problem.
4. Comprehensive Progress Report (required for *renewal* and *supplemental* applications): Describe progress on this project since its beginning, or since the comprehensive progress report submitted with the last renewal application. Do not exceed 12 pages of single-spaced type, including pages for summary charts, graphs, or tables. The progress report should include the following:
   a. Period: Give beginning and ending dates for the period covered by the report.
   b. Summary: Summarize in not more than 200 words the results of work during this period.
   c. Detailed Report: Describe progress relative to the research objectives for this period, whether or not the work has been published.
   d. Publications: List all publications and completed manuscripts which have resulted from this project during the period covered by the progress report.
   e. Staffing: List all professional personnel who worked on this project, their titles, and their periods of appointment.
B. Specific Aims: List specific objectives for the total period of requested support.
C. Methods of Procedure: Give details of the research plan, including a description of the experiments or other work proposed; the methods, species of animals, and techniques it is planned to use; the kinds of data expected to be obtained; and the means by which the data will be analyzed or interpreted. If clinical studies are involved give details of responsibility for patient selection and patient care. Include, if appropriate, a discussion of pitfalls that might be encountered, and of the limitations of the procedures proposed. Point out any procedures, situations, or materials that may be hazardous to personnel and the precautions to be exercised.

Insofar as possible, describe the principal experiments or observations in the sequence in which it is planned to carry them out, and indicate, if possible, a tentative schedule of the main steps of the investigation within the project period requested.

D. Significance: What is the potential importance of the proposed work? Discuss any novel ideas or contributions which the project offers. Make clear the health-related implications of the research.

E. Facilities Available: Describe the facilities available for this project including laboratories, clinical resources, office space, animal quarters, etc. List major items of equipment available for this work.

Sample Proposal: Polarization-Spectroscopic Study of Visual Polyenes

The investigation of the excited *electronic states* of the *visual polyenes* and related molecules using a new spectroscopic technique called molecular *two-photon polarization spectroscopy* is proposed. The technique provides a measure of absolute two-photon absorption cross sections and is extremely sensitive to excited electronic states, even those which do not fluoresce. It can also be used to determine wavelength-dependent two-photon *fluorescence quantum yields*.

The method should provide important new information concerning symmetry, energy level location and electronic mixing of these states, and may shed light on the pathways through which the initial optical excitation gets converted to structural alterations in the visual chromophore.

A.1 INTRODUCTION AND OBJECTIVES
This is a new proposal seeking support for investigating the excited electronic states of visual polyenes utilizing a very new spectroscopic technique which promises to provide important new information concerning the symmetry, energy level location and electronic mixing of these states. Such information may ultimately be useful in elucidating the photophysical mechanism of vertebrate vision.

To date, our effort has been directed toward the development of the spectroscopic technique which we call molecular two-photon polarization spectroscopy (MTPPS), and we have carried out some preliminary studies concerning this new method. Currently, additional studies are being supported by grants from the American Chemical Society–Petroleum Research Fund and the National Science Foundation. The former is not renewable and provides only minimal funds necessary to the catalysis of a new research effort. The latter provides funds for the development of some of the instrumentation and its application to a variety of small molecules of high symmetry, and does not duplicate the present proposal.

A.2 BACKGROUND

Linear Polyene Spectroscopy   Linear polyenes, which represent model compounds for the visual chromophores, have been studied in considerable detail for the last 50 years. This work has most recently been reviewed by Hudson and Kohler and by Honig and Ebrey.

The development of two-photon spectroscopy has sparked renewed interest and controversy into the study of these molecules within the past decade. Problems arise due to the difficulty in obtaining level orderings for the low-lying electronic states (and, in some cases, in observing certain states at all). Nevertheless certain general trends have been revealed. For example, the lowest excited singlet state in linear, all-*trans* polyene chromophores is usually of ^1A_g rather than ^1B_u symmetry, at least for the longer chains (four to six double bonds). For shorter polyenes, the picture is less clear: the ^1A_g state has not been observed in either hexatriene, which was studied using thermal lens spectroscopy, or butadiene, studied by both multiphoton ionization and thermal lens spectroscopy. The ^1A_g state has been observed in diphenylhexatriene, and very recently, the existence of a ^1A_g state has been inferred for two cholestadienes from fluorescence measurements.

Many two-photon studies of linear polyenes measure the strength of the two-photon resonance by recording the intensity of the sample fluorescence. The interpretation of such spectra is complicated by a fluorescence quantum yield which is wavelength-dependent—retinal, for example—so that it is necessary to correct these spectra in order to obtain accurate two-photon absorption cross sections. Unfortunately, the only reported fluorescence quantum yields are for single-photon excitation. It has generally been assumed that the quantum yield for one-photon excitation is identical to that for two-photon excitation. The assumption is that there exists sufficient mixing of the excited states, so that no matter how a system is excited to a given energy, the relaxation pathway is invariant. Similar assumptions are needed to interpret thermal lens and multiphoton ionization spectra.

Recent Developments in Two-Photon Spectroscopy   Two-photon spectroscopy, which has blossomed over the last decade, is a technique which can be used to probe vibronic states of molecules which are inaccessible through classical one-photon spectroscopy, owing to new selection rules (e.g. $g \leftrightarrow g$, $u \leftrightarrow u$, $\triangle J = \pm 2$).

A problem associated with two-photon spectroscopy is the difficulty in making direct absorption measurements with high sensitivity. A number of important indirect methods have been developed, including detection of fluorescence from the populated excited state, detection of acoustic waves generated by the thermal degradation of the absorbed energy, detection of thermal lensing associated with a temperature gradient in the sample due to heating from the absorption of light, and detection of ions formed by photodissociation or photoionization of the sample molecules. Of these methods, the most sensitive and most widely applicable is fluorescence detection, although for weakly luminescing states, other methods must be used.

During the past four years, a number of researchers have made ingenious use of the polarization properties in multiphoton and double-resonance phenomena to devise sensitive detection methods for measuring these processes. These various techniques come under the titles polarization spectroscopy, Raman-induced Kerr effect (RIKES), Bjorklund-Liao effect, and elliptical polarization state alteration (ELLIPSA). Our own work in this area has involved the first demonstration of the Bjorklund-Liao effect in a molecular system (carbon disulfide). As applied to molecular systems, we call this technique molecular two-photon polarization spectroscopy (MTPPS).

Within the last year, a further improvement called optical heterodyne detection (OHD) has been developed. The sensitivity of RIKES and MTPPS can in many instances now exceed the sensitivity of fluorescence detection. These improvements are not applicable to ELLIPSA, since it is a single-beam technique, so that OHD-MTPPS is at present the most sensitive of the two-photon polarization-spectroscopic techniques. It has a further advantage of possible resonance enhancement of spectra, in which one of two laser beams is tuned near a one-photon resonance. The most important feature of this method is that it provides a direct measure of two-photon cross sections, independent of the manner in which the absorbed energy is degraded by the system.

A.3 RATIONALE

Polarization spectroscopy offers a method for obtaining absolute two-photon absorption spectra, and so bypasses the problems of the indirect detection techniques. By comparing such a direct spectrum with a fluorescence-detected spectrum, it would be possible to directly obtain the two-photon fluorescence quantum yield and thus test the assumption concerning the mixing of electronic states alluded to above. If full mixing exists, the one- and two-photon yields should be identical. Partial mixing should be apparent from differences in the two quantum yields. Degree of mixing may depend on the nature of the molecular environment. One way of testing this possibility is to compare fluorescence yields in different solvents and at a variety of temperatures.

In addition, the technique in its most highly developed form has a sensitivity which can exceed that of fluorescence detection, yet the excited state need not fluoresce at all. Thus it is a technique well suited to the search for missing excited states.

B. SPECIFIC AIMS

1. *Construction of an OHD-MTPPS spectrometer* We currently have an MTPPS spectrometer based on the original design of Liao and Bjorklund, utilizing two pulsed dye lasers. In the improved configuration due to Owyoung and Levenson, one of these lasers is replaced by a continuous wave (cw) dye laser. We shall modify the current instrument to provide the improved sensitivity offered by the OHD detection and characterize the resulting instrument.

2. *General survey of two-photon spectra* With this improved instrumentation, we shall proceed to make a systematic study of series of linear polyenes to confirm previous observations, to search for missing states, and to obtain improved energies, spacings and orderings of electronic levels.

3. *Wavelength-dependent two-photon fluorescence quantum yields* A convenient feature of the OHD-MTPPS spectrometer is that it can be used to simultaneously record fluorescence spectra. Thus, a simple ratio between OHD-MTPPS signal and fluorescence intensity provides the two-photon fluorescence yields as a function of wavelength quite simply and accurately. Comparison with one-photon fluorescence yields is planned, as well as a study of the dependence of quantum yield on solvent and temperature, in order to determine the nature and extent of electronic state mixing in linear polyenes.

C. METHODS OF PROCEDURE

Sample preparation and control The particular compounds to be studied include the series of unsubstituted all-*trans* polyenes, the series of all-*trans* α,ω-diphenylpolyenes, all-*trans* retinal and retinol. All of these compounds are commercially available with the exception of all-*trans* 1,3,5,7-octatetraene, which must be synthesized. Standard purification techniques include recrystallization and chromatography. Most of the compounds will be studied in solution, using a variety of solvents: cyclohexane, benzene, MCH/IH (methylcyclohexane/isohexane), EPA (diethylether/isopentane/ethanol), and 3MP (3-methylpentane). Butadiene and all-*trans* 1,3,5-hexatriene can be studied as either pure gases or liquids. Temperature of samples will be controlled via jacketed sample cells, with liquid coolants appropriate to the temperature range of interest. Experiments in glasses at 77K will be carried out using a windowed Dewar and liquid nitrogen cooling.

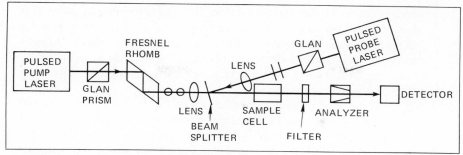

FIGURE 12-3   Conventional arrangement for MTPPS

Data collection and reduction   Figure 12-3 shows the schematic experimental arrangement for molecular two-photon polarization spectroscopy (MTPPS). An intense circularly polarized dye laser beam at frequency ω_1 interacts with the sample, and induces optical activity in this normally achiral medium. The plane-polarized probe laser at ω_2 responds to this induced optical activity by having its plane of polarization rotated or by becoming slightly elliptically polarized. These changes are monitored by measuring the transmission of the probe beam through a crossed polarizer. Thus, only in the presence of induced optical activity does light reach the detector. Most importantly, this transmission is intense only in the vicinity of molecular resonances either at $\omega_1 + \omega_2$, which is a two-photon absorption resonance, or at $\omega_1 - \omega_2$, which is a Raman resonance.

We presently employ an arrangement in which both lasers are pulsed lasers, although great improvement in sensitivity is achieved by using the configuration shown in Figure 12-4. In that case, the probe laser is continuous wave (cw), a Soliel-Babinet compensator is inserted to fully control the polarization state of this beam and to cancel cell-window birefringence, and the analyzing polarizer is

FIGURE 12-4   Experimental arrangement for OHD-MTPPS

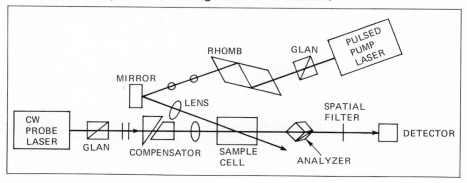

rotated away from total extinction. The interference between this background transmission and the signal transmission linearizes the detected signal and increases the sensitivity. This method is known as optical heterodyne detection (OHD). A spectrum is recorded by scanning either laser over a certain wavelength range and plotting detector signal versus $\omega_1 + \omega_2$.

Because of intensity fluctuations of the lasers, effective signal averaging is essential. This is accomplished with a sample-and-hold circuit followed by an analog-to-digital converter which integrates the signal and digitizes it. The signal is then fed into a minicomputer and all further processing is carried out digitally. The interface which performs this processing was built this past summer by research assistant and Ph.D. candidate George Smith. This minicomputer also controls stepping motors which tune the dye lasers, and plots the resulting spectrum on an x-y recorder.

D. SIGNIFICANCE

The understanding of how light triggers the visual process must start with a firm knowledge of the nature of the electronic states which become populated upon absorption of light. Although much is known about the nature of these states, the degree of interaction of states of differing symmetry is less well characterized. The application of the new technique of polarization spectroscopy should clarify this question and thus shed light on the pathways through which the initial optical excitation gets degraded and finally converted to structural alterations in the visual chromophore.

E. FACILITIES

The facilities at the Institute are well suited to all phases of the proposed research. Our laser laboratory is equipped with a variety of lasers including a 1-MW nitrogen laser and two pulsed tunable dye lasers. This laboratory is also equipped with an optical table, and an array of polarizing optics and photodetectors. Signal processing equipment includes a PET minicomputer interfaced to a terminal, an x-y recorder, and two stepping motors and detectors. Specialized mounts can be fabricated in the Institute's machine shop. We also have about 200 square feet of preparative laboratory space, equipped with ample glassware and equipment for sample preparation. Departmental facilities which will be available to this program include two Perkin-Elmer fluorescence spectrometers (MPF-2A), two Spex double monochromators and a Cary 14 absorption spectrometer. The principal investigator's laboratory also contains sufficient office space for four research assistants.

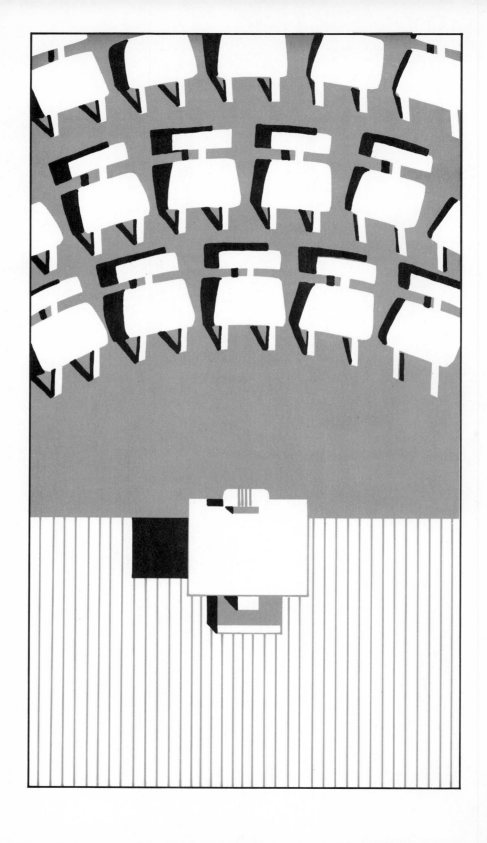

FOUR

Oral Presentation and and Short Forms

13

Preparing and Giving a Speech

It is easy to be correct but incomprehensible. . . .
Old Saying

It was an afternoon session at a professional meeting. The speaker walked to the lectern, gave the opening remarks, and turned off the lights. After the first three slides, heads began to nod and bob. By the sixth slide—an extremely detailed one, impossible to read beyond 10 feet—a quarter of the audience was dozing. Others sat with eyes glazed, their faces composed into the polite, zombielike expressions of people who aren't following a word of the explanation. The speaker, who had launched his talk with a certain amount of flair, wilted.

This scene is not imaginary; in fact, it is not even extreme. You can observe eyes glazing and heads nodding during technical speeches at professional conferences and corporate workshops, university seminars and industrial conventions.

Anyone who's ever given a technical speech can deliver one truth: it is easy to be correct but incomprehensible.

Usually the fault is not in the technical content of the speech. The speaker has the facts at hand, and the explanations are comprehensive. Rather, the problem lies in the technique—erratic eye contact, uncertain manner of delivery, massive doses of slides—and in broad miscalculation of audience interest and background.

Talking to a group is part of the job of any professional. One to two speeches, technical briefs, or seminars a year are typical for scientists and engineers beginning their careers, and the number of talks increases as the years advance. But typical beginners are not well prepared for this job; instead, they stand before the group, nervous, uncertain of how to establish an appropriate tone, aware of the gap between the information they are presenting and the amount their audience is absorbing.

The guidelines in this chapter are directed at making technical presentations not only correct but also comprehensible—on target for the group you are addressing and the reaction you seek from that group.

Before You Begin

Before you write the first word, whether your topic is a new product or research results, think about two things: your audience and your purpose. The two are fundamental to your speech.

Audience   Who will be listening to you? If there are doctors in the group, you may not get the reaction you want if you quote Christopher Marlowe: "Be a physician, Heap up gold." If you decide to recount a witty exchange between Szilard and Bethe, its impact will be lessened if you have to explain who they are.

Before you start, you need to think about who is in the audience, why they are there, and what they know already.

Regardless of your topic, the way to develop it is dictated almost entirely by audience background. This is particularly true for technical subjects, which by definition draw on highly specialized experiences.

Thinking about audience background does not necessarily mean you have to speak to the lowest common denominator. Your audience may range from people in management only peripherally involved in your area to workers in the field; but if you are aware of these disparate backgrounds, you can decide on an effective way to present the material despite the fact that both ends of the spectrum are there. For example, you may decide on a general presentation so that most people will understand you, but also include two highly technical points. If you begin with a general discussion, you can present the two points as highly technical, and the bulk of the audience will attend while you explain the points even though the subject is not within their area. While they won't understand this section of the talk, or will understand it only incompletely, it is acceptable to include highly specialized detail if you do so within the pattern of a clear general explanation.

Purpose   Beginning speakers almost always encompass too wide a field in their speeches. Instead, pinpoint what you have to say in one idea and then develop this idea slowly and methodically in the time allotted.

In other words, before you write a word, decide on what idea you want your listeners to take out the door with them. Then arrange your arguments and visual accompaniments to support this idea.

This is a difficult notion for beginning speechmakers to accept. Instead of concentrating on developing one point, they try to get in as much as possible on their subject, and in seeking to "cover" a large area, they do just that—they cover it from view, rather than uncover it so that the audience will understand the point. If you are lecturing to a university class where the audience has read much of the background information in advance and is taking notes as you talk, it may be possible to explain many technical points in one sitting. And, of course, there are extraordinary occasions presided over by extraordinary people. Julian Schwinger, a physics professor and former student of J. Robert Oppenheimer, spent a marathon eight hours explaining quantum electrodynamics, and at least one of his listeners, Oppenheimer, understood. But for the ordinary audience, such strategies won't work.

There is a great difference between reading information and absorbing spoken information. In printed text, the reader can return to tables, to graphs, to difficult ideas. There is time to go back and ponder. This possibility does not exist in speaking, and that makes all the difference.

Perhaps you've heard the slogan: one idea to a paragraph. This can be modified for an oral presentation to: one idea to a speech.

What is the idea? It may be the particular behavior of a molecule bombarded by light, or a new type of windshield wiper. In 30 minutes—if you have that much time—you may give five or six arguments supporting or developing the point. Complicated information that requires study and restudy should be printed and distributed as a handout, to be pondered later by the audience. When you're on your feet and talking, you should concentrate on covering one basic idea that is elaborated by a variety of techniques. *Decide on that idea before you begin.*

Writing Out the Speech

Impromptu speeches are those made "off the top of your head"— that is, they are speeches made without benefit of manuscript. The speaker, armed with experience and seasoned by years of standing before groups, simply rises and delivers a clean, profes- sional speech. Unfortunately, most people who do not have an earlier, written version of their speech begin to ramble, giving impromptu and undue emphases.

Writing out a speech will prevent this kind of disorganiza- tion. It's a basic step in preparing a technical talk. Bear in mind, however, that writing out a manuscript does not mean delivering it by reading the text word for word. The manuscript is the first step in a successful oral presentation rather than the final one. Here are steps for writing out a manuscript:

1. *Begin with an outline. Shape it to the time allotted.* Let's say you have 30 minutes. Divide the presentation into an introduction, body of the text, and conclusion. If you take 3 minutes for the introduction, and 3 minutes for the conclusion, you have 24 minutes left. Decide now how many ways you want to elaborate on or explain your point. List them under the main discussion topic. If you have six examples or elaborations, that's 3 minutes each.

    I. Introduction: Statement of argument
    II. Body: Technical support for argument (maximum of six examples or elaborations)
        1.
        2.
        (Restatement of points 1 and 2 and relationship to argu- ment.)

   3.
   4.
   5.
   (Restatement of points 3, 4, 5 and relationship to argument.)
   6.
   III. Conclusion: Restatement of argument

2. *Putting aside the introduction and conclusion, write out each of the points in the body of the text.* You may need more than three minutes to expand an item if the point turns out to be more complicated than your initial estimate suggested. That means you'll have to reduce the total number of points you're using to back up the argument. You may be able to make only three or four elaborations.

3. *As you write, begin thinking about the visual accompaniments you may use.* These will take part of the time allotted for explanations. If you decide to use slides, overhead transparencies, tagboard, or other visuals, indicate references to them as you write.

4. *Return to the introduction.* Write a clear statement of the argument. Follow it with a "road map"—either all of the major divisions or the first subtopic you will discuss.

5. *Cast a critical eye over the speech.* Arrange and rearrange argument for persuasiveness and logic. Remember that the internal logic of the document is probably much clearer to you, the writer, than to your uninitiated listener. As you revise, bear in mind the difference between written and oral presentation. You'll need to restate points from time to time, and you'll also need to recap your arguments periodically. Finally, go over this checklist.

Checklist: First Draft of a Speech

1. *Content*: Have you included all necessary information?
2. *Visuals*: Have you made tentative provisions for the visuals in the text?
3. *Comprehensibility*: Do you need to adjust the pace by expanding examples or adding a summary so that the explanation will be understandable?

Rehearsing

There are two ways you may deliver the speech: extemporaneously or reading directly from the manuscript.

Extemporaneous Speaking   This is the more useful of the two methods in most corporate, industrial, and professional settings. Extemporaneous delivery does not entail memorizing the speech word for word. Instead, the speaker takes each topic within the speech and practices delivering the information until it can be spoken rather than read. The only text actually carried by the speaker is a skeleton outline with key words and slide lists, plus statistics, quotations, or other items that need to be quoted verbatim.

This mode has many advantages over manuscript reading. First, of all, the rhythm and pace of the talk will be closer to those occurring in natural speech: the speaker who talks rather than reads tends toward shorter sentences, more repetition, use of contractions, and other natural speech rhythms. Further, spoken delivery permits good eye contact. You, the speaker, can add explanations if the group seems confused, or edit information if the group turns out to be more sophisticated than anticipated. Voice, tone, and emphasis can be varied in relation to audience response.

Manuscript Reading   It is hard for most listeners to attend to someone reading a speech. There's little eye contact and little variation in pace or tone since the reader is not guided by audience response. There are some exceptions, though: Franklin D. Roosevelt, for instance, was famous for his lively reading style.

If you must read the manuscript, practice so that you can look up regularly and at length.

Practicing Extemporaneous Delivery   Read through your text two or three times until you're comfortable with the arguments. Then practice the speech out loud, without reading it, section by section.

Saying the speech out loud works well for most people. Do not try to get each section word for word. Instead, try delivering all the details within one section. If you fumble, find a simpler way to state the point. Use an index card for any details such as figures or quotations that need to be read. Remember, the section does not have to be word-perfect. You may phrase a statement one way during practice, another way during delivery. That's not significant; what's important is a clear way of stating each point.

Some people use tape recorders, videotape recorders, or the mirror while they are practicing. Others are paralyzed with self-consciousness by such maneuvers. Tape and video recorders are fine—so long as they support rather than inhibit your performance.

After you can say each point aloud, go through the entire speech. Make up a skeleton outline in which you have two or three words or phrases to remind you of each major point. This outline will be useful when you are speaking: it will prevent your losing the order of points or omitting major topics in the course of the speech.

Check this skeleton outline against your list of visual aids, and coordinate the two by numbering the visuals and inserting these numbers in the skeleton outline. Figure 13-1, for instance, shows a section of a speech. The author has taken out key words and placed them to the left. These are the cue words; they could be transcribed to an index card to remind the speaker of the content and order of points. Figure 13-2 shows the list another speaker took to the podium. Slides and transparency notations are boxed.

Clutching a full script in hand while speaking is usually a bad idea—you may find yourself succumbing to the security of reading it. Instead, take only (1) the outline, with key words and slides indicated, and (2) index cards with anything that must be read verbatim. When the time comes, reach for the card and read the quote or the statistic. Otherwise, *address the audience directly*.

On Machinery

"And these are the data," said the speaker, putting the transparency on the stage of the projector. It flashed on the screen   upside down. . .

"I think we're having some trouble here," said the speaker, as the slide machine jammed, and he wasn't sure how to fix it. . .

"As you can clearly see," said the speaker, pointing to a spot on the screen. He was using his ball-point pen, and the shadow of his arm obscured most of the slide. Then he tried using his finger, but that was worse. . .

- ı -

INTRO

This afternoon, I would like to discuss two aspects of
optical activity in liquids: firstly, an application of the
natural optical activity ~~of~~ certain liquids and solutions, and [*exhibited by*]
secondly, optical activity induced by intense pulses of circularly
polarized light in ~~m~~ormally isotropic achiral liquids.

LORD

I will first describe a novel, inexpensive device which
employs solutions of sucrose in water, that can be used as a tunable
polarization rotator for incident uv and visible ~~lader~~ radiation.
Because the active medium is a liquid, such a liquid optical
rotatory device, for which we have coined the term "LORD", is
extremely resistant to damage due to intense incident light, and
will therefore be useful for many high power laser applications.

CONVENTIONAL MATERIALS

Crystals exhibiting optical activity have been the conventional
substrates for such devices, but because of the rotatory dispersion
in these materials, each wavelength of interest requires a different
crystalline plate cut to the appropriate thickness, and these
materials are subject to permanent internal damage at high laser
intensities.

EQUATIONS

On slide 1, we see the equations needed to describe the
polarization due to optically active liquids and solutions. [*rotation*]
Note that the observed rotation angle Θ is linear in both the
concentration and the pathleng~~h~~h, which gives tunability
directly by either using an adjustable pathlength cell containing
the solution, or by changing the concentration of the solution.
Because of rotatory dispersion in liquids, α, ~~the specific~~ [*The specific rotation [α] depends on the particular optically active material.*]
is a function of wavelength, and the tuning is required to
compensate this dispersion.

ORD OF SUCROSE

The next slide shows an optical rotatory dispersion or ORD
spectrum of a dilute solution of sucrose in water. Note that as
the ~~optical~~ absorption band is approached from longer wavelengths, [*electronic at ~200 nm.*]
the rotatory power increases rather dramatically. ~~With~~ From this
spectrum, we were able to prepare a sucrose solution of the
appropriate conce~~m~~tration and pathlength to act as a 90° polarization
rotator for a frequency doubled ruby laser at 347nm. (The pathlength
used was 10 cm, and the corresponding concentration was 1.22 M)
The sucrose was purified , and a solution was prepared and filtered
directly into a 10 cm pathlength quartz cell.

FIGURE 13-1   Section of a speech. The author has taken out key words and
placed them to the left. The key words and slide notations can be placed on
index cards and used during the speech.

To avoid these situations, take the machinery out, set it up in
conditions that duplicate those for your speech, and do a trial
run. For information to bear in mind when you do this, see the
chapter appendix following the exercises.

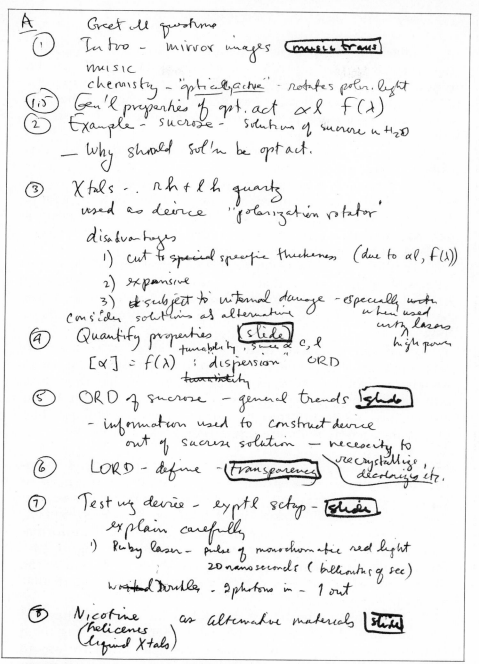

FIGURE 13-2 Outline for a speech. Slides and transparency notations are marked.

Delivery Using Slides or Transparencies

A peculiar thing happens when people use slides and transparencies. Instead of reading from a manuscript, they read from the slides. They bury their heads in the slides in the same way that shy speakers use manuscripts to escape looking at the audience. To avoid this, *do not talk to the slides or transparencies.* Talk to the audience.

Step to the side of the screen and face the audience. This is difficult to do. Your illustrations are behind you, and there will be a strong tendency to turn away toward the screen.

However, you need to maintain eye contact with the group. Do this by standing to the side of the illustration and using a pointer. In this way, you can indicate details on the screen without turning away from the group.

Try electric pointers that project an arrow on the screen, or collapsible metal pointers that fit in a pocket or briefcase when not in use. A pencil or index finger won't work. You'll cast a shadow on the screen, obscuring the data just when someone needs to look at it.

Furthermore, do *not* turn the lights off. It's a sure way to send a portion of the audience to sleep, and to frustrate those who want to take notes. Instead, experiment so that you have to reduce only the light over rows immediately in front of the screen. If you are using an overhead projector, turn it off when not in use. The glare and machine noise are distracting.

Organization   A rough rule is two minutes per slide. Remember that the heart of a speech is variety, and that you need to change what is in front of your listener to create a less passive experience. If the slide takes longer than two minutes to explain, it may be too complicated. In this case, try to divide the information so that you have two or three separate slides. In Figure 13-3 for instance, the speaker has used three slides to show how the principle of superposition can be used to describe a particular optical phenomenon.

The problem with slides is that unless one is careful, they end up controlling the content of the speech. One starts using them with the best of intentions; they are a simple, attractive way to illustrate technical presentations. But those of you who have sat through speeches where the slides sailed past—too fast, too complicated, too many—know that slides can be disastrous. Take care to simplify and focus their presentation.

PRINCIPLE OF SUPERPOSITION:

The linearly polarized probe beam can be
considered as a superposition of right
and left circularly polarized components
of equal magnitude:

$$\uparrow = \circlearrowright + \circlearrowleft$$

Therefore, the polarization experiment can
be considered the superposition of the
following two experiments:

(Slide 1)

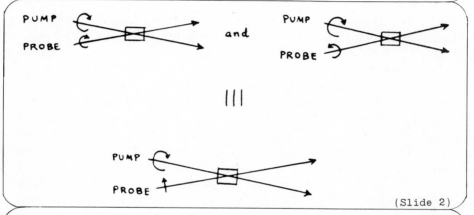

(Slide 2)

Since $\langle\delta\rangle_{cc} \neq \langle\delta\rangle_{\circlearrowleft c}$, the probe beam in each
individual experiment is depleted by different
amounts due to two-photon absorption.

But

$$\circlearrowright + \circlearrowleft \neq \uparrow$$

Therefore, some component of the net probe
beam will leak through the analyzer.

(Slide 3)

FIGURE 13-3 Divide complicated information into a series of slides. In this
case, the speaker has taken one idea—how the principle of superposition can
be used to describe a particular optical phenomenon—and presented it in a
series of three slides.

You might also be sure that you are not in the position of a colleague who commented, "I'm not sure what I'll talk about. I'll just follow the slides." Avoid this manner of presentation. Instead, write an introduction and a conclusion that are free-standing—that can exist independent of the visuals. Then use readable slides in the body of the text if they will aid your talk, but remember that they should be used to illustrate points rather than as the points themselves.

Blackboards, Easels, and Tagboards

The blackboard has advantages. For one thing, it slows the speaker down. It's harder to rush through complicated illustrations, as speakers routinely do with slides, when the speaker has to draw each figure laboriously. The board has another advantage: if you draw a simple figure, outline, or equation, you can add to it as you talk. If, for instance, you are explaining how to read a weather map, you can add each notation as you introduce it rather than present the entire map at once. The effect is similar to that achieved with transparencies when you add successive details through overlays.

Two pieces of advice if you use a blackboard: (1) Stop talking while you're writing. (2) Add illustrations with some sort of plan so that you'll have a coherent display at the end rather than an unrelated series of notes.

Companies usually have an alternative to the blackboard—an oversized note pad called a *flipchart* (often as large as 24 × 24 inches) sitting on an easel. Illustrations, outlines, equations, or key words may be prepared in advance and the flipchart used to illustrate the talk, or the illustrations may be done during the talk. The paper surface is easier and quicker to write on than a blackboard, particularly if you use a felt-tipped pen. Speakers often tear off each page as they finish and tape it to the wall. In this way, up to 20 pages can be displayed for reference during the talk.

Tagboards, prepared in advance for display during the talk, can also be useful. Like slides, they should have large lettering that is visible beyond the first few rows. If the board is sturdy, it can be placed on an easel during the talk. In a well-known lecture series, the physical chemist Norm Colthup interprets infrared spectra using a series of hand-lettered boards which are displayed during the talk.

Audience Participation

As a speaker, you need to imagine what you want your audience to be doing while you're talking. This is a prosaic but necessary consideration. For instance, if you want them to take notes, you'll need to arrange appropriate desks and lighting.

You also need to think about what you *don't* want them to do. For instance, demonstrations in front of the group are effective, while demonstration models passed from hand to hand are not. The model may be dropped by the person in third-row center, three people will reach for it, and the distraction will spread. Props are effective, but are best demonstrated by the speaker who should, incidentally, be amply prepared with spare parts for any type of equipment that could break.

Questions If you are allowing time for responses to your talk, you'll need to prepare for questions and inevitable challenges that accompany critical discussions. Certain types of questions —misunderstandings by the audience, requests for further information—are easily fielded if you have prepared. Skilled speakers often imagine before a talk what questions they will be asked, and then check to make sure they have concise answers at hand. Questions involving controversial issues are harder to handle. Some will be irrelevant. An occasional listener uses a question as an opportunity to deliver a speech on an entirely different issue. "Yes, that certainly seems to be a problem" is a reasonable response to such rhetoric, rather than getting involved in discussing a side issue. For questions that challenge the speaker and present an alternative interpretation, it's probably best to (1) rephrase the question to be sure you've understood it, (2) acknowledge that there are differences of opinion on this issue, and (3) reiterate your own position. "Yes, I'm familiar with that data. My interpretation, as I argued, is quite different." Avoid becoming defensive.

Polishing Your Delivery

The way you look at the audience, your manner of speaking, even your manner of standing while you talk are vital to a technical speech. All three of these areas can be vastly improved by practice.

Eye Contact   You can't stare at people, but you do have to look at them while you're talking. To understand how strange it is for an audience when the speaker avoids eye contact, try this game. First, stare at a friend. After 40 seconds, the friend will become intensely uncomfortable—unless both of you have begun laughing to relieve the discomfort. Then resume talking to your friend, but as you talk, look up at the ceiling, then at the floor. Don't look at your friend. After a minute, you'll both understand how peculiar the experience is. Yet many people don't look at the audience; instead, they stare at the ceiling, the floor, the walls, and this considerably lessens their impact as speakers.

Instead, practice looking at your audience, shifting your gaze from one member of the group to another. There will always be three or four persons interested in what you're saying. Return to them when you need feedback, and otherwise try to address yourself to each person in the room. Watch out for a natural inclination to address only one person as the target—students tend to talk solely to the teacher, employees only to the supervisor.

Voice   Bob and Ray, the comedians, have a routine in which Bob, the energetic but unsuspecting interviewer, walks up to a man in the street and asks his name. The man replies, "Harold . . . [pause of 20 seconds] P . . . [pause of 20 seconds] Whitcomb." "And where do you come from, sir?" asks Bob, his voice picking up speed. "From . . . Lands . . . Falls"—at this point the frantic Bob supplied, "New York." "New York," continues the man on the street, who then reveals he is the president . . . and . . . recording . . . secretary . . . of Slow . . . Talkers . . . of . . . America.

If you speak . . . too . . . slowly, you'll irritate the audience. Most speakers, though, don't tend in this direction. Instead, they either speed up or avoid the entire issue by mumbling. Practicing a speech until it can be delivered extemporaneously is a good first step in learning to control your voice and keep it within a normal range.

Once you have learned the talk, you'll find you are naturally changing your rate from time to time to give emphasis, and this change will be useful in keeping the audience attentive. Skilled speakers learn that variation is important in all aspects of the speech—from eye contact and the visual displays to tone and rate of speech.

Most people have no trouble projecting their voice for an audience of up to 200 people. Following the venerable advice to pitch your voice to the person in the back row, you can easily get along without amplification until the audience reaches over 200. From that point, you may need a microphone. If you have to use a mike, try to use one you can clip to your shirt or wear around your neck. If you use a stationary model attached to the lectern, your voice will rise and fall as you step to the side to discuss the slides, and if it is a hand-held mike, you may end up with the mike in one hand and the pointer in the other, an awkward situation.

Bearing   You'll want to move, and for good reason—muscle activity releases tension, and most speakers are tense. Go right ahead and relieve the tension, but do so in a measured way, by stepping forward to make a point, or by using your arm in a natural gesture that accompanies what you're saying.

This is easier said than done. Instead of standing calmly in front of the group, beginning speakers tend to dribble basketballs, form fig leaves, scratch their head or ribs, or engage in other nervous motions. One speaker in a group took his necklace out and began nibbling on the medallion as he talked, another developed an unaccountable itch on his scalp, a third threw imaginary frisbees.

Try to keep these nervous mannerisms to a minimum. Above all, *do not pace*. It makes everyone nervous. One speaker mesmerized the group by a pattern of one-two-three, tap, back-two-three, tap. People's heads began bobbing as they marked time, waiting for the inevitable accent mark of the tap.

The Speech as a Whole

A 30-minute speech can be divided as follows:

1. *Opening* (first three to five minutes): Some speakers begin with a joke—a mistake if you don't have a good joke or a professional's knack for delivering the punch line. Others begin with a topical anecdote—for instance, a news item on their subject. Still others start with an allusion to the occasion, the nature of the audience, or some other personalized reference to the group and purpose. I have seen speakers introduce talks with a dedication to an outstanding historical figure in the field—showing a slide of the figure in the laboratory (see Figure 13-4)—or with a related topic that illustrates the principle of the speech (see Figure 13-5).

These openings are tricky, however, and if you are uncom-

FIGURE 13-4   This slide of R. W. Wood, a pioneer in optics, was shown in the introduction of a lecture on present-day spectroscopy. (*Courtesy AIP Niels Bohr Library.*)

fortable to begin with, a wall of unsmiling faces just after you've told your anecdote is not likely to relax you. If you want to begin with an anecdote, a topical allusion, a reference to the occasion, a joke, or a quotation, be sure that you are willing to live with the results if the lead doesn't work.

Otherwise, stick to that which is essential in any introduction: state the subject and define any terms. This is more than adequate for any talk. To sum up: (1) State your central point, (2) give an example if necessary, (3) define any unfamiliar terms, and (4) follow with a road map. This sort of clear-cut, businesslike introduction will be appreciated by most of your audience.

It is particularly important not to neglect the introduction if you are showing slides. Avoid the tendency to dive right in and to let the slides dictate the content of the speech. Don't sacrifice the introduction. The listener needs it to establish a foundation for the rest of the speech.

2. *Body of speech* (20 minutes): Whether you use slides and transparencies, or simply speak directly to the audience, allow two to three minutes to make each argument. Remember, your

B.W. XXV. (I)

FIGURE 13-5   This facsimile of Bach's mirror figure was used by a speaker in the introduction to a lecture on symmetry. Follow the shapes of the melodies on either side of the dotted line and you will see that they are mirror images of each other. The speaker used the fact that the two pieces of music, while intimately related, are indeed different compositions to illustrate properties of mirror-image (chiral) molecules.

audience does not have the advantage of reading. They cannot stop when they come to a puzzling item, pause over it, or refer to an earlier section as they could if the information were printed.

As you proceed, use transitional words and phrases to help the listener along.

At two or three points, give an internal summary. Restating the points as you develop them will be an aid to the listener.

Look out at the audience, not at your notes or the screen. If you use an outline, coordinate it with your visuals in case you lose your place.

If you use slides or transparencies, don't simply flash them—explain them.

There is a variety of techniques you can use to keep the audience attentive. Pause. Look around before making a point. Change the tempo from time to time. Use a gesture or a step forward to emphasize a point. Some speakers employ demonstrations or hold up objects relevant to the discussion.

If possible, present the argument in puzzle order. That is,

instead of giving the answer, pose the situation, and gradually work your way to the solution. If you are clever about this, you'll do it in such a way that the audience will get there one jump ahead of your statement of the solution. This will give them the pleasure of solving the puzzle, add a little flair to the presentation, and make the speech a less passive experience.

Watch the clock. The first time you get up to speak, you may find that, like the person at the opera who didn't much care for it, you will look at your watch after what feels like two hours and discover that only five minutes have passed. But as you become more accustomed to speaking, you'll find you tend to exceed your time, particularly if you find ways to explain points in an interesting and lively way. Your audience will follow what you're saying, and you won't notice how quickly the moments have gone.

Dividing the speech into sections, represented by key words in your outline, will help you avoid this. You can look down, see how much you have to go, and how much time is left. In this way you can easily judge if you are going to end too soon, or, as is more often the case, exceed your allotted time.

3. *Closing* (last three to five minutes): Don't apologize! Novice speakers finish their talks, look up, realize they're done, and are suddenly smitten with nervousness. "Well," they say uncertainly, "I guess that's all." And they shuffle off with an air of apology at having taken everyone's time, in a sudden embarrassment at the silence and attention directed at them. Don't do this. Crush any tendency to sound apologetic. Instead, wind up with a brisk summary of your central point. Include an upbeat anecdote or quotation if you have one that illustrates the gist of the talk. Then call for questions. Answer them pleasantly and don't be defensive.

Summary: A Checklist

If you are studying in a group, use this checklist as a basis to evaluate each other's speeches. Be pleasant in your comments—it won't help a nervous speaker if you ruthlessly criticize him or her for playing with a ring or some other personal object while talking. But one of the best ways to improve quickly is to have constructive, courteous feedback from members of the group.

EVALUATION OF A TECHNICAL TALK

Speech	Good Features	Features That Could Use Improvement
Organization		
1. Introduction (Is it adequate to establish a foundation for the talk? Were essential terms defined? Was the thesis stated clearly?)		
2. Body of talk (Was adequate time allowed for each important point? Were there internal summaries? Transitional words? Was it possible to follow the explanation?)		
3. Conclusion (Was there a restatement of the thesis? Was the ending positive rather than apologetic?)		
Presentation		
4. Eye contact, voice, bearing, gestures, timing (Did the speaker look at all members of the group? Was the pace brisk or lethargic? Were voice, hearing, and gestures used effectively?)		
5. Visuals (Were they legible? Was each one explained adequately? Were they too complicated?)		
6. Unusual aspects (Good introduction? Lively format? Unusual illustrations? Upbeat ending? Effective eye contact?)		

Exercises

1. Prepare a five-minute speech on *one* of the following subjects. Use a blackboard, tagboard, flipcharts, or other appropriate visuals.

   Polishing specimens in metallurgy
   Reading a weather map
   Solar hot-water systems
   Three basic football tackles
   Bending glass tubing
   Observing constellations in the winter sky
   How (an oscilloscope, a flourescent activator, another instrument) works

Coal gasification
How to dissect a fetal pig
Use of a soldering iron
Tacking a sailboat
One or two aspects of the physics of a guitar, violin, piano, or
   other musical instrument
Black holes
High-speed photography (What is the shape of a raindrop?)
Fuel-injection ignitions
The formation of lichen
Mitochondria
Pheromones
Another technical topic of your choice

2. Expand your five-minute talk to ten minutes. Do so by selecting two to three technical details and developing them within
   the basic topic. If possible, use either slides or transparencies to
   illustrate your talk.

Appendix

Working with Transparencies and Slides

Overhead Projectors

1. Unlike a slide projector, the overhead projector (OP) must be placed close to
   the screen, usually within 6 to 12 feet. At 6 feet, a 10×10 inch transparency
   will be 40×40 inches, at 12 feet it will be 96×96 inches.
2. If possible, position the OP so that the audience has an unobstructed view.
3. The OP should face the screen squarely. Otherwise the picture will be
   distorted. Sometimes the table on which the OP rests will be too low or the
   screen too high. This will result in *keystoning*—in projecting an image that is
   broader at the top than at the bottom. To avoid keystoning, tilt the screen
   forward. If the screen is fixed, raise the level of the OP.

Transparencies

1. If you are preparing transparencies by hand, use a central area no larger than
   7×10 inches. In this way, distortion along the edges will not affect the text.
2. Use special transparency marking pens, available in bright colors and dense
   black. Ordinary felt-tipped pens appear to work well on application, but
   within hours the ink tends to bead until the text is almost invisible. Plain lead
   pencils and wax pencils also work, although they are not as effective as the

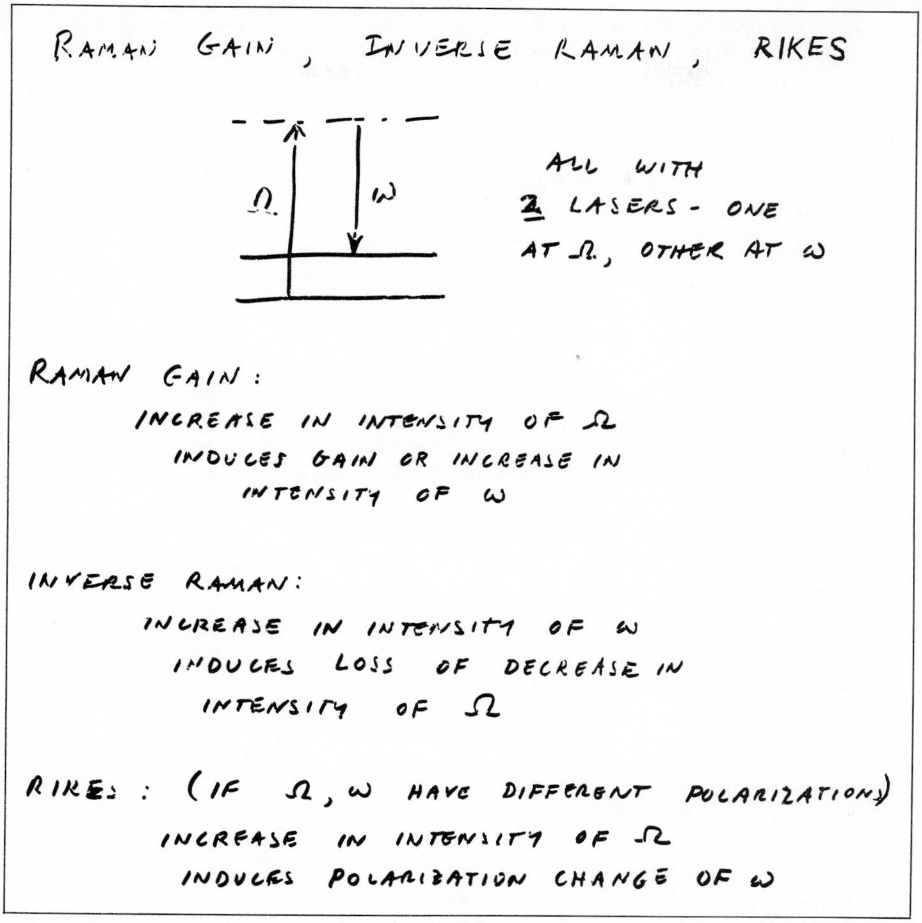

RAMAN GAIN , INVERSE RAMAN , RIKES

ALL WITH
2 LASERS - ONE
AT Ω, OTHER AT ω

RAMAN GAIN :
    INCREASE IN INTENSITY OF Ω
    INDUCES GAIN OR INCREASE IN
    INTENSITY OF ω

INVERSE RAMAN :
    INCREASE IN INTENSITY OF ω
    INDUCES LOSS OF DECREASE IN
    INTENSITY OF Ω

RIKES : (IF Ω, ω HAVE DIFFERENT POLARIZATION)
    INCREASE IN INTENSITY OF Ω
    INDUCES POLARIZATION CHANGE OF ω

FIGURE 13-6   Simple, hand-drawn illustrations can be prepared effectively on transparencies for OPs.

special pens. With proper pens, simple, hand-drawn illustrations can be prepared effectively on transparencies for OPs (Figure 13-6).

3. You can also prepare transparencies using the newer generation of copying machines by taking out the regular paper and loading the machine with transparencies. Pages of books or any typed copy can be duplicated in this way.

4. With some preparation, you can overlay transparencies, first placing one on the stage of the projector, then placing additional ones on top of the original to add information progressively. This is an effective technique, somewhat similar to beginning a sketch on the board and gradually adding details as you talk.

5. Transparencies are hard to handle. They accumulate static electricity and stick to one another. Many a speaker reaches for one, picks up two instead,

and has to separate them and peer at the transparencies to see which is the correct one. Instead, separate them with blank sheets of paper. This will allow you to see which image you're about to project. It will also prevent the transparencies from clinging to one another.

Slides

Transparencies can be prepared at the last minute, but slides usually require at least a day's lead time.

Preparation:
1. For sharp reproduction, supply the original rather than a photocopy if you are having drawings, graphs, or text copied. If you are preparing material for slides on your own, use white paper and keep to a central area of 7 × 10 inches. If you are doing your own letters, try to keep them large—a minimum of 3/16 inch. This is particularly important for symbols. There is a tendency to make the numbers in graphs large, with the accompanying symbols for units so small they are unreadable in the audience. If you are typing, use a carbon ribbon—the impression is denser and more uniform than that given by cloth ribbons.
2. Try to keep the illustrations uncomplicated. Don't present a slide with 15 columns of tabulated data. Instead, edit the table, picking out data you need and presenting it simply.

> A table of the sort pictured on page 232 is inappropriate as a slide; it is too complicated and too small, although it would work well in a textbook, where the reader could study it at leisure.
>
> You may be familiar with the rule: One idea to a speech. The public speaking corollary is: *One idea to a slide.*

3. Keep wording brief and the letters large.
4. Make sure none of the slides is inverted. Go through the entire run to guarantee this elementary step.
5. Have an extra bulb on hand. Make sure you know how to replace the bulb if the original one burns out or explodes.
6. Make sure you know what to do if the slide tray jams.
7. If you plan to use colored slides, be forewarned of some visibility problems. Albert Rocklin, Senior Research Chemist at Shell Development Company, has this to say in a letter he wrote to the editor of *Chemical and Engineering News*:

> "May I have the first slide." Frequently this ushers in a period of discomfort as the room is plunged into darkness and I try to read what is projected on the screen. To a great extent the fault lies with the lecturer whose ignorance of, or unconcern about, slide legibility can undermine an otherwise good presentation, but some of the blame must be shared by ACS [American Chemical Society].
> The ACS instructions to lecturers suggest colored slides, with preference for those with light printing or dark background. There are several reasons why this is guaranteed to promote illegibility. Most people have imperfect vision, even with corrective lenses, but it may not be

noticed because in good illumination the iris of the eye closes to a small opening which minimizes focusing errors. But the darkened screen in the darkened lecture hall is like the optometrist's examining room where the iris is opened wide to show those errors at their worst. They certainly show up in the lecture hall to the point that I and many others like me cannot read the slides.

The problem is compounded by slides with printing of different colors on a dark background. Eyes do not focus different colors in the same plane. This chromatic aberration is not noticeable in good illumination, but the effect is greatly exaggerated in dim light, where the blue end of the spectrum gives a viewer the impression of being nearsighted, and the red end farsighted. The effect is that printing in one color may be clear while another color on the same slide will be blurred. The situation becomes worse as we get older and our ability to change focus diminishes.

14

Letter Writing

Dear Faculty Member: Please read this letter to the end
no matter how bored you are . . .
Opening of a letter

In 1482, Leonardo da Vinci wrote one of the most famous job application letters of all time. Employing a minimum of flourish in the salutation, he went on to propose his qualifications with a clarity of expression that has not dimmed in 500 years.

"Most illustrious Lord," he wrote his prospective patron, Ludovico Sforza, "I have plans for bridges, very light and strong. . . . I have plans for making cannon, very convenient and easy to transport." He continues, "I can execute sculpture in marble, bronze or clay, and also printing in which my work will stand comparison with that of anyone else whoever he may be," and ends, "I offer myself as ready to make trial of them in your park or in whatever place shall please your Excellency."

Here is the entire **letter** [1]:

Most Illustrious Lord, having now sufficiently seen and considered the proofs of all those who count themselves masters and inventors of instruments of war, and finding that their invention and use of the said instruments does not differ in any respect from those in common practice, I am emboldened without prejudice to anyone else to put myself in communication with your Excellency, in order to acquaint you with my secrets, thereafter offering myself at your pleasure effectually to demonstrate at any convenient time all those matters which are in part briefly recorded below.

1. I have plans for bridges, very light and strong and suitable for carrying very easily, with which to pursue and at times defeat the enemy; and others solid and indestructible by fire or assault, easy and convenient to carry away and place in position. And plans for burning and destroying those of the enemy.

2. When a place is besieged I know how to cut off water from the trenches, and how to construct an infinite number of bridges, mantlets, scaling ladders and other instruments which have to do with the same enterprise.

3. Also if a place cannot be reduced by the method of bombardment, either through the height of its glacis or the strength of its position, I have plans for destroying every fortress or other stronghold unless it has been founded upon rock.

4. I have also plans for making cannon, very convenient and easy of transport, with which to hurl small stones in the manner almost of hail, causing great terror to the enemy from their smoke, and great loss and confusion.

5. Also I have ways of arriving at a certain fixed spot by caverns and secret winding passages, made without any noise even though it may be necessary to pass underneath trenches or a river.

6. Also I can make armoured cars, safe and unassailable, which will enter the serried ranks of the enemy with their artillery, and there is no company of men at arms so great that they will not break it. And behind these the infantry will be able to follow quite unharmed and without any opposition.

7. Also, if need shall arise, I can make cannon, mortars, and light ordnance, of very beautiful and useful shapes, quite different from those in common use.

8. Where it is not possible to employ cannon, I can supply catapults, mangonels, *trabocchi*, and other engines of wonderful efficacy not in general use. In short, as the variety of circumstances shall necessitate, I can supply an infinite number of different engines of attack and defence.

9. And if it should happen that the engagement was at sea, I have plans for constructing many engines most suitable either for

attack or defence, and ships which can resist the fire of all the heaviest cannon, and power and smoke.

10. In time of peace I believe that I can give you as complete statisfaction as anyone else in architecture in the construction of buildings both public and private, and in conducting water from one place to another.

Also I can execute sculpture in marble, bronze or clay and also painting, on which my work will stand comparison with that of anyone else whoever he may be.

Moreover, I would undertake the work of the bronze horse, which shall endure with immortal glory and eternal honour the auspicious memory of the Prince your father and of the illustrious house of Sforza.

And if any of the aforesaid things should seem impossible or impracticable to anyone, I offer myself as ready to make trial of them in your park or in whatever place shall please your Excellency, to whom I commend myself with all possible humility.

Leonardo's letter is exemplary—direct, to the point, leaving no question in the reader's mind either of the applicant's background and objectives, or the fit between those objectives and the job offered.

Contrast the simplicity and decisiveness of that letter with this one:

Dear

As you are no doubt aware, ERC is now open. But since we estimate about two or three weeks' delay in bringing the center to full utilization, I wanted to give you an idea of the move in progress. The temporary inconveniences hopefully will meet with your forbearance and ultimately the result will fulfill your expectations.

During this week the staff will move in to the new facility, and on 13 Wednesday September the facility will open. In this initial period, the Center will remain open from 12:00 to 5:00. By the end of the week of 22 September we shall be in place and well on our way to a normal, 8:00 a.m. to 5:00 p.m. schedule, and repairs can be handled centrally and in a more efficient way than by the present, scattered system. No doubt the changes will necessitate a shared patience. Let me thank you in anticipation of your cooperation and ask you to address any questions you might have to the Electronic Repair Center Staff at Ext. 8766-7

Sincerely,

This letter certainly does necessitate a shared patience. The message is clear—there's a new Electronic Repair Center. For the first three weeks, the hours will be limited; after that, service will be in full swing.

Why didn't the writer say that, simply and directly? Instead, there are useless phrases ("as you are no doubt aware"), redundancy ("estimate a delay at about two to three weeks"), and inflated language ("utilize" for *use*, "facility" for *building*, "in this initial period" for *first*).

In addition, there are the sorts of nervous tics endemic to letter writing, such overcourteous, fulsome phrases as "Let me thank you in anticipation" "The temporary inconveniences hopefully will meet with your forbearance." This sort of hemming and hawing is common at the ends of letters when people, unsure of how to end gracefully, overdo the closing.

Are there simple ways to avoid writing letters like this?

Ten Suggestions for Letter Writing

1. Get to the Point You should get to the point as quickly and as clearly as possible. Letters are best kept to one page, two at most. In this one-page slot of two to four paragraphs, you need to land immediately and securely on the point—"I have plans for bridges, very light and strong" rather than "Pursuant to your request of August 26 on the matter of Inley Steel Option 46." Save space and emphasis for your message, not for such throat clearings as "Please be advised that."

Audience This is always the fundamental question in writing: Whom are you addressing? The question is easier to deal with in letters than in articles, for you can reasonably expect one person rather than a multitude to be attending. Think about the other person—what he does for a living, how much time she has to spend, what he or she wants to know—and be guided accordingly.

Objective Why are you writing the letter? In the same way that you prepared for reports, state audience and objective to yourself in one sentence, "I am writing this for   [audience]   so that   [objective] .

Style Each writer develops his or her own voice, and this voice will show clearly in letters, traditionally a more personal form of address. The range of styles, of the sound of the writer's voice on paper, is as wide for letters as it is for any other form of prose. It's wise, though, to remember that in technical and scientific correspondence a premium is placed on a dry, objective style. The flourishes that are common in sales correspondence—beginning a letter, for instance, with a question—are generally out of place in technical writing.

Applying for a job as an engineer, you would be violating all the conventions if you began, "Are you looking for an engineer who can write?" They may be looking for just that, but a more traditional style is the route to that job.

Sound Openings   *The New Yorker* has a feature called "Letters We Never Finished." Here are the openings of some letters I never finished:

> Dear Faculty Member:
> Please read this letter to the end no matter how bored you are.
>
> Dear Sir:
> You probably think this letter is just another piece of junk mail.
>
> Dear Sir:
> Don't throw this letter away, no matter how much you want to.
>
> Dear Sir or Madam:
> I know you have many claims on your attention. . . .

These sorts of openings provide much unintended amusement for the recipient.

Here, in contrast, are some openings that are sound—that get to the point quickly—given a particular audience and objective.

> Here is the reprint you requested on lactic fermentation in yeast.
>
> The enclosed booklet, particularly pages 7 to 11, answers the questions you addressed to our office 18 July.
>
> The chemicals you ordered were shipped yesterday, 8 July.
>
> I'm pleased to enclose the information on thin layer chromatography you requested.

Should you be concerned about how original your opening is? Probably not. Originality is much more important in sales letters than in general technical correspondence. "I am applying in response to your ad of 18 October" may be trite, but it tells the reader immediately the objective of the letter and is therefore a serviceable beginning.

Instead of originality in the opening, concentrate on getting the message across simply and clearly, with as little fuss as possible.

Let's look at the openings of a series of letters recently received for a job; all are in response to the same ad:

(1) Dear Dr. Findlater:

I hereby apply for the position of assistant professor of chemistry. [one-page letter]

(2) Dear Dr. Findlater:

I have recently read with interest in *Science* that there is an academic opening in the field of biochemistry at State University at Hempstead. I have been actively involved in the field of physical biochemistry for the last seven years and should like to be considered for the position that is available at State University at Hempstead. [two-page letter]

(3) Dear Professor Findlater:

Your recent correspondence concerning the availibility [sic] of a new faculty position in your department has been brought to my attention. I am very interested in this position and wish to be considered as an applicant. [two-page letter]

(4) Dear Dr. Findlater:

I would like to apply for a faculty position in your department, advertised 21 December in *Science*. Presently I am an assistant professor of biochemistry at Caltech. I enclose my curriculum vitae, statement of research plans, and a list of equipment in my laboratory purchased through my research grants. [end of letter]

Do all of these applicants get to the point quickly and clearly? Part of the information here should be (1) the name of the job, and (2) where it was advertised. As a rule, it's important to link your letters to any prior correspondence or events that are relevant.

Example 1 does not identify the ad. Example 2 identifies the ad, but takes many more words than necessary to do so. "I have recently read with interest that there is an academic opening in the field of biochemistry at State University at Hempstead" is essentially the same as "should like to be considered for the position that is available at State University at Hempstead." The information on the writer's background belongs in a later paragraph and could be condensed to "I recently read with interest in *Science* that you have an academic opening in biochemistry for which I should like to be considered," or even more simply, "I should like to apply for the faculty position in biochemistry advertised in the 21 December issue of *Science*."

Example 3 does not specify the advertisement or the faculty position. Availability is misspelled.

Example 4 is brief, complete, and to the point.

An opening statement should

Link the letter to any necessary prior information
State the objective directly and clearly

2. Avoid Letterese   Letters are an interesting literary form because the letter has invented its own jargon, creating unto itself an array of awkward, impenetrable expressions. Linguists may one day study such turns of phrase as "taking cognizance of your letter of." In the meantime, here is a list of words and expressions to avoid, with alternatives in the right-hand column.

Abeyance, hold in	Wait
Affix your signature	Sign
Afford an opportunity	Have the opportunity
As of this date	Today
Attention is called to the fact that	(Delete)
Attached please find; attached herewith, hereto	Attached
Cognizant; cognizance; taking cognizance of	(Rewrite)
Earliest practicable date	(Say when)
Effectuate	Effect
Endeavor to ascertain	Try to find out
Fullest possible extent	Utmost
In compliance with your request	As requested
In view of the fact that	As

Predicated on the assumption   (Delete)
    that
Utilize   Use

3. Use a "You" Approach   Organize the letter so the spotlight is on the reader, not the writer. Consider, for example, the difference in emphasis in these two openings:

(1) I am writing to propose a course in plant management at State University at Hempstead. I know a great deal about the area both as a practicing engineer and as a consultant, and would be interested in such a position.

(2) Are you interested in offering a course in plant management this fall at State University at Hempstead? Such a course might attract considerable business from nearby companies, particularly since your school is well known for its management course.

Example 1 uses an "I" approach; the emphasis is on the *writer's* background and needs. Example 2 uses a "you" approach; the emphasis is on the *reader's* background and interests.

The focus in a letter should be on the reader, not the writer. To write in the context of one's own needs—"Your recent correspondence concerning the availability of a new faculty position in your department has been brought to my attention. I am very interested in this position and wish to be considered as an applicant"—rather than the reader's needs is to pick up the telescope from the wrong end. If you want to talk about yourself, set the stage by placing the information firmly within the context of the other person's objectives. This is far more important in a letter than in conversation. It's possible to be a bore in person when one's quarry can't escape and must pretend to listen; the same tactics won't work in a letter which can be directly and unceremoniously dumped in the trash.

4. Keep It Short   One page usually is plenty for letters. Resist going to two pages unless it is essential. Use short words, short sentences, and short paragraphs.

In his essay "Politics and the English Language" George Orwell advised, "Never use a long word where a short one will do." That doesn't mean "avoid long words" for a long word may be exactly the one you seek. It means merely that every word should tell, and long words—such as *implement, utilize, disseminate, effectuate,* and the like—should be avoided if a short one will do the job just as nicely.

English began as a muscular, vigorous language. With the Norman conquest, the language became polysyllabic. The longer words were associated with the new French rulers, the shorter words with the Angles, Saxons, and Jutes—the people of Germanic origin who had abruptly become the Normans' servants. A tradition developed where *perspired* was better than *sweat,* where the long word was considered more genteel than the short.

Avoid fanciness for its own sake. Stick to simple, direct language. As to sentence and paragraph length, be aware that the longer the sentence, the more difficult it will be for a person to understand it. You're more likely to get the message across in short sentences. Of course, if you make each sentence short and choppy, or write in the manner of a first-grade primer, your reader will also have difficulty.

Nonetheless, an eye to shorter sentences is useful in letter writing if you want to avoid going over the head of your reader. Readability formulas are useful here. These are crude but reliable measures of how difficult prose is; most work by counting the number of words in a sentence and the number of syllables in the words. The longer the words and sentences, the more difficult the passage is for the reader.

Robert Gunning's Fog Index is a handy tool for estimating the reading level of a letter. To try it, choose a 100- to 150-word sample.

1. Divide number of words by number of sentences. This yields average number of words per sentence.
2. Count words of three or more syllables (except for proper nouns). Divide this number by the total number of words in the sample. The answer is the percentage of difficult words in the sample.
3. Add average number of words in a sentence to percentage of difficult words.
4. Multiply the total by 0.4. This gives a Fog count. A count of 10 means the passage should be easy reading for the average tenth grader.

Sample Application   Here is a famous letter from Einstein to President Roosevelt [2]. What is its reading level?

Albert Einstein
Old Grove Road
Nassau Point
Peconic, Long Island
August, 1939

F. D. Roosevelt
President of the United States
White House
Washington, D.C.

Sir:

Some recent work by E. Fermi and L. Szilard, which has been communicated to me in manuscript, leads me to expect that the element uranium may be turned into a new and important source of energy in the immediate future. Certain aspects of the situation which has arisen seem to call for watchfulness and, if necessary, quick action on the part of the Administration. I believe therefore that it is my duty to bring to your attention the following facts and recommendations:

In the course of the last four months it has been made probable—through the work of Joliot in France as well as Fermi and Szilard in America—that it may become possible to set up a nuclear chain reaction in a large mass of uranium by which vast amounts of power and large quantities of new radium-like elements would be generated. Now it appears almost certain that this could be achieved in the immediate future.

This new phenomenon would also lead to the construction of bombs, and it is conceivable—though much less certain—that extremely powerful bombs of a new type may thus be constructed. A single bomb of this type, carried by boat and exploded in a port, might very well destroy the whole port together with some of the surrounding territory. However, such bombs might very well prove to be too heavy for transportation by air.

The United States has only very poor ores of uranium in moderate quantities. There is some good ore in Canada and the former Czechoslovakia, while the most important source of uranium is Belgian Congo.

In view of this situation you may think it desirable to have some permanent contact maintained between the Administration and the group of physicists working on chain reactions in America. One possible way of achieving this might be for you to entrust with this task a person who has your confidence and who could perhaps serve in an inofficial capacity. His task might comprise the following:

a) to approach Government Departments, keep them informed of the further development, and put forward recommendations for Government action, giving particular attention to the problem of securing a supply of uranium ore for the United States.

b) to speed up the experimental work, which is at present being carried on within the limits of the budgets of University laboratories, by providing funds, if such funds be required, through his contacts with private persons who are willing to make contributions for this cause, and perhaps also by obtaining the cooperation of industrial laboratories which have the necessary equipment.

I understand that Germany has actually stopped the sale of uranium from the Czechoslovakian mines which she has taken over. That she should have taken such early action might perhaps be understood on the ground that the son of the German Under-Secretary of State, von Weizsäcker, is attached to the Kaiser-Wilhelm-Institut in Berlin where some of the American work on uranium is now being repeated.

> Yours very truly,
> [Signed] Albert Einstein

Apply the Fog Index to the letter by completing each step:

Step 1. Number of words (end of second paragraph)
Step 2. Number of sentences.
Step 3. Average number of words per sentence (Step 1 divided by Step 2)
Step 4. Number of difficult words (three or more syllables)
Step 5. Percentage of difficult words (Step 4 divided by Step 1)
Step 6. Sum of word average and difficult word percentage (Step 3 plus 5)
Step 7. Fog Index (Step 6 multiplied by 0.4)

5. Use Lists   For example, use lists whenever you can within a letter. This allows the reader to tick off points when responding. Here's an example of a well-organized letter using a list.

Dr. R. Smiley
Chemistry Department
State University at Hempstead
Hempstead, NY 11553

Dear Dr. Smiley:
My purpose in writing you is threefold:

1. To send you the completed work on the assignments for your ACS course, Gas Chromatography—Mass Spectrometry.
2. To take advantage of your assenting to my request to comment on the enclosed abstract of my dissertation.
3. To ask for information about the courses you will be teaching in the fall at State University at Hempstead.

I look forward to your evaluation of the enclosed papers. A return envelope is included for your convenience.

Thank you for an enjoyable and productive session.

This letter simplifies the respondent's job. Dr. Smiley can draft an answer, assemble the documents, and then check the original letter to make sure the job is done. To make the process more efficient, some people underline or box key words, or put a scratch outline in the margin of each letter they receive before they respond, particularly if they are going to dictate an answer.

6. Do a Scratch Outline First If the letter is complicated, you might want to do a scratch outline before you respond. You can put it in the margin or at the end of the letter to which you're responding. It will help you keep to the point; it's also a good checklist to guarantee you've included all intended information.

For example, Dr. Smiley might have annotated the preceding letter as follows:

Dr. Ronald Smiley
Chemistry Department
State University at Hempstead
Hempstead, NY 11553

Dear Dr. Smiley:
My purpose in writing you is threefold:

Assignment OK see attached 1. To send you the completed work on the assignment for your ACS course, Gas Chromatography–Mass Spectrometry.

Note to Contact Scheir, U. Va. 2. To take advantage of your assenting to my request to comment on the enclosed abstract of my dissertation.

Enclose Brochures 3. To ask for information about the courses you will be teaching in the fall at State University at Hempstead.

I look forward to your evaluation of the enclosed papers. A return envelope is included for your convenience.

Thank you for an enjoyable and productive session.

Here is a second letter. This one is an interoffice letter to members of the Chemistry Department.

12 November 1980

Dear Colleagues:

At the last staff meeting, an ad hoc committee was chosen to recommend merit raises to the administration. To aid the committee, each faculty member is invited to submit a brief memorandum presenting activities and/or successes which the committee might consider. Emphasis might appropriately be on the recent past, particularly the calendar year 1979.

The faculty established the following ranking of activities:

1. Successful research, reflected in theses, publications, and grants
2. Good teaching
3. Service to the department
4. Service to the university

If you wish to submit a memorandum, please have it reach me by Friday 4 January.

This early submission is necessary because of the several steps in the procedure, involving the committee, department head, and dean.

This letter will be useful for the recipient, who can use it as a guide in responding.

7. Layout Both of the preceding letters have attractive layouts. There is an abundance of white space, created by indenting; both are easy to read. As a courtesy to the reader, arrange letters so that they are not a wall of print. Generous margins and indentation for lists will aid in this. Simple tables also add to an attractive layout, as does organizing the letter so that the reader can respond quickly.

For example, the following information can be presented in two ways. Which way will make the respondent's job easier?

Mr. I. M. Gotcliff
MSI Instruments
30 Marlowe Drive
Cambridge, Mass.

Dear Mr. Gotcliff:

Our laboratory is in receipt of an invoice from you, number L34570, for $105.80 for two anerobic cells at $52.90 each. These were type LJ-28 Thunberg. In addition we later ordered four more cells presumably at the same price. This invoice was L35462. The first invoice, for your records, was dated 1 July, the second 2 September. But the second invoice was for $422.86.

Inasmuch as it is our understanding that the rate for the service was $52.90 per cell, we are therefore enclosing a check for $423.50, as according to our accounting this is the sum owed. Enclosed herewith is a check for that amount. If it is not satisfactory and the additional charge arises other than from error, kindly inform us by March 1, supplying complete details and justification for the additional charge. Otherwise the enclosed remuneration will be presumed to be in the correct amount.

Mr. I. M. Gotcliff
MSI Instruments
30 Marlowe Drive
Cambridge, Mass.

Dear Mr. Gotcliff:

We have received two invoices for LJ-28 Thunbergs totaling $528.66. We calculated the sum owed at $423.50. Here is the information you will need to follow our calculation.

Purchase Order No.	MSI Invoice No. and Date	Unit Price and Quantity	Amount of Purchase Order	Amount MSI Invoice
C1060	L34570 (7/1/80)	$52.90 (2)	$105.80	$105.80
C1067	L35462 (9/2/80)	$62.90 (6)	317.70	422.86
		Total	$423.50	$528.66

Let us know promptly if there is any reason for the additional charge; otherwise we'll assume it is a billing error and that the enclosed check for $423.50 is correct.

8. Be Specific in the Closing State clearly either what you will do next or what you expect of your respondent. Don't be vague.

Vague Closings	*Specific Closings*
It would be good to get together soon.	I will telephone 15 October to arrange an appointment.
	Are you free for lunch 18 October? I will telephone to find out.
Please answer promptly.	Please have the form reach me by Friday, 4 January. The early submission is necessary because of the several steps in the procedure, involving the committee, department head, and dean.

9. Check Details for Accuracy   Have you gotten the person's name right? Is the title correct? Did you enclose all the documents you intended? Did you check spelling? Misspellings are glaring in letters and are guaranteed to produce an effect opposite to the one intended. For instance, this letter was received by the director of a technical writing program from a man who wanted to teach in the program. Can you see why he wasn't granted an interview?

Please reply to:

Richard Hornestay
114 W. 92 Street
New York, NY 10025
PL 2-3546

16 August 1980

Prof. J. Gold
Director, Technical Writing Program
State University at Hempstead
Hempstead, NY 11553

Dear Prof. Gild:

Would you be interested in a business or commercial writing course for the Fall semester?

Aimed at the nonprofessional writer, the course would unravel the intricacies of the "you" approach, guide students in the stragety of effectively writing memoranda, presentations, reports, and letters that sell in terms of the reader's interest.

The enclosed data highly my communications and writing experience; experience that includes annual reports, capability

reports, market newsletters, consumer and trade magazine articles, financial column writing, etc.

If you are interested, I will be happy to talk with you at your
convenience.

10. Don't Shoot from the Hip   If the letter contains material
that is delicate or that could have repercussions for yourself or
your company, let it sit overnight. In the morning, you may want
to modify it considerably.

Courtesy in Letter Writing

Despite the barrage of third-class, computer-generated mail that
arrives every morning, letters remain a personal vehicle. They are
a place for courtesy; inquiries about business affairs, children, or
health are not out of place if the correspondent is on that footing
with the recipient.

Avoid recriminations, injured pride, and finger shaking in
letters, no matter how tempted you may be to engage in them.
Such expressions as "As I thought I'd already made clear," and
"As should be apparent" will probably evoke the opposite reaction
from the one you desire. The person receiving the letter may
become more irritated and less likely to do as you wish. If, for
instance, you are doing funded research at a university, your
money will be handled by the university's business or grants
office. They typically add 50 percent to the cost of the grant as
overhead charges for processing the money. If they make mistakes in their record keeping, it won't help to remind them that
you are in essence paying their salary.

If you are handling a complaint—either your own or one
addressed to you—start with the positive news. This will help
maintain a pleasant tone in the letter. Also, since people like good
news, it will ease the bad news that follows. Thus, if the business
office has continued to bill you incorrectly for two months with
what you view as extraordinary and genuinely galling inefficiency,
begin with a compliment on some other area of administration if
it is timely and true. You might write as follows:

Thank you for prompt processing of the bill to Landau. They are
demanding, and I appreciate the extra service you gave. Another problem has come up. Your charges for the past two months

for scientific products have included an item, Number 056879, for glass products. I have no record of our ordering such products, and I've checked with my graduate assistant. Could you backtrack and see if we are actually supposed to be charged for these? I'll have Roger call tommorrow, 14 May, to check with you.

Courtesy is not only important in complaints; it also counts when there's an apology to be made. Although it's not necessary to grovel, it is a courtesy to the reader to apologize simply and directly when necessary and then get on with the point. Instead of the passive, "It will be found that," or the royal "we," as in "We are sorry to inform you that," try, "I regret we will be four weeks late with the shipment" or "I apologize for not answering your letter sooner. Yes, we do have the technical information services requested."

Address the reader directly when possible. Say "you will find" rather than "it will be found that." Refer to yourself rather than using an impersonal passive: "I made an error" rather than "Errors have been made." Use "we" when you speak for the organization, "I" when you speak for yourself.

Dictation

Talking your writing is a respectable way to get the news across. The Greeks and Romans composed aloud—Cicero, for example, apologized for not writing a letter because he'd had a sore throat.

Using a dictating machine can save a lot of time: average writing speed is about 25 words per minute, in contrast to 100 words per minute for dictating.

It's a knack that is acquired through practice. The typical pitfalls in dictating are (1) a tendency to repetition and (2) lack of organization. Here are guidelines.

1. Make an outline before you dictate.
2. Develop a simple form for the typist on which you can put the name of the recipient, title, company, and address. The form should also specify the kind of stationery, the date, and the distribution, if any. A sample cover sheet to accompany dictation might look like this:

☐ Letter   ☐ Memo   Type of stationery:

Recipient

Name _____

Title, Company _____

Address _____

Date _____

Subject or Reference Line _____

Distribution _____

On Cover Letters and "No" Letters

Cover Letters Cover letters, or letters of transmittal, are typical in technical writing since they accompany the reports, specifications, vitae, or other papers that are the main documents shuttling back and forth in the communications network. A letter of transmittal should state the point and then give an exceedingly brief digest of the attached document.

For instance, a letter of transmittal with a technical report should encapsulate the report in a few sentences, giving precedence to the conclusions or recommendations. In a job application, it is the enclosure—the résumé or vita—that will be of main interest to the employer; however, the attached letter should briefly state one's background, suggesting one's unique qualifications for the job.

For example, if the transmittal letter accompanies a résumé, state the job you are applying for immediately so the recipient can check the files. "I am applying for the job of assistant professor in Chemistry, advertised in the 14 January issue of *Science*." Address the point briefly and clearly. In this case, state your background briefly, as well as your reason for applying. "I am presently a postgraduate in biochemistry at the University of Ohio, where I've published three articles on fiber proteins in conjunction with my adviser, Dr. Xerrenia." Close without letterese, proposing a plan when appropriate. "Enclosed is a vita, including articles published, grants coauthored, and equipment purchased through grants." In this case, it would be presumptuous to ask for an appointment, but in many instances it would be correct to write, "May I have an interview at your convenience?"

There's temptation to cram into the letter far too many details of the report, résumé, or document you are attaching. Try to resist this temptation. Instead, *confine a letter of transmittal to one page*. In summary:

1. Refer to any necessary previous documents.
2. State the point.
3. Encapsulate the enclosed documents in a few sentences. If it is a report, give conclusions and/or recommendations. If it is a vita, give your particular qualifications for the job in a nutshell.

For a sample cover letter and corrections see the chapter appendix.

Letters That Say "No" The artist Devis Grebu drew a cartoon of a man stretched on a table, having a tattoo inscribed on his back. When one reads the tattoo, one discovers a letter to Mr. Grebu, rejecting drawings he submitted to a competition.

Rejection letters sting. If you are writing one, try to ease the impact. For instance, if you are not going to interview a person for a job, a courteous answer might be, "Dear (Name), I appreciate your interest in the position. Unfortunately, we are interviewing only candidates with a strong research focus on inorganic chemistry. Your application is excellent, but the biochemical focus makes it beyond the range of people we will interview. I wish you good luck during the coming year, and hope to see you at national meetings."

Summary

1. Avoid letterese.
2. Avoid hemming and hawing both at the beginning— "Herewith you'll find attached"—and at the end—"Asking your grateful cooperation, I remain. . . . "
3. Keep the letter short, the sentences short, the paragraphs short.
4. Pay attention to (*a*) organization and (*b*) tone. Use lists or subheads to help organize the text. Make the margins and indentations generous. Maintain a courteous, personal tone.
5. Speak directly and clearly to the reader. Use a positive, "you" approach.
6. If the letter is complicated, do a scratch outline first, particularly if you plan to dictate it.

7. If the matter is sensitive, let the letter sit overnight.
8. Before it goes out, check to make sure it is both neat and accurate. If you are sloppy about letters, you are unlikely to inspire confidence about your abilities in other areas.
9. The parts of the letter should do the following: The beginning should connect the letter to any relevant prior events and then state the point. The middle should address the point briefly and clearly. The end should propose a specific plan when appropriate.

For a sample letter and corrections, see the chapter appendix.

Literature Cited

1. E. MacCurdy (ed.), *The Notebooks of Leonardo da Vinci*, vol. 2, Reynal & Hitchcock, New York, 1938, pp. 1152–1153.

2. Reprinted by permission of Dr. Otto Nathan, executor of Einstein's literary estate.

Exercises

1. Criticize this letter. Afterward, rewrite it according to the guidelines in the chapter.

November 5, 1980

Dear Faculty Member:

Please read this letter to the end no matter how bored you are. It has been said that "Information is anything which clarifies the amount of uncertainty." Some of your uncertainty can be solved by a new service we've installed: access to on-line computer information retrieval systems. We have a trained staff to provide this service.

Why use an on-line computer terminal, you may ask. In the modern world of today, it doesn't make sense any more to do without a computer and we have one right on the spot in the library. The computer will be useful for the generation of a bibliography. It is possible to use one to track down facts that are or have been elusive. It can remove part or all of the tedium from a literature search, and much, much more. Please read the attached to find out details and then contact us soon.

2. Criticize this letter, both for effective and for poor techniques. Afterward, correct the less effective aspects.

Dear Out-of-State Applicant:

The Committee on Admissions regrets to inform you that it will not be able to act favorably on your application for admission to our next entering class at Hogate Medical College.

Unfortunately, the volume of rejection letters precludes a description of the reason(s) for our decision on each application. And if we could tell you, in a number of cases we would not because the decisions have, wholly or in part, been based on information given to us in confidence or on the subjective judgements of Committee members.

As you can see, this is a form letter with a simulation of signature below. Considering the time and effort you devoted to the submission of your application, we recognize and apologize for the inappropriate nature of this reply. But when we contrasted the need for more than 4000 personal replies with our relatively small secretarial staff, it was obvious that a form letter would be the best that we could.

I hope you have gained admission to another medical school.

Sincerely yours,

3. Check the classified ads in a newsletter or other publication in your field. If you are a chemical engineer, for instance, look in *C & E News*. Find an ad for a job for which you may be qualified. Write a cover letter and résumé to answer the add. (Dictate the materials if appropriate.)

4. Arrange to exchange cover letters and résumé with your classmates. Get their reactions to strong and weak aspects of your work.

5. Collect three or four letters from your files. If you are studying in a group, copy these letters for the class. Analyze them for (*a*) style, (*b*) author's purpose, (*c*) tone, and (*d*) structure.

6. Your materials research laboratory needs a research metallurgist. The person will need to maintain and repair high-performance electron microscopes, design and construct experimental apparatus, and supervise students in the use of instruments. The person must have a B.S. in physical science or engineering plus experience in electron microscopy. The salary is negotiable and the position is available now. You,

Professor _____, are head of the committee to fill this position. You are at State University at Hempstead.

(a) Write an ad.

(b) Your ad is very successful, and 47 people respond. Now write (1) a general letter acknowledging their response and explaining your plan for interviewing, (2) a letter of invitation to those chosen to be interviewed, and (3) a letter of rejection to those you do not choose to interview.

Appendix

Sample Letters and Corrections

Dr. Richard Armour
Direction, Quality Control Assurance
Lincoln Laboratories
Pearl, New York

Dear Dr. Armour:

I hereby[1] apply for a job[2] as auditor in your laboratory.

I feel[3] that my academic backround[4] and experience makes[5] me qualified for this position.[6] Enclosed is a vita.

Sincerely,
Ruth Gianini

Corrections

[1]Avoid such letterese as "hereby."

[2]Where was it advertised? Was the writer referred by someone?

[3]Focus should be on Armour's needs, not on the writer's needs.

[4]Misspelling.

[5]Subject-verb agreement error. Should be *make.* ·

[6]Vague. What specifically is the writer's academic background? A major in biology? A Ph.D. in biochemistry?

Dear

To avoid major disruption during the course of our business day, strategies are presently being developed[1] to assist INTER-FACE employees in getting to the workplace[2] if faced with the New York City transit strike scheduled for April 1, 1980.

For the purpose of formulating carpools,[3] please submit the attached form. At a later date[4] you will be provided[5] with employees who live in your area. Additionally you will receive information relative to[6] parking facilities,[7] including capacity, rates, and hours of operation. Tips on making carpooling successful will also be provided.[8]

We[9] look forward to your response. If you have any questions we'll be more than happy to respond.[10]

Corrections

[1]"are presently being developed"—unnecessary passive.

[2]"workplace": Is this where we work, perhaps? Wordy. Rewrite, "getting to work."

[3]"For the purpose of formulating carpools." How do you formulate a carpool?

[4]"at a later date" = later.

[5]Unnecessary passive.

[6]"relative to" = about.

[7]"facilities"—redundant.

[8]Unnecessary passive.

[9]Keep voice consistent.

[10]Fulsome ending.

15

Résumés

Corporations call them résumés, the government calls them personal data sheets, and in academia they are curricula vitae, or CVs. The most popular general term is *résumé*, from the French *résumer*, "to summarize." A résumé is a summary of one's qualifications. Typically it is prepared and submitted by an applicant who mails the résumé in response to a job offering. The interviewers read the cover letters and résumés, and then decide whether or not to schedule an interview.

The length and focus of the résumé depend on your qualifications and the type of job for which you are applying. A second-year undergraduate may wonder whether to include the summer job at a supermarket, while the graduating senior may be concerned with presenting details of a double major.

There are, however, certain basics you can use when preparing a résumé—guidelines on how to get started, how to categorize information, and how to assemble an attractive final product.

Getting Started

Assemble notes under basic categories: career objective, educational background, work experience, special skills and activities. Consider these questions as you begin to brainstorm:

1. What is your *career objective*? Do you want to distinguish between short-range and long-range goals?
2. What is your *educational background*?
3. What is your *work experience*?
4. What are your other *special abilities or activities*?

This part of résumé writing is personal and exploratory. Write down all the things about yourself that you think may be important for getting the job. Look through records, think about the past. Include all items for each category that may be useful. Later you can sift and evaluate.

Basic Categories

Identification　Name, address, telephone number. Formats for the identification vary. Some people prefer the information flush left, others center it. Most capitalize the letters of their names. For two addresses, it is usual to center one's name, and then give academic address to the left and permanent address to the right. Here are two examples.

JULIA MONDAY

Academic Address	Permanent Address
252 White Road	44 Wycoff Street
Scotch Plains, New Jersey 07076	Brooklyn, New York 11201
(202) 475-6998	(212) 273-8661

RALPH BLESSER
147 Rand Street, Apt. B-8
Richmond, Virginia 23226
Telephone: (804) 285-2626

Professional Objective　This category is optional. Some applicants feel that if they list an objective, it will restrict the use of the résumé, and result in their having to prepare a different résumé for each interview. Others reject the objective for a different reason: they think it is redundant when a résumé is manifestly in response to an advertised position.

Despite these holdouts, however, most entry-level applicants state their objective at the top of the résumé since, in general, interviewers expect such a statement.

Some suggestions for preparing the objective: (1) When appropriate, divide your statement into immediate and long-term goals. (2) Make the statement sufficiently general so that it does not exclude a variety of jobs. Otherwise, you will need to rewrite the résumé for each position.

The heading for this and other categories can be centered (crossheading) or placed to the left (side heading). Some people use all capitals, others use initial capitals or capitals and lowercase. Pick a format that suits your taste. Once you've decided, however, be consistent throughout the résumé. Don't switch from all capitals in one heading to initial capitals in another heading. Here are some examples.

Career Objective

An entry-level position in design or development as a mechanical engineer. Future educational goals include M.B.A. degree with concentration in management.

Professional Objective Summer position using skills achieved in aerospace engineering program.

PROFESSIONAL OBJECTIVE Challenging position in mechanical engineering working with rotating equipment.

OBJECTIVE A career involving the application of industrial engineering principles where I can contribute to the organization while growing professionally.

OBJECTIVE Part-time employment in entry-level mechanical engineering position.

PROFESSIONAL OBJECTIVE
Immediate Goal. A part-time position in which my skills in engineering, mathematics, physics, and computer programming can be applied to problem solving.

Long-Term Goal. Research and development in aerospace/mechanical engineering.

PROFESSIONAL OBJECTIVE
Challenging position in chemical engineering. Special interest in computer-aided design and technical writing.

Education   Most applicants put this heading after objective. Certain information is essential: degrees you have earned or will earn, dates, institute awarding degree. Information you may want to add includes class standing schoolwide, class standing within major, grade point average within major, or grade point average overall, if any of these figures are to your advantage. Students who do not feel listing a grade point average is to their advantage often include instead courses which interested them or projects they completed on special assignment.

Information about high school education is optional. Students with exceptional achievements in high school or lower-level college students may want to include this listing. Usually, however, the longer the time since high school graduation, the less necessary the information.

Examples

EDUCATION   B.S., Mechanical Engineering (to be awarded June 1981)
State University at Hempstead
GPA: 3.0/4.0. Class standing: Top 25 percent

Meadowland High School, Richmond, Virginia (1973–1977)
Member, National Honor Society

EDUCATION   B.S., Industrial Engineering (expected June 1981)
Rochester Polytechnic Institute
Grade Point Average in Major: 3.2/4.0
Overall Grade Point Average: 3.0/4.0

EDUCATION   State University at Hempstead, Hempstead, New York
Received B.S.M.E. June 1981. My program included several graduate courses in machine analysis and in advanced mechanics and vibration. For my senior project I developed a Fortran software package for the analysis and design of machines incorporating four-bar linkage systems.

EDUCATION   Aerospace Engineering
1978–Present   State University at Hempstead
B.S. expected June 1983.
In addition to the aerospace sequence, I have taken electives in Fortran and PL/1.

Honors and Awards   This category follows education, and is optional. If you do not have information for this slot, simply omit it. If, however, you have honors and awards to announce, make sure you identify them clearly. Do not modestly announce you are the recipient of a Texas State Sp 3, and then leave the reader to figure out what the award means.

Instead, explain each honor explicitly.

Examples

HONORS AND AWARDS Dean's list, six semesters, 1978–1981.
Bronze medal, awarded by Long Island Math Fair, 1980, for project in heuristic learning using a computer program simulating a chess game.

Honors and Awards
State University of New York: Dean's list, 1978, 1979.
Member, Pi Tau Sigma, honorary mechanical engineering society
Member, Sigma Xi, honorary science society.

Special Skills   Some applicants place special skills immediately after career objective, since they want these to get maximum attention. Thus, for instance, if you have extensive programming ability and you want the interviewer to know this, the information may be made into a list and entered as a special skill. Others place the category after education since the subjects may be related. Some people omit the category entirely, using instead divisions such as "Extracurricular Activities" or "Interests."

Example

SPECIAL SKILLS   Programming ability: PL/1. PLC, PLAGO, Fortran. Minicomputer experience: PDP 8 and 11 Machine and Assembly. Microprocessor experience: Motorola M6800

Work Experience   Undergraduates typically put their education first and work experience second, since they usually have more of the former than the latter. Those with extensive job histories may prefer to put work experience first if the change in emphasis is advantageous.

It's customary to start with one's most recent job, and work back. Essential information for each job includes title, place of employment, and dates. Usually you'll want to follow this listing with a thumbnail sketch of your job, concentrating on the tasks for which you were responsible.

If you are an undergraduate, you may confront the problem

of deciding which part-time jobs to list, especially if none had a technical focus. If you have little or no technical experience, you might treat each of your part-time jobs individually, stressing your duties and responsibilities. While they may not be in your field, the jobs show your ability to apply yourself and can therefore serve a useful part in the résumé.

Examples

Work Experience

Summer 1981   Engineering aide
R & V Consulting Engineers
Worked on design and planning of power distribution and electrical equipment; performed calculations of electrical risers and loads; drafted various types of building plans, including electrical work.

Summer 1980   Office assistant
Bursar's Office, Polytechnic Institute
Entered statistical information into ledgers; pulled and filed cases for microfilming.

WORK EXPERIENCE

9/81–Present
Part-Time   Filing clerk, University Library, Akron University
Principal duties consist of putting away periodical files, books, and magazines, and clipping articles from newspapers and magazines.

9/81–Present
Part-Time   Crew member, Fast Food, Inc., Akron
Varied duties include working at register, cooking on grill, doing inventory, and working soda and dairy machines.

Summer 1981   College aide, Mathematics Department, Akron University
Light typing, diversified filing, telephone messages.

Professional and Extracurricular Activities   One student discovered at a job interview that his experience as business manager of the school newspaper was important to his prospective employer, who viewed it as useful training. That's not an unusual experience: professional and extracurricular activities are a relevant part of the résumé. The category in which you put campus or professional activities will vary according to your strengths. If, for instance, you have a mixture of professional activities, but few campus involvements, you may simply want to use the heading

"Activities." If you have something to say about each division, however, two separate headings would be better.

Examples

Activities

President, Student Chapter, American Society of Mechanical Engineers, 1980

Member, Co-op Program, State University of New York, 1978–1980

EXTRACURRICULAR ACTIVITIES

Member, Chinese Student Association; Member, Photography Club

Member, Student Chapter, Institute of Electrical and Electronics Engineers

In addition, I designed and built a solar electric generator as a project with three other members of the IEEE student chapter. We presented the generator at the Student Exposition on Energy Resources, 1979.

Other Interests or Abilities   What about your ability to speak and read Russian? that chess championship? your position in the Queensboro Orchestra? your interest in hiking? There is a place for these, too, on some résumés, usually near the end in a category such as "Special Interests" or "Other Activities." This category is, however, rarely used in a résumé designed for an academic position.

Personal Data   This is not required on résumés: there is no obligation to state date of birth, for instance, or marital status. You may, however, want to state your citizenship or the fact that you are willing to relocate.

References   Do not include the names and addresses of your references on the résumé. Instead, offer to furnish such information on request only.

Summary

The résumé should reflect you—who you are, where you've been, where you want to go. Its shape will emerge from the items you decide to stress. Graduate students, for instance, may rely heavily on courses that they took and the special projects they accomplished. On the other hand, an undergraduate in a co-op program who developed an extensive work experience may stress the category "Engineering Employment."

For an undergraduate, one page should be adequate; in fact, you will probably want to shape and mold the information to this handy length. Graduate students and those with longer histories of employment may find that their résumés expand with time, although they can usually be trimmed and shaped at all points so that they maintain a sharp focus.

If your typing or proofreading skills are weak, get a professional to type your résumé. Typing a résumé is not a job for an amateur. The appearance is important, and an electric typewriter produces a more uniform product just as a good copying machine produces more attractive duplicates. After you have the résumé typed professionally, proofread it carefully. Are the headings uniform? Or is one underlined and another not underlined? Are the dates accurate or were digits transposed? Is the spelling correct? If you can't proofread, ask a friend to do so before final corrections are made.

There is no need to have the résumé professionally printed. Typeset résumés, as well as such excesses as résumés on gilt-trimmed paper or brightly colored stock, are risky: there's a good chance you'll annoy rather than impress the reader. A crisp, straightforward presentation is the safe route, properly typed, proofread, and copied on a high-quality machine (preferably offset) that gives good definition to the reproduction.

Sample Résumés

RUTH CHIN
143 Wooster Street
New York, N.Y. 10024
(212) 643-4214

Career Objective

Entry-level position in mechancial engineering. Future educational goals include M.B.A. degree.

Education

B.S.M.E., State University of New York, Albany, N.Y., to be
    awarded June 1982.
    Grade Point Average: 3.2/4.0.

Engineering-Related Employment

American Motors. Body Engineering Specialist. Reviewed
    problem descriptions written by test engineers with
    design engineers to determine whether changes were
    necessary; managed reviews of prototype vehicles at
    various stages for design engineers. (Co-op program,
    Fall 1981).

American Motors. Engineering Assistant. Developed records
    of usage of high-strength, low-alloy steels in production
    vehicles; prepared summary of aluminum alloy usage.
    (Co-op program, Fall 1980).

Honors and Awards

Dean's List, 1979, 1980, 1981. State University of New York.
Member, Pi Tau Sigma, honorary mechanical engineering
    society.

Activities

Treasurer, Student Chapter, American Society of Mechanical Engineers, 1980.
Member, Co-op Program, State University of New York,
    1979–Present. (In this program, students with academic
    averages above 2.8 may be selected to work for one
    semester each year in an industrial job.)

RICHARD MARTINEZ
4412 Franklin Street
Richmond, Virginia 23226
(804) 285-1806

PROFESSIONAL OBJECTIVE
Summer position using my educational skills achieved in Aerospace Engineering.

EDUCATION
1978–Present

Aerospace Engineering, Virginia Technical College; B.S. expected June 1982.

In addition to the Aerospace sequence, I have also taken electives in Fortran and PL/1.

Cumulative Grade Point Average: 3.43/4.00.

1974–1978

St. Christopher's High School

National Honor Society; Science and Math Honors

Second Place: Virginia State High School Science Expo (1977) for nuclear energy display.

HONORS AND AWARDS
Mathematics Medal, 1981, State Virginia Technical College

Academic Scholarship, 1978–present; Virginia Technical College

Dean's List (1979–present)

WORK EXPERIENCE
Summer 1980

Engineering Assistant, Martin Abelow, Consulting Engineers, Inc.

Worked on design and planning of power distribution and electrical equipment layout; performed calculations of electrical risers and loads; drafted building plans.

Summer 1979

Laboratory Assistant, Laboratory of Professor N. Flannery, Virginia Technical College

Worked on debugging and simplifying computer programs.

PROFESSIONAL SOCIETIES
Member, American Institute of Aeronautics and Astronautics

Member, Sigma Gamma Tau (Aerospace Engineering Honor Society)

REFERENCES FURNISHED UPON REQUEST

This résumé is for a student applying for a writing position. He has had no professional experience, but has an excellent educational background. Therefore he's stressed his courses, picking out skills he learned that will make him employable. His part-time, nonwriting employment is listed but not stressed. This résumé is two pages instead of one.

RALPH KLEIN
42-19 Monument Avenue
Hillsdale, New York 11780
(516) 424-8113

Objective
Trainee position as science writer.

Education
M.S., Specialized Journalism
State University of New York, August 1981
Grade Point Average 3.75/4.00

B.S., Biology
Columbia University, June 1979
Grade Point Average 3.00/4.00

Major Courses and Topics Covered in Master's Program
Reporting on Medicine and Science Wrote weekly news stories based on original research in *New England Journal of Medicine*. Instructor: James Wright, Science Editor, *Globe*.

Advanced Science Reporting Wrote three feature-length articles based on interviews with experts. Instructor: Hilda Lief, Science Editor, *World Record*.

Graphics and Production Techniques Studied all aspects of printing, layout, and mechanicals. Instructor: Ralph Kincaid, Art Director, *Science Illustrated*.

Technical Report Writing Wrote abstracts, technical descriptions, and technical reports. Instructor: Dr. William Schmidt, State University of New York.

Medical Public Relations Took comprehensive course including press releases, press conferences, and related literature.

Instructor: Professor R. Zdanowicz, President, Z-R Associates.

Special Project   Prepared a medical public relations kit for a genetic engineering company. Kit included press releases, interviews, outline for a press conference, and background information.

Related Science and Math Courses

As an undergraduate, I took courses in genetics, embryology, cell biology, and cell physiology; three semesters of math (calculus and statistics); three semesters of physics; six semesters of chemistry (organic and physical). I also took one semester of Fortran. While an undergraduate, I worked as a laboratory assistant for Dr. Melmer on biochemical research to determine protein molecular weights.

Part-Time Employment

Manager
Radio Shack, Lafayette (August 1978–Present)
Duties   Taking care of cash, supervising part-time help, maintaining quick and reliable service to customers, and ordering supplies for next business day.

This résumé was written as part of an application for a summer job by a student with no technical experience. Accordingly, she presented her part-time jobs in a way designed to emphasize the skills she did acquire.

JUDITH BERGSTEIN
4113 Sheldon Drive
Alexandria, Virginia 22312
(703) 484-1111

Professional Interest

    Aerospace Engineering

Education

1980–Present   B.S. Candidate in Aerospace Engineering, Virginia Technical Institute.
    Major courses completed: Calculus, Physics, Graphics, Statics, Dynamics, and Fortran IV. College Average: B.

1976–1980   St. Gertrude's Graduate. Concentration in mathematics.
    Class standing: Top 20 percent

Work Experience

1980–Present   Virginia Savings Bank
    Part-time teller
    Learning basic banking procedures and how to work under pressure.

Summer 1979   Millers Department Store
    Salesperson
    Did pricing, stocking, and inventory. Learned how to relate to people courteously.

This résumé was prepared by a senior prior to scheduling of job interviews.

RICHARD WEBSTER

Academic Address	*Permānent Address*
590 Pride Avenue	43 West Eighth Street
Redwood City, California	Los Angeles, California
Telephone (714) 434-1212	Telephone: (213) 866-8012

Objective

A career in industrial engineering in which I can contribute to the organization while growing professionally.

Education

1979–Present   California Polytechnic
Redwood City, California
Bachelor of Science in Industrial Engineering—June 1982
Average in Major 3.4/4.0. California Polytechnic Scholarship recipient. Earned 85 percent of educational expenses.

Honors and Activities

Vice-President, Student Chapter of American Institute for Industrial Engineers at California Polytechnic.
Member, Tau Beta Pi, Industrial Engineering Society.
Dean's List each academic semester.

Employment

1979–Present   Management Trainee in Industrial Engi-
(Part-time)   neering
Charles Lee, Inc.
Devised and recommended plans which increased productivity; prepared volume forecasts and cost control reports.

1979–Present   College aide, Department of Management,
(Part-time)   California Polytechnic.
Assist in office operations; light typing.

Personal

United States Citizen
Fluent in English and German.
Extensive travel in Germany and Austria.

This résumé was prepared by a college junior seeking a summer job.

LUCILLE HASTINGS
441 Court Street
Scotch Plains, New Jersey 07076
Telephone (609) 484-1234

Professional Objective

Immediate Goal Part-time position in which my skills in engineering, mathematics, physics, and computer programming can be applied to problem solving.

Ultimate Goal Research and development in interrelated problems of aerospace and mechanical engineering.

Education

College New York College, 1979–Present
Program in aerospace engineering
GPA: 3.00/4.00

High School St. Mary Woods, 1974–1978.
Member, National Honor Society.

College Activities

Student member, American Institute of Aeronautics and Astronautics
Radio Club
National Society of Black Engineers

Employment

Spring–Summer 1979 Graphics Assistant. RW Associates, Inc.
Light drafting and pictorial representations of products

Spring–Summer 1978 Parham Community Library Assistant
Light typing and filing; originated community bulletin board.

Special Skills

Proficiency in Fortran.

Appendixes

Appendices

A

Keeping a Laboratory Notebook

I especially recommend the writing of those who are expounding difficult subjects and are determined to make themselves understood.

P. B. Medawar

In 1959, Gordon Gould filed an application for a laser patent. But he didn't get it. Instead, in 1960, Charles Townes and his brother-in-law, Arthur Schawlow, were awarded the basic laser patent.

Gould went to court, claiming he was the inventor of the laser and therefore entitled to the rights. Gould's challenge was based in part on a page from his research notebook. The page had a sketch, a statement of the main idea, and a derivation of the acronym LASER—light amplication of stimulated emission of radiation.

In October 1977, after a series of litigated oppositions, Gould was granted a patent for optically pumped laser amplifiers. The world market has been estimated at between $100 and $200 million.

323

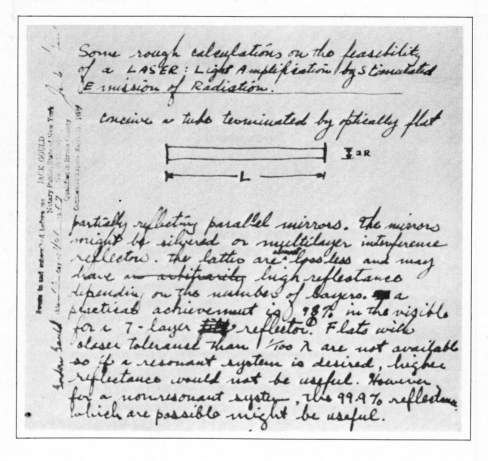

Gould's case is one example of the role of notebooks in patent law. Notebooks serve as valuable documents:

1. They are vehicles for organizing and focusing the thinking of the writer.
2. They are primary records in patent law.
3. They provide complete, accurate records of ongoing work.
4. They are receptacles for detailed procedural information that may not be available in highly compressed journal articles.

They may also protect not only the inventor but the public as well. If properly maintained, they are a record of success and failure, a safeguard against error and carelessness in such important areas as the testing of drugs and chemicals.

For Authentication: Purpose and Format

If you plan on using a notebook to authenticate a discovery, you'll need to develop an orderly method for entering the information. It's true that some people jot down their notes on table napkins and the backs of interoffice memos. This may be the only way if inspiration strikes during a business lunch or in the middle of a meeting. But the method has serious drawbacks for those planning to submit records in court. And the situation is not far-fetched. In a laboratory, patents are always a possibility. If you have an idea—and you want to prove it is yours exclusively—you'll need proper documents.

To satisfy demands for a first instance of invention, the notebook typically should supply this information:

Conception of invention, date, name of persons
First sketch or drawing
First written description
First disclosure to others
First test of invention

The manner in which the information is entered and witnessed—the format—is extremely important in laboratory notebooks.

General requirements for the format are summed up in the well-known *Good Laboratory Practice* (GLP) regulations of the Food and Drug Administration. Here is the GLP protocol [1]:

> All data generated during the conduct of a nonclinical laboratory study, except those that are generated by direct computer output, shall be recorded directly, promptly and legibly in ink. All data entries shall be dated on the day of entry and signed or initialed by the person entering the data. Any change in entries shall be made so as not to obscure the original entry, shall indicate the reason for such change, and shall be dated and signed or identified at the time of the change.

Exact procedures vary from company to company. However, there are general guidelines that you can follow despite slight variations within particular industries:

1. Use a *bound* notebook. Loose-leaf pages are not acceptable.
2. Make sure that the pages are *numbered in advance*.
3. *Do not remove any pages* or any part of a page. Pages missing

from a notebook will seriously weaken a case in the Patent Office or a case that goes to court for litigation.

4. Record all entries directly and legibly in solvent-resistant black ink.

5. *Do not leave blank spaces on any page.* Instead, draw either diagonal lines or a cross through any portion of the page you do not use.

6. Date and sign what you have written *on the day of entry.* In addition, most companies require that each notebook page be read, signed, and dated by a *qualified witness,* one who is not directly involved in the work performed, but who understands the purpose of the experiment and results obtained.

7. Extra materials such as graphs and charts should be inserted, signed, and witnessed in the same way as other entries.

8. *Never use correction fluid or pasteovers of any kind.* If you decide to correct an error, place a single line through the mistake, sign and date the correction, and give a reason for the error. Use a cross-reference if necessary. However, even the practice of drawing a line through numbers entered in error is discouraged in many companies. Instead, workers are asked simply to make a new entry correcting the error when this is possible.

In a University Setting

E. Bright Wilson tells the story of the astronomer Le Monnier, who observed Uranus several times before its identification as a planet by Herschel. Le Monnier saw Uranus, but decided it was a fixed star, not a planet. "This," Wilson points out, "was probably due in part to the fact that he wrote his measurements on scraps of paper, including a paper bag originally containing hair powder" [2].

This anecdote points up the importance of laboratory notebooks in research groups. Here they are perceived primarily not for their uses in patent law but as devices scientists should use for their own good, since notebooks are far more reliable than either their memories or odd bits of paper.

There may, of course, be the issue of a patent; and in this case, entries should be witnessed and care taken with materials added at a later date.

However, in a university setting, notebooks often function primarily as the natural spot to record daily events within the framework of long-range goals. For instance, a researcher may spend two or three days preparing a compound prior to the actual experiment, or a week doing laboratory work for a blood-clotting material. Details of the work will not appear in the published paper, which will of necessity be short. Indeed, the most telescoped section of such papers is often the procedure. Yet there may be some detail of manipulation or apparatus of interest to another worker.

The laboratory notebook is the perfect place to enter all details of procedure. They can then be indexed for other students or workers by volume and page number. Entries and references should be such that, years later, it is possible to tell what apparatus was used and under what circumstances.

In some research laboratories, the director and staff prepare an annual report based on the notebooks. Each person is responsible for abstracting different major headings from the notebooks. However, the key to using notebooks efficiently in this way is a proper table of contents. Otherwise, it's very difficult to retrieve the information. To guarantee a good table of contents, most labs leave the first 10 or 20 pages blank, with the formal log commencing on page 11 or 21. The table of contents is maintained each day, or after a series of similar experiments is completed. The usual format is a list kept in the front by subject and page number. This relatively simple procedure will save a great deal of time later when the search begins for a piece of information.

What to Include

The question of what should be entered and what omitted is crucial. In determining the answer, Wilson points out that, "it should be extremely salutary . . . trying to figure out something from another's book. All references to apparatus, places, times, books, papers, graphs, and people should be sufficiently explicit to be understandable years later" [3].

He adds that it should be possible to take "each scientific paper and show just where every figure, description or statement in it is backed up by original observations in the laboratory notebook, and exactly why the final and original numbers differ, if they do."

The notebook is not a place for polished writing. Don't, for instance, enter recalculated data. Rather, enter data in its primary form. In one laboratory, for instance, a worker had the habit of performing all the calculations separately, and then entering only results. This made it difficult to detect error that was the result, for instance, of digits transposed during a calculation.

Instead, be as detailed as possible so that someone else can duplicate what you've done by reading your account. This means putting in the contradictions as well as the successes. If there is a conflict, enter a description of it rather than omit it. The negative results may be important for another worker at another time.

Summary

Pasteur is credited with saying that "chance favors the prepared mind."

For many people, writing serves to prepare their minds, for when they know they will soon need to write, they become more observant. And when they begin to write, they find that the writing itself helps to organize and shape their thinking.

You may be able to use a notebook to develop a prepared mind: it's a natural place in a laboratory to allow writing to help crystallize understanding.

It may also be useful as a journal or *aide mémoire*. The journal is enshrined as a technique for many literary writers. It is here that they record details that later turn out to have significance, here that many look to refresh their memories. The same functions can be served by a scientific notebook—to capture a thought that might otherwise be forgotten, to hold a full and accurate rendition of events.

If properly kept, notebooks save time in the laboratory. They can be the local reference for procedures, for instructions, for recipes that are too complicated and lengthy to be affixed to small bottles—for dozens of necessary details that may be handily recorded, indexed, and retrieved.

Literature Cited

1. "Good Laboratory Practice Regulations," Nonclinical Laboratory Studies, *Federal Register*, vol. 43, no. 247, December 22, 1978, p. 58.185.
2. E. Bright Wilson, Jr., *An Introduction to Scientific Research*, McGraw-Hill, New York, 1975, p. 130.
3. Ibid., p. 132.

Exercises

1. In the library, locate copies of the notebooks of Leonardo da Vinci. How do these serve as a scientist's notebook? Give examples.
2. In the library, locate copies of Faraday's notebooks. Choose a selection and discuss how the author uses his journals as a record of his observations. Give examples.
3. If you are a member of a research group, choose a major heading from the laboratory notebook and then prepare an abstract based on this heading.
4. If you are a member of a research group, make a copy of the table of contents of your current laboratory notebook. Is it adequate? Discuss strengths and weaknesses.
5. If you presently keep a notebook, bring a copy of several pages to class (unless the notebook is confidential). In a group, discuss the criteria you used to determine whether or not to enter information.

B

Prosefalls

Only use semicolons; to connect independent clauses.
Old Saying

Here is a quick test of grammar and usage. All examples are taken verbatim from technical reports written either by under-graduates or by working engineers and scientists. Can you spot the mistakes? (Answers appear at the end of the chapter.)

1. Furthermore, the ratio of carvone to menthone, which is directly related to the levels of spearmint leaf and pepper-mint leaf in the blend was not consistent with the predicted control batch value.

2. Two samples were received for analysis; one from batch 29 that had low flavor, and another from batch 27 that was organoleptically acceptable.

3. Mydrex 100 is more stable to oxygen than the current frying oil, Mydrex 100/500, therefore, both oils are compared in the experiment.

4. Stringent as always, the human cell vaccine is only in its testing stage by the FDA.

5. The job fair is a means by which students can compliment their on-campus interviews through direct contact with company representatives.

6. When aiming the timing light at timing marks, be careful of the turning fan, also keep all wires away from the fan.

7. I would like to thank the following people for the many hours they afforded me during my visit; Mr. J. Lee, Plant Engineer, Ms. S. Shaw, Quality Control Supervisor, and Ms. M. Bright, Chemist.

8. The devices include pump sprays, Freon aerosols, pressurized rubber balloons and hydrocarbon propellants. The last was initially considered most promising, but they are flammable and incompatible with food products.

9. The administration building, with its dingy windows and deep‚ gray paint, house the administrative offices, including the infamous "fishbowl."

10. Roger's Hall was once a razor blade factory, and this accounts for it's seamy appearance.

Affect or *effect*? *The series is* or *The series are*? This chapter offers a troubleshooter's guide to common mistakes in grammar, punctuation, and usage. The chapter is not comprehensive; rather, it is a list of those errors encountered most persistently in undergraduate and professional writing.

Included are four pitfalls of grammar—modification, subject-verb agreement, antecedent agreement, and parallelism; trouble spots in the use of semicolons, colons, dashes, parentheses, apostrophes, and quotation marks; distinctions in the use of numbers written as words or as symbols; and 10 usage demons.

Grammar: Four Trouble Spots

1.1 Misplaced Modifiers   A misplaced modifier is a word, phrase, or clause placed so that it modifies the wrong word.

Wrong	*Right*
In our laboratory we have developed a new material for the space program that is polymeric.	In our laboratory we have developed a new polymeric material for the space program.

To avoid this solecism, keep modifiers as close as possible to the words they modify. In the above example, for instance, the clause *that is polymeric* modifies *material*, not *space program*.

Dangling participles are the most common instances of misplaced modifiers, although adjectival phrases, prepositional phrases, and appositives can also be dangled. Such phrases are said to dangle if they fail to modify the subject of the sentence.

Wrong	*Right*
To be considered for a job, a typing test must be taken.	To be considered for a job, applicants must take a typing test.
Long a mecca for conservationists, we are all concerned about the severe cutbacks in funds and services the Jamaica Bay Wildlife Refuge has suffered recently.	Long a mecca for conservationists, the Jamaica Bay Wildlife Refuge has suffered a severe cutback in funds and services—a situation that concerns us greatly.

There are, however, acceptable danglers in technical writing; that is, there are cases where the reference is so general that the introductory phrase does not have to agree with the subject. For example, the following sentence is acceptable.

Substituting in Equation (3-5), $x = a + c$.

1.2 Subject-Verb Agreement   A verb should agree in number with its subject. In other words, if the subject is plural, the verb should be plural.

If you have trouble, (1) imagine the subject next to the verb, (2) ignore any intervening phrases, (3) decide whether the subject is singular or plural, and (4) match the verb to the subject.

Consider the following examples:

Wrong	*Right*
The tedium of commuting—the long waits for trains, the unexplained failures and delays, the endless peering down the tracks—*are* familiar to all those who live on the periphery of the city.	The tedium of commuting—the long waits for trains, the unexplained failures and delays, the endless peering down the tracks—*is* familiar to all those who live on the periphery of the city.
In the library *is* a well-lit work area, tables and chairs, and recent periodicals.	In the library *are* a well-lit work area, tables and chairs, and recent periodicals.

The value of the gases *are* measured by the oxygenator bypass every 20 minutes.	The value of the gases *is* measured by the oxygenator bypass every 20 minutes.

Words such as *contents, couple, group, dozen, number, series, majority,* and *pair* are collective nouns. When a collective noun refers to the group as a whole, it takes a singular verb.

Wrong	*Right*
The series *have* been arranged in order of decreasing size.	The series *has* been arranged in order of decreasing size.

If you use *each* or *every* to modify the subject, use a singular verb.

Wrong	*Right*
Each desk and chair *come* with a lamp.	Each desk and chair *comes* with a lamp.

Use a singular verb with or/nor constructions.

Wrong	*Right*
A good lamp or overhead light *were* necessary.	A good lamp or overhead light *was* necessary.

1.3 Antecedent Agreement Pronouns should match the words to which they refer (antecedents). Thus, if the antecedent is plural, the pronoun should be plural. If the antecedent is singular, the pronoun should be singular.

Wrong	*Right*
With *their* dingy windows and deep gray paint, the administration building houses the Bursar and the Registrar.	With *its* dingy windows and deep gray paint, the administration building houses the Bursar and the Registrar.

1.4 Parallel Construction In parallel construction, all of the items in the series have the same grammatical form. Here is an example of parallel form; the author is William Harvey:

The organ is seen now to move, now to be at rest; there is a time when it moves, and a time when it is motionless.

In the first clause, the phrases "to move" and "to be at rest" are parallel because they are expressed in the same grammatical form—in this case, they are both infinitives. In the second clause, "when it moves" and "when it is motionless" are parallel.

The organ is seen *now to move*
　　　　　　　now to be at rest

There is *a time when it moves,* and
　　　　　　a time when it is motionless.

Items joined by *and, or, nor, but, not only . . . but also, both/and, either/or, neither/nor* should be parallel.

Wrong	*Right*
A time not for action but words.	A time not for action but for words.
	not　　　*for action*
	but　　　*for words*
A skilled manager not only works well with his staff, but also he does not compromise his values.	A skilled manager not only works well with his staff but also does not compromise his values.
	not only　　*works* well with staff
	but also　　*does not compromise* his values.

Use parallel construction in definitions:

Wrong	*Right*
To corrode is wearing away.	To corrode is to wear away.

Use parallel construction for items in a series. Thus, either use an article before all items in a list, or before the first item only.

Wrong	*Right*
The procedure, the results, conclusions, and recommendations.	The procedure, the results, the conclusions, and the recommendations.
	or
	The procedure, results, conclusions, and recommendations.
To observe, to classify, deduce —these are great pleasures for the scientist.	To observe, to classify, to deduce—these are great pleasures for the scientist.
	or
	To observe, classify, deduce— these are great pleasures for the scientist.

If you use a simple outline format in your reports or memos, keep the items in parallel form. In the left-hand column of the following example, items A and B are phrases; C is a complete sentence. Correct so that either all three items are phrases or all three items are sentences.

Wrong	*Right*
Program Advantages	The program will provide these advantages:
A. Intensive exposure to new speakers from many disciplines	A. Intensive exposure to new speakers from many disciplines
B. An enhanced reputation for the sponsoring agency	B. Enhanced reputation for the sponsoring agency
C. The ultimate goal of increased sales will be realized.	C. Increased sales

or

Program Advantages
A. There will be intensive exposure to new speakers.
B. The sponsoring agency will derive an enhanced reputation.
C. The ultimate goal of increased sales will be realized.

Punctuation

2.1 Apostrophe

1. Use *'s* to form the possessive of singular nouns.

   Polytechnic's courtyard.

2. Usage varies if the noun ends in a sibilant sound (the sound of a *s* or *z*). In most cases, simply add *'s*.

   The waitress's table
   Louise's book

   But there are exceptions. To form the possessive of names ending in a sibilant sound, the style in technical writing is to add only the apostrophe.

   Gauss' equations
   Bayes' theorem
   Stokes' law

3. Use only the apostrophe to form the possessive of plural nouns ending in *s* or *es*.

   Two months' delay

   For all other plural nouns, add *'s*.

   The children's department.

4. It's = it + is. *It's* is a contraction of *it* plus *is*. Some people confuse *it's*, the contraction, with *its*, the personal pronoun. The latter, like other personal pronouns *your, our, their*, does not require an apostrophe to form the possessive.

   If you have trouble with this construction, replace *its/it's* with the words "it is." Does the resulting sentence make sense? If not, use the possessive, *not* the contraction.

2.2 Colon   The colon is used properly as a salutation in letters and to set off long quotations. It is also used correctly in sentences where it has the sense of *as follows*. There is one peculiarity of its usage that surprises some students. It cannot be used directly after the verb *to be* or after a preposition. Instead, it must be separated from the verb *to be* by a phrase such as *as follows* or *as shown in the following*.

Wrong	*Right*
The people on the team were: George Sanders, research operations; Henry Pilar, computer science; Ruth Smalow, biochemistry.	The people on the team were as follows: George Sanders, research operations; Henry Pilar, computer science; Ruth Smalow, biochemistry.
	or
	The following people were on the team: George Sanders, research operations; Henry Pilar, computer science; Ruth Smalow, biochemistry.
The meetings were held at: Evanston, Illinois; Cedar Rapids, Iowa; and Sioux City, Iowa.	The meetings were held at Evanston, Illinois; Cedar Rapids, Iowa; and Sioux City, Iowa.

2.3 Commas

1. Use commas to set off nonrestrictive clauses. A nonrestrictive clause is parenthetical. It gives information but is not essential. If it is deleted, the sentence will still be meaningful. In

contrast, if a restrictive clause is deleted, the meaning of the sentence is greatly altered. Beginning writers tend to put in the first comma in nonrestrictive clauses but to omit the second one.

Wrong

Furthermore, the ratio of carvone to menthone, which is directly related to the level of spearmint leaf and peppermint leaf in the blend was not consistent with the predicted or control batch value.

Right

Furthermore, the ratio of carvone to menthone, which is directly related to the level of spearmint leaf and peppermint leaf in the blend, was not consistent with the predicted or control batch value.

2. Do not use a comma to connect independent clauses.

Wrong

Whem aiming the timing light at timing marks, be careful of the turning fan, also keep all wires away from the fan.

Right

When aiming the timing light at timing marks, be careful of the turning fan; also keep all wires away from the fan.

"Also keep all wires away from the fan" is an independent clause. If necessary, it could exist as a sentence by itself. Do not connect independent clauses with commas. Instead, either (1) use a period, or (2) use a semicolon if the two independent clauses are closely connected in meaning.

Wrong

The activity on bromopyruvate was decreased, however, the activity on pyruvate was enhanced.

Right

The activity on bromopyruvate was decreased; however, the activity on pyruvate was enhanced.

"However, the activity on pyruvate was enhanced" is an independent clause. Either make two separate sentences, or connect the two independent clauses with a semicolon.

3. Use a comma to separate three or more items, phrases, or clauses in a series. The final or serial comma before *and/or/nor* is optional, but you should be consistent in whatever style you choose. Either of the following is correct.

The samples from batch 27, from batch 29, and from batch 31 were received for analysis.

The samples from batch 27, from batch 29 and from batch 31 were received for analysis.

4. Use a comma in a compound sentence to separate long independent clauses joined by *and/or/nor/but*.

> Most people request references in bibliographic form, and it is cheaper to have these delivered off-line than to have the citation list printed on-line.

The comma is optional if the sentences are short.

5. Use a comma to set off introductory dependent clauses.

> When introducing the model and unit, please specify the brand.

6. As a rule, use commas between adjectives preceding a noun when each adjective modifies the noun independently—that is, when you could, if you wished, use the word *and* between the adjectives.

> A complex, detailed procedure

(The procedure is complex *and* detailed.)

In technical writing, however, you'll often find that commas are omitted in strings of adjectives preceding nouns.

> a 5-hp 230-V dc shunt motor

2.4 Dashes   These useful punctuation marks can function as weak colons or as strong parentheses. (In typescript a dash is indicated by typing two hyphens, not one.)

1. You may use dashes for technical definitions inserted within general text, as shown in the following examples.

> Using integrated circuits—tiny slices of pure silicone embedded with traces of impurities—engineers condensed the functions of a roomful of vacuum-tube equipment into a portable plastic box.
>
> Users can buy their games packaged on ready-to-use tapes or "floppy disks"—circles of flexible Mylar plastic that record programs much like tapes but allow easier access—or they can program their own games using books or their imagination.
>
> Ellen Ruppel Shell

2. You may use dashes to set off parenthetical phrases if you wish to lend them more emphasis than if they were either enclosed in parentheses or set off by commas.

> If he insists upon visiting the plant—and I hope he won't—then please let me know well in advance.

> Diesel particulates have been shown to cause mutations in human cells—an effect linked to cancer—and indeed some believe that unless its emissions can be better controlled, the diesel is in danger of being legislated out of existence.
>
> John Heywood

3. You may use dashes to set off parenthetical remarks with commas within them.

> It was a three-step procedure—first at Lindenwood, New Jersey, then in Ravenwood Laboratory, and finally at Englewood Cliffs—and it took several years to develop.

4. You may use dashes to set off a summary statement.

> Step one in Lindenwood, step two at the Fairbanks plant, step three in Englewood—these are the routine stages in the process.

2.5 Parentheses   Use parentheses for technical definitions, figure citations, acronyms, abbreviations, and asides.

> In the course of a heart attack (myocardial infarction), the damaged muscle cells release specific isoenzymes.

> Combustion is fast, permitting much of the exhaust gas to be recirculated to reduce combustion temperatures and consequent emission of nitrogen oxides (NO_x).

> The scientific investigation of UFOs (unidentified flying objects) continues.

> The Footsie (see Figure 1) is a red, plastic children's toy.

2.6 Quotation Marks   Do not use quotation marks to appear quaint or colloquial. Do not use quotation marks to apologize for your choice of language. If you are uneasy about an expression, omit it. Putting quotation marks around the word or words will not solve the problem. For example, the following sentences illustrate an ineffective use of quotation marks.

> Please forgive the hastiness of this report. The deadline "caught me with my pants down."

> Some people may find this information "old hat," but I think it has applicability.

Use quotation marks, however, for inexact usage that helps you to make your point.

> Skilled writers refer to this situation as "data poisoning."

2.7 Semicolon

1. If you wish, use a semicolon to separate independent clauses if the information is connected logically. Consider the following example from Twain's *Huckleberry Finn.*

> After supper she got out her book and learned me about Moses and the Bulrushers and I was in a sweat to find out all about him; but by and by she let it out that Moses had been dead a considerable long time; so then I didn't care no more about him, because I don't take no stock in dead people.

2. Use a semicolon to separate phrases or clauses that have commas within them.

Confusing	*Clearer*
Attending the meeting were V. S. Anderson, Vice President, Elliot Arnold, Second Vice President, Citizen's Bank, Enold James, Chemist, Metropolitan Transit Authority.	Attending the meeting were V. S. Anderson, Vice President; Elliot Arnold, Second Vice President, Citizen's Bank; Enold James, Chemist, Metropolitan Transit Authority.
The units were 300 mm deep, 200, 300, or 400 mm long, and 250 mm high.	The units were 300 mm deep; 200, 300, or 400 mm long; and 250 mm high.

3. Do not use a semicolon to stand for the words *as follows*. If you can use these words, the correct punctuation is a colon.

Wrong	*Right*
Two samples were received for analysis; one from batch 29 having low flavor, and another from batch 27 that was organoleptically acceptable.	Two samples were received for analysis: one from batch 29 having low flavor, and another from batch 27 that was organoleptically acceptable.

Ten Usage Demons

3.1 Affect/Effect

Effect (noun) = result
Effect (verb) = to cause; to bring about
Affect (verb) = to act upon

Effect is the noun. One way to remember this is to think about the classic couple, cause-effect, both of which are nouns.

Light has an *effect* on matter.
The high-intensity light beam did not *affect* the substance.
The laser beam did not *effect* a change in the substance.

3.2 Complement/Compliment

To compliment = to praise
To complement = to complete or balance

The staff *complimented* us on our performance.
Two angles are *complementary* if, when put together, they form a
straight line.
If two *complementary* colors are merged, the result is white
light.

3.3 Continual/Continuous

Continuous = Uninterrupted
Continual = Done in rapid, but not necessarily unbroken, succes-
sion

Most movies have *continuous* showings.
Variables can be either *continuous* or discrete.
His work record was plagued by *continual* absence.

3.4 These data/This data *Data* is the plural of *datum* and
generally takes a plural verb.

These data were obtained through a series of experiments.

3.5 Fewer/Lesser *Few* is used with that which can be counted. *Less* is used with amount or degree.

Fewer students will enroll in colleges in the 1980s, and therefore
there will be less income for the universities.
Those with fewer than eight packages may use the express line.

3.6 Further/Farther *Farther* refers to physical distance. *Further* is used for argument, for degree, and for time.

We need to move farther from the city.
We need to investigate the issue further.

3.7 i.e./e.g.

i.e. = abbreviation of Latin *id est*, "that is to say"
e.g. = abbreviation of Latin *exempli gratia*, "for example"

The overall air-fuel ratio of such a stratified charge engine is considerably higher (i.e., the mixture is leaner) than in a conventional gas engine.

3.8 Imply/Infer

Imply = suggest
Infer = conclude

The speaker implies, the hearer infers.

He implied Tulley was responsible for the poor handling of waste disposal.

From his manner, I inferred his intense disapproval of Tulley's toxic waste policy.

3.9 Principle/Principal

Principle (noun) = a rule, law, or code of conduct
Principal (adjective) = most important
Principal (noun) = leader, head, person in authority

Her *principles* are said to be uncompromising.
He is the *principal* investigator in the project.
She is said to be a *principled principal* investigator.

3.10 Unique

Unique = one of a kind

An object either is or is not unique. The subject does not admit such qualifications as *very unique, quite unique, virtually unique*, or *pretty unique*.

Numbers: Numerals or Spelled Form?

According to one chemist, the best rule of thumb is "Almost everything is written with a numeral."

In practice, most numbers in technical and scientific writing are expressed in numerals. There is only a handful of cases where this practice is not followed:

1. If a number begins a sentence, write it as a word. If the number beginning the sentence is accompanied by a unit of measure, both should be spelled.

Wrong	*Right*
5 mg was added.	Five milligrams was added.
14 people attended.	Fourteen people attended.

If you don't like beginning with a written number, recast the sentence.

There were 14 people at the meeting.
I added 5 mg.

2. If you have two adjacent numbers, spell one of them.

Wrong	*Right*
5 5-W bulbs	Five 5-W bulbs
143 3d Avenue	143 Third Avenue

3. Consult a stylebook in your field for rules on numbers without units. For nontechnical matter any number below 100 (if not accompanied by a unit of measurement) is usually written out; for technical matter words are used for any number under 10. Many publications follow this rule: Use words for any number under 10 (cardinal or ordinal) that is not followed by a unit of measurement.

Wrong	*Right*
Only 1 came.	Only one came.

If you do have two numbers in the same sentence, however, remember to cast them in the same form.

Wrong	*Right*
The second and 18th tests were successful.	The second and eighteenth tests were successful.

Exercises

Correct these sentences.

1. There is an automatic brake system which has 2 backup systems on its own, so there is no way the elevators could free fall more than a few feet without the automatic brake stopping it.

2. Stopping at every floor, it takes 10 minutes to ascend to the eighth floor and back down to the lobby 3 times; or about

3:33 minutes for a round trip, and these calculations are based on the elevator which is the fastest in the bank.

3. I would change the controls making all the elevators fully automatic, then I would change the motors.

4. Although he did state that the plan for modification of all the elevators was in process, he could not give farther details.

5. The school is in a converted factory, and the elevator with many passengers jammed in at the peak times between classes are noted for overcrowding.

6. Polytechnics' courtyard is quite small.

7. After adjusting the timing, tighten the distribution locking screw, then repeat Step 2 as a check.

8. Do not grasp the stick, hold it lightly between the thumb and fingers.

9. The second step is most important, start at one side of the fixture.

10. The handset has two perforated ends, one contains a microphone and the other has a speaker.

11. Start by inserting AR1 then bring the same end through BL 1.

12. Crossing into Tennessee, Nashville was nearer.

13. His reasons for declining were the following: the overwhelming size of the debt; that the company was mismanaged; and finally he had so little time to do the job.

14. After carefully stirring the interphase, nuclei were pelleted by centrifugation.

15. Upon breaking out the case of sherry, the first bottle emptied in a flash.

16. Instead of losing your reader in a welter of detail, he is introduced gradually and logically to the subject.

17. The series have been set for the week of 8 April.

18. An intensive program of 65 courses are offered this semester.

19. The mail arrives through rain, sleet, and through snow.

20. As soon as we met, I realized she was intelligent, lively, and she worked hard.

21. He worked not only on reapportionment legislation, but also was an ardent reformer of voting rights.

Here is a quotation from Bertrand Russell. Which phrases are parallel? Why do you think the author used parallel form in this way?

That Man is the product of causes which had no prevision of the end they were achieving; that his origin, his growth, his hopes and fears, his loves and his beliefs, are but the outcome of accidental collocations of atoms; that no fire, no heroism, no intensity of thought and feeling, can preserve an individual life beyond the grave; that all the labors of the ages, all the devotion, all the inspiration, all the noonday brightness of human genius, are destined to extinction in the vast death of the solar system; and that the whole temple of Man's achievement must inevitably be buried beneath the debris of a universe in ruins—all these things, if not quite beyond dispute, are yet so nearly certain, that no philosophy which rejects them can hope to stand. Only within the scaffolding of these truths, only on the firm foundation of unyielding despair, can the soul's habitation henceforth be safely built.

Test Answers

1. Furthermore, the ratio of carvone to menthone, which is directly related to the levels of spearmint leaf and peppermint leaf in the blend, was not consistent with the predicted control batch value.

   Rule: Use commas to set off nonrestrictive clauses. See Section 2.3.

2. Two samples were received for analysis: one from batch 29 that had low flavor, and another from batch 27 that was organoleptically acceptable.

   Rule: Use a colon in the sense of *as follows*. See Section 2.2.

3. Mydrex 100 is more stable to oxygen than the current frying oil, Mydrex 100/500; therefore, both oils are compared in the experiment.

   Rule: Do not use a comma to connect independent clauses. See Section 2.3.

4. Rewrite sentence so that the phrase *stringent as always* is followed by *the FDA*. A possible answer is as follows: "Stringent as always, the FDA is only beginning its tests of the human cell vaccine."

   Rule: Place modifiers as close as possible to the words they modify. See Section 1.1.

5. The job fair is a means by which students can complement their on-campus interviews through direct contact with company representatives.

   Rule: *To compliment* is "to praise." *To complement* is "to balance." See Section 3.2.

6. When aiming the timing light at timing marks, be careful of the turning fan; also keep all wires away from the fan.

   Rule: Do not connect independent clauses with a comma. See Section 2.3.

7. I would like to thank the following people for the many hours they afforded me during my visit: Mr. J. Lee, Plant Engineer; Ms. S. Shaw, Quality Control Supervisor; and Ms. M. Bright, Chemist.

   Rules: (1) Use a colon in the sense of *as follows.* (2) Use a semicolon to separate phrases or clauses that have commas within them. See Sections 2.2 and 2.7.

8. The devices include pump sprays, freon aerosols, pressurized rubber balloons, and hydrocarbon propellants. The last were initially considered most promising, but they are flammable and incompatible with food products.

   Rule: Verbs should agree in number with the subject. See Section 1.2.

9. The administration building, with its dingy windows and deep gray paint, houses the administrative offices, including the infamous "fishbowl."

   Rule: Verbs should agree in number with the subject. See Section 1.2.

10. Roger's Hall was once a razor blade factory, and this accounts for its seamy appearance.

    Rule: Personal pronouns (your, it, our, their) do not require an apostrophe to form the possessive. See Section 2.1.

Index

Abstracting and indexing services, 108, 125, 129–138
Abstraction, 6
Abstracts, 159–178
    commercial, 169–171
    definition of, 160
    format of, 160
    indicative, 161
    informative, 161–164
    in journal reports, 192, 193
    in laboratory notebooks, 327, 329
    in memo reports, 189–190
    in proposals, 242
    purpose of, 159–160
    samples of, 164–169, 185
Acknowledgments, 187
Acronyms, 5–6, 30
Adjectives:
    in physical description, 45
    in process description, 47
    punctuation of, 338
Affect, effect, 340–341
Agreement:
    of pronoun and antecedent, 333
    of subject and verb, 332–333
Ambiguity, 4–5
Analogy, 86–87, 92, 102
Analysis by function (see Process description)
Analysis by structure (see Physical description)
Antecedent, agreement with pronoun, 333
Apostrophe, used in possessive, 335–336
Appendixes, 189, 194

Aristotle, 145
Audience analysis:
    in instructions, 66
    in letters, 285
    in proposals, 235
    in scientific writing, 5–7, 9–24
    in speeches, 256, 271, 275

Bach, Johann Sebastian, 271
Bar charts, 214, 229, 231
Beringer, F. Marshall, 114, 116
Bernard, Robert, 14–19
Bibliography, 188
Biddle, Wayne, 36, 37, 39
Bloomfield, Leonard, 4
Bob and Ray, 272
Brevity, 5, 8, 146, 285, 289–290
Bullets, 187
"Bureaucratese," 150
Buried verbs, 152

Callouts, 219–221
Captions:
    in graphs and charts, 216–217, 228–232
    in illustrations, for instructions, 72–73
    in photographs, 221
Carroll, Lewis, 7, 85
Cause-effect pattern, 93–95, 103
Changnon, Stanley, 20–24
Charts, 213–218, 230–233

Chemical Abstracts, 160
Chemical & Engineering News,
    49–54, 60
Chronological order:
    in instructions, 76
    in process descriptions, 47, 55
Circular definition, 29
Citation index, 126, 142
Clarity, 146–153
Classification, 98–101, 103
Clauses, punctuation of,
    336–338, 340
Closings:
    in letters, 295–296
    in speeches, 263, 271, 276
Colon, 336
Colthup, Norman, 270
Column heads, 225, 227, 233
Commas, 336–338
Comparison, contrast, 35–36,
    87–90, 103
Complement, compliment,
    341
Compound sentence, punctuation
    of, 338
Comprehensibility, 66, 67, 76
Computerized search services,
    109, 125–126, 129–135
Conferences, scientific, proceedings
    of, 139
Consistency in language of
    science, 4
Continual, continuous, 341
Correction fluid, use in lab
    notebooks, 326
Cowan, David, 171
Crick, Francis, 5, 130, 131
Current Contents, 125,
    139–141
Curricula vitae (*see* Résumés)

Dangling modifiers, 332

Dashes, 338–339
Data bases for library research
    (*see* Computerized search
    services)
Data, datum, 341
Data poisoning, 114–115
da Vinci, Leonardo, 282–284,
    329
Deductive order, 96–98, 103
Definition(s):
    academic, 34
    acronyms used in, 30
    analytical, 32
    circular, 29
    by class and differentiation,
        30–31
    by example, 35
    expanded, 33–34
    importance of, 29
    by list of properties, 32–33
    logical, 30–31
    operational, 31
    parallel construction in, 334
    in physical description, 41, 43
    in process description, 47
    by synonym, 33
    use of parentheses in, 339
    using comparison, contrast,
        35, 36
    using dashes in, 338
    using etymology, 31–32
    wordiness in, 29–30
Dependent clause, punctuation
    of, 338
Deprisco, Robert, 77
Description:
    detail within, 47, 50, 55, 56
    as extension of definition, 41
    interrelationship of physical and
        process analysis, 41–42
    physical, 44–46
    process, 46–53
    technical versus literary,
        42–43

Detail, use of: depending on
    audience background, 16–19
  in description, 47, 50, 55, 56
Drafts of papers, techniques for
    writing, 113–118

Editing, 116–118
Einstein, Albert, 291–292
Eliot, T. S., 2, 41, 107
Encyclopedias, use of, 126–128
Engineering Index, 135–136
Enumeration, 98–101, 103
Examples, use of, 35, 45, 148
Exploded views, 219, 229

Faraday, Michael, 4, 8
Fewer, lesser, 341
Figures, list of, 184
First drafts, techniques for,
    113–115
Flipcharts, 270
Flow in reports, 200
Fog Index, 290
Footnotes:
  in reports, 187
  in tables, 225, 227
Freuchen, Peter, 61–63
Further, farther, 341

Good Laboratory Practice
    regulations, 325
Gould, Gordon, 323
Graphs and charts, 213–218
Guides to the literature of science,
    128–129
Gunning, Robert, 290

Haldane, J. B. S., 95
Hall, Donald, 146
Handbooks, use of, 128
Harper's Magazine, 36, 39
Headings:
  in business reports, 184–186
  in instructions, 76
  in reports, 199
  in résumés, 307
  in revision, 117
Heisenberg, Werner, 2, 6
Herschel, Sir William, 326

I.e., e.g., 341
IEEE Spectrum, 14–19
Illustration, 212–233
  callout of, 218–220
  captions for, 216, 228
  combining figures within, 218
  exploded views, 219, 229
  graphs and charts, 213–218
  in instructions, 68–75, 218–220
  labeling, of, 213
  as part of description, 43–44
  photographs, 220–221
  in process description, 55
  tables, 222–228
Imperatives, use in instructions, 76
Imply, infer, 342
Independent clause, punctuation
    of, 337, 338, 340
Indexing and abstracting services,
    108, 125, 129–138
Inductive order, 95–96
Inflated language, 145, 148–152
Instructions:
  chronological order in, 76
  use of illustrations for, 218–220
  writing of, 65–84
Internal summaries in speeches,
    275
Its, it's, 336

Jargon, 147
Jeans, Sir James, 86–87
Johnson, Samuel, 8, 30, 153
    154, 159
Journals (*see* Laboratory notebooks)

Labeling of illustrations, 218–221,
    229–231
Laboratory notebooks, 323–329
  definition of, 3
  format for, 325–328
  function of, 324
Language of scientific prose, 4–5
Layout:
  in letters, 294–295
  in reports, 200
Leads:
  in instructions, 68, 75
  in letters, 286
  in process descriptions, 50, 55
  in reports, 199
  in speeches, 273–274
Leeuwenhoek, Anton, 2–3
Leonard, John, 67
Letter writing, 282–304
  audience for, 285
  brevity in, 289–292
  closings of, 295–296
  courtesy in, 297–298
  cover letters, 299–300
  dictation of, 298–299
  layout of, 294–295
  letterese, 288–289
  "no" letters, 299–300
  openings in, 286–288
  outlining in, 293–294
  as reports, 191–192
  style of, 285–286
  "you" approach in, 289
Levi, B. G., 16–19
Library, use of, 124–142
List of figures, 184

List of symbols and
    abbreviations, 184
List of tables, 184
Lister, Joseph, 98, 164–169
Litchman, William, 116
Literature search, techniques
    for, 108
    (*See also* Library, use of)
Lockhead Information Systems,
    129, 132

McGraw-Hill Dictionary of
    Scientific and Technical
    Terms, 38–39
McGraw-Hill Encyclopedia of
    Science and Technology,
    32–33, 40, 44, 45, 99–102
Mathematical Reviews, 161
Meaningless language, 151–152
Medawar, P. B., 141
Memo-reports, 189–191, 203–208
Miller, David B., 96–98
Modifiers:
  dangling, 332
  misplaced, 331–332
Moore, Marianne, 1, 4

National Institutes of Health,
    247–249
National Science Foundation,
    243–247
Nature, 96–98, 130
Negative statements, 153
Nestorian pattern, 92–93
New York Times, 89–93
New Yorker, The, 286
Newsweek, 19–20
Newton, Sir Isaac, 159, 179
Nicholson, Garth, 35–36
Nominalization, 152

Nonrestrictive clause, commas
 and, 336–337
Notebooks (*see* Laboratory
 notebooks)
Numbers:
 numerals versus spelled forms,
  342–343
 in tables, 228
 in technical description, 45

Objective, determination of:
  in letters, 285
  in memo-reports, 191
  in reports, 183
  in scientific writing, 7
  in speeches, 261–262
Objective tone, 4–5, 45, 148, 151
Offprints, use of, 108–109
Openings, standard formats, 109
Oppenheimer, J. Robert, 261
Oral presentation (*see* Speeches)
Orwell, George, 148–149
Outlines, use of, 110–113
  in letters, 293–294
  parallel form in, 334–335
  in speeches, 262, 266, 267
Overhead projector, 265–267,
 278, 279
Overview, use of, 50, 55, 56

Parallelism, 333–335
Paraphrase, use of, 196
Parentheses, 339
Parenthetical phrases, punctuation
 of, 338–339
Passives, 147–148, 151–152
Patent documentation (*see*
 Laboratory notebooks)
Patent information, sources of,
 139–140

Patterns of writing (*see* Rhetorical
 patterns)
Photographs, 220–221
Physical description, 41–45,
 56–63
Physics Today, 16–19
Pie charts, 214–215, 233
Popular Electronics, 9–14
Possessives, apostrophes and,
 335–336
Principle, principal, 342
Problem-solution pattern, 90–92
Proceedings of scientific
 conferences, 139
Process description, 41–42, 46–63
Pronouns in agreement with
 antecedent, 333
Proposals, 234–254
Punctuation:
 apostrophe, 335–336
 colon, 336
 comma, 336–338
 dash, 338–339
 parentheses, 339
 quotation marks, 339
 semicolon, 340

Quotation, legitimate versus
 illegitimate use of, 197–198
Quotation marks, 339

Readability formulas, 290
Redundancy, 149
Reference list, 188–189, 193
Report writing:
 business reports: back matter,
  188–189
  body, 184–188
  definition of, 3
  format for, 183–187

Report writing: business reports
(*Cont.*):
front matter, 184
parts of, 182–183
contract reports, 194
crediting sources in, 194–198
journal reports, 192–193
letter reports, 191–192
memo reports, 189–191, 203–208
progress reports, 180–181,
200–201
purpose of, 179
style in, 180
trip reports, 181, 201–202
types of, 180–182
Research Corporation, 181
Research services (*see* Library,
use of)
Résumés, 305–319
Review volumes, scientific, 138
Revision, need for, 8
(*See also* Drafts of papers,
techniques for writing)
Rhetorical patterns:
analogy, 86–87, 92, 102
cause-effect, 54, 93–95, 103
classification, 98–101, 103
comparison, contrast, 87–90, 103
deductive order, 96–98, 103
definition, 29–40
description, 41–63
enumeration, 98–101, 103
inductive order, 95–96
Nestorian order, 92–93
problem-solution order, 90–92
Rhetorical stance, 5–7, 66
Roosevelt, Franklin Delano,
291–292

Schwartz, Harry, 89–90, 93–94
Schwinger, Julian, 261
Science, 20–24, 171, 177, 178
Science 80, 46–48, 54

Scientific American, 35–36
Scope line, use in memo-reports,
191
Search services, computerized,
125, 129–135
Secondary sources, use of, 108,
129–139
Semicolon, 340
Sentence, length of, 290–292
Series, punctuation of, 337–338
Sforza, Ludovico, 282
Slides, use of, during speeches,
265–269, 274, 280–281
Smith, Sydney, 146
Solomon, Leslie, 9–14
Speeches, 259–281
audience analysis, 260–261,
271, 275
bearing during, 273
blackboard, use of during, 270
central idea, development of,
261–262
closings for, 263, 271, 276
comprehensibility of, 259–260
delivery of, 271–276
extemporaneous mode, 264–265
eye contact during, 272
flipchart as aid, 270
impromptu mode, 262
internal summaries in, 275
manuscript reading of, 264
openings of, 273–274
outlining of, 262–263
overhead projector, use of,
during, 265–267, 278, 279
puzzle order in, 275
rehearsing for, 262–265
slides, use of during, 265–269,
274, 280–281
timing of, 276
transparencies, use of during,
265–269, 275, 278–280
voice during, 272–273
Steinem, Gloria, 107
Stockton, William, 6

Stub column, 225
Style:
  brevity, 146
  "bureaucratese," 150
  clarity, 146-153
  inflated language, 145-148, 152
  jargon, 147
  in letters, 285-286
  meaningless language, 151-152
  negative statements, 153
  nominalization, 152
  redundancy, 149
  in scientific prose, 4-5, 7-8
  wordiness, 145-146, 148-153
Subject, agreement with verb,
  332-333
Successive locator, 218-220
Swift, Jonathan, 147, 234
Symbols and abbreviations, list
  of, 184
Synonyms, used in definition, 33
Systematic Buzz Phrase Projector,
  150
Szent-Gyorgi, Albert, 154

Table of contents, 184, 186,
  327, 329
Tables, 222-228
  list of, 184
Thomas, Lewis, 2
Time, 95-96
Title, use of, 68, 74, 198-199, 225

Tone in reports, 199
Topic sentences, 177
  (*See also* Leads)
Transitional words:
  in process description, 53-54
  in revision, 117
  in speeches, 275
Transparencies, use of, during
  speeches, 265-269, 275,
  278-280

Unique, 342

Verbs:
  agreement with subject, 332-333
  in instructions, 68, 76
  passive, 147-148, 151-152
  in process description, 47
Visuals, use of (*see* Illustration)
Vitae, curricula (*see* Résumés)

Webster, Bayard, 94-95
White, E. B., 101, 153
Wilson, E. Bright, Jr., 108, 124,
  326, 327
Wood, R. W. 5, 274
Wordiness, 145-146, 148-153
Writing, process of, 107-123